Death in Second-Century Christian Thought

Death in Second-Century Christian Thought

The Meaning of Death in Earliest Christianity

BY JEREMIAH MUTIE

◆PICKWICK *Publications* · Eugene, Oregon

DEATH IN SECOND-CENTURY CHRISTIAN THOUGHT
The Meaning of Death in Earliest Christianity

Copyright © 2015 Jeremiah Mutie. All rights reserved. Except for brief quotations in critical publications or reviews, no part of this book may be reproduced in any manner without prior written permission from the publisher. Write: Permissions. Wipf and Stock Publishers, 199 W. 8th Ave., Suite 3, Eugene, OR 97401.

Pickwick Publications
An Imprint of Wipf and Stock Publishers
199 W. 8th Ave., Suite 3
Eugene, OR 97401

www.wipfandstock.com

ISBN 13: 978-1-4982-0164-3

Cataloguing-in-Publication Data

Mutie, Jeremiah

    Death in second-century Christian thought: the meaning of death in earliest Christianity / Jeremiah Mutie

    xvi + 228 p. ; 23 cm. Includes bibliographical references.

    ISBN 13: 978-1-4982-0164-3

    1. Death—Religious aspects—Christianity. 2. Death—Religious aspects—Christianity—History—2nd century. 3. Christian literature, Early. I. Title.

BR63 M874 2015

Manufactured in the U.S.A.

This book is dedicated to the memory of my father, Mr. Job Mutie Musoi, who went to be with the Lord on 26 August 2009, the very day that I, for the first time, made my full incursion into the research of the meaning of death in early Christianity. I believe that Paul's words became true of my father that day:

Ἐμοὶ γὰρ τὸ ζῆν Χριστὸς καὶ τὸ ἀποθανεῖν κέρδος—Phil 1:21

Contents

Preface | ix
Acknowledgments | xi
List of Abbreviations | xiii

CHAPTER 1 Introduction | 1
CHAPTER 2 The Concept of Death in the Apostolic Fathers | 54
CHAPTER 3 The Concept of Death in Valentinian Gnosticism, Apologists, and Polemicists | 100
CHAPTER 4 Treatment of the Dead in the Second Century | 156
CHAPTER 5 Conclusion | 191

Bibliography | 197
Index | 217

Preface

THE CONCERN OF THIS book is the concept of death in second-century Christian thought. It addresses the question of how second-century Christians understood death as evidenced by their writings as well as their attitudes towards the dead. The need for the study is the lack of adequate treatment of the subject of death in this crucial period in the history of Christianity. The discussion focuses on the works of the earliest second-century Fathers (the Apostolic Fathers), the apologists, and the polemicists.

The thesis of this work is that second-century Christians carefully selected, adapted, and utilized existing views on death from the Old Testament, Greco-Roman culture, and the documents that eventually became the New Testament to present a distinctively Christian concept of death commensurate with their level of progressive revelation. This selective adaptation involved rejection of some ideas, modification of others, as well as reinterpretation of others. They reinterpreted Old Testament views of death to reflect the new situation of Jesus' post-resurrection, arguing for a paradoxical view of death that sees it, on the one hand, as a reality to be contended with, and, on the other hand, as a defeated foe whose presence does not stop the believer's fellowship either with Christ or with other believers.

A review of relevant literature reveals two competing views concerning the scholarly understanding of death in second-century Christian thought. On the one hand, conceptions of death in this period are a complete contrast to Greek concepts of death. On the other hand, it is argued that views of death in second-century Christian thought show the evidence of complete Hellenization of the Greek concepts. Although there is some truth in both of these views, both cannot be entirely true because they are opposites.

An examination of the relevant Old Testament, New Testament, and Greco-Roman data reveals that there are significant conceptual similarities (terms and metaphors) with the second-century understanding of death. However, an examination of the relevant second-century writings and practices reveals significant conceptual differences as well on the subject of death. This study proposes that these similarities and differences can be accounted for on the principle of a critical adaptation, modification, and the utilization of existing views on death to present a Christian view of death in light of the level of revelation held by second-century believers.

Acknowledgments

ALTHOUGH I AM PERSONALLY responsible for the contents of this book, I am extremely grateful to all those who came alongside me during the process of writing my dissertation of which this book is a revision. First, I am very grateful to my dissertation readers, Dr. D. Jeffrey Bingham, Dr. Glenn R. Kreider, and Dr. Linda M. Marten for their deep questions, critiques, and helpful suggestions that provoked me to greater reflection and clarity in the research and presentation of my findings in this work. Dr. Bingham's questions and critiques led to the refinement of the thesis of my argument. Drs. Kreider and Marten offered extremely helpful suggestions on how to present my research findings in a readable manner. Dr. Richard Taylor's comments were of immense help in the production of the final form of this work especially on matters of style and grammar. My friends Dr. Michael Svigel, Beau Bishop, and Deena Pryor proofread the entire book for me. I could not have completed the book without your support and encouragement. Thank you all.

I could not have completed my PhD studies without the loving support of numerous family members and friends who remained a source of constant moral, spiritual, and material support throughout the entire program of study. Above all, this particular project would not have been completed without the loving support of my wife Eunice. Thank you for your love, support, and insurmountable sacrifice for all these years. I will never know the depth of humility that you put in as you bore with me during this very important time of our life. My children, Jackson and Cynthia, kept prodding me to "finish your book so that we can go to the beach!" Thank you all very much. My mom Monicah and my parents-in-law, Mr. and Mrs. Jackson Muli, were a continued source of encouragement. I am also extremely grateful for the grace and support that I received from the staff at Pickwick Publications. Mention must be made of my tireless editor, Dr. Robin Parry and my very keen typesetter, Calvin Jaffarian. God bless and reward you mightily.

Finally, many other friends and churches have generously supported me along the way. May the Lord bless and reward you mightily in ways that surpass all human wisdom and understanding.

Soli Deo Gloria

List of Abbreviations

THE APOSTOLIC FATHERS

Barn.	*Letter of Barnabas*
1 Clem.	*1 Clement*
2 Clem.	*2 Clement*
Did.	*The Didache (The Teaching of the Twelve Apostles)*
Diogn.	*Epistle to Diognetus*
Herm. Mand.	*Shepherd of Hermas, Mandate(s)*
Herm. Sim.	*Shepherd of Hermas, Similitude(s)*
Herm. Vis.	*Shepherd of Hermas, Vision(s)*
Ign. *Eph.*	Ignatius, *To the Ephesians*
Ign. *Mag.*	Ignatius, *To the Magnesians*
Ign. *Phld.*	Ignatius, *To the Philadelphians*
Ign. *Pol.*	Ignatius, *To Polycarp*
Ign. *Rom.*	Ignatius, *To the Romans*
Ign. *Smyrn.*	Ignatius, *To the Smyrnaeans*
Ign. *Trall.*	Ignatius, *To the Trallians*
Mart. *Pol.*	*Martyrdom of Polycarp*
Pol. *Phil.*	Polycarp, *To the Philippians*

THE APOLOGISTS AND NAG HAMMADI TRACTATES

Haer.	Irenaeus, *Adversus haereses*
1 Apol.	Justin, *First Apology*
2 Apol.	Justin, *Second Apology*
Dial.	Justin, *Dialogue with Trypho*
Gos. Phil.	*Gospel of Philip*
Gos. Truth.	*Gospel of Truth*
Interp. Know.	*The Interpretation of Knowledge*
Treat. Res.	*Treatise on the Resurrection [Epistle to Rheginos]*
Tri. Trac.	*Tripartite Tractate*

SECONDARY SOURCES

BDAG	Bauer, Walter et al., eds. *A Greek-English Lexicon of the New Testament and Other Early Christian Literature*, 3rd ed. Chicago: University of Chicago Press, 2000.
BJRL	*Bulletin of the John Rylands University Library of Manchester*
CH	*Church History*
Comm.	*Communio*
FRLANT	*Forschungen zur Religion und Literatur des Alten und Neuen Testaments*
HNT	*Handbuch zum Neuen Testament*
HTR	*Harvard Theological Review*
ICC	International Critical Commentary
JAOS	*Journal of the American Oriental Society*
JBL	*Journal of Biblical Literature*
JQR	*Jewish Quarterly Review*
JR	*Journal of Religion*
JRS	*Journal of Roman Studies*
JSNT	*Journal for the Study of the New Testament*

JTSA	*Journal of Theology for Southern Africa*
NIDOTTE	*New International Dictionary of Old Testament Theology and Exegesis*. Edited by W. A. VanGemeren. 5 vols. Grand Rapids: Zondervan, 1997
NovT	*Novum Testamentum*
NTS	*New Testament Studies*
RHPR	*Revue d'histoire et de philosophie religieuses*
RSR	*Recherches de science religiuse*
SC	*Sources chrétiennes*
ST	*Studia theologica*
TDNT	*Theological Dictionary of the New Testament*. Edited by G. Kittel and G. Friedrich. Translated by G. W. Bromiley. 10 vols. Grand Rapids: Eedrmans, 1964–76
VC	*Vigiliae christianae*
TS	*Theological Studies*
WTJ	*Westminster Theological Journal*
WUNT	*Wissenschaftliche Untersuchungen zum Neuen Testament*
ZNW	*Zeitschrift für die neutestamentliche Wissenschaft und die Kunde der älteren Kirche*

CHAPTER 1

Introduction

THE NEED FOR THIS STUDY AND SCHOLARLY DISCUSSION

IN HIS INTRODUCTION TO a discussion of the question of life and death, John Hick, in 1978, offered a chilling regret concerning the state of theological discussion on the matter compared to the same in the secular world. He wrote:

> It is a curious feature of the present time that a boom in secular interest in the idea of a life after death seems to be matched by a recession in high level of theological interest in that possibility. There is today a wave of popular non-religious concern about death and about a post-mortem existence, expressed in parapsychology, occultism, thanatology, and talk of mediumship, reincarnation, out-of-the-body experiences and the reports of those who have been revived after having been clinically dead. And yet at the same time some of the best Christian thinking today is inclined to deemphasize the idea of the life to come, even to the point of virtually abandoning it as an element in the Christian message.[1]

Indeed, according to the Roman Catholic theologian Terrence Nichols, this gloomy situation has not changed much in recent years. Writing about the attitude towards death and afterlife in the present times, Nichols, in 2010, observed:

1. Hick, "Present and Future," 1.

> Increasingly, pastors do not talk about afterlife. Often they simply offer brief slogans, such as "He is with God now." I once asked a pastor in my athletic club what he told his flock about the soul after death. His response was "Our [sic] theologians tell us not to talk about it." This seems to be the case in mainline Protestant churches and is becoming true in some Catholic churches. It's even more true in our popular culture. I ask people if anyone ever brings up the topic of death and afterlife at a party. Of course not, they laugh; people don't talk about it.[2]

But has the church been that much disinterested in the question of death and the afterlife since her inception? How did, for example, Christians who were closest to the apostles of Jesus Christ deal with the question of death?

Modern scholarship has dealt with the question of the early church's concept of death by offering two key answers. Since the approach to the study of the Fathers' concept of death has always been in relationship to their theological and cultural milieu, these answers have also been presented against that background. The first of these two answers became clear in the interchange between Oscar Cullman and Harry A. Wolfson in the famous Ingersoll Lectures on Human Immortality at Harvard University in the mid-1950s.[3]

On the one hand, Oscar Cullmann, although focusing on death and resurrection in the New Testament, contended that in the thought of the Fathers, the concept of death was a complete contrast to that of their immediate milieu, the Greco-Roman culture. Exposing the view that he had vehemently argued in both *Christ and Time* and *Immortality of the Soul or Resurrection of the Dead?* Cullman argued in his 1955 Ingersoll Lecture entitled "Immortality of the Soul or Resurrection of the Dead? The Witness of the New Testament," that there is a radical difference between the early Christians' view of death and that of the Greeks.[4] In order to argue his case, Cullmann brought to the attention of his readers what he saw as the complete contrast between the attitude shown towards death by both

---

2. Nichols, *Death and Afterlife*, 10.

3. The Ingersoll Lectures on "The Immortality of the Man" were established at Harvard University in 1894 by Caroline Haskell Ingersoll in honor of the wishes of her father, George Goldthwaite Ingersoll. For more introductory information, see Stendahl, "Introduction," in *Immortality and Resurrection*, 1–8.

4. Cullmann, "Immortality of the Soul," 18. See also Cullmann, *Immortality of the Soul*, Cullmann, *Christ and Time*.

INTRODUCTION

Socrates and Jesus. On the one side, he sees Socrates' death, as reported by Plato, as a "beautiful death." He writes:

> The death of Socrates is a beautiful death. Nothing is seen here of death's terror. Socrates cannot fear death, since indeed it sets us free from the body. Whoever fears death proves that he loves the world of the body, that he is thoroughly entangled in the world of the senses. Death is the soul's great friend. So he teaches; and so, in wonderful harmony with his teaching, he dies—this man who embodied the Greek world in its noblest form.[5]

Cullmann immediately contrasts this with the attitude towards it and the death of Jesus Christ, the epitome of all Christian deaths in early Christianity. According to him, Jesus was extremely fearful of his death. "He was really afraid," he writes of Jesus.[6] "Here is nothing of the composure of Socrates," he continues, "who met death peacefully as a friend."[7] Why was Jesus so much afraid of death, according to Cullmann, while Socrates was not?

The answer lies in the contrasting views of death that were held by the Greeks and the Christian view of death.[8] Since the Platonists saw the body as a prison or tomb in which the soul (ψυχή) longed to be freed (hence, the famous saying: σῶμα σῆμα—"the body is the tomb"—was often quoted in Platonism), death was seen as something beautiful. On the other hand, Jesus and early Christians understood death as the complete destruction of the body and the soul, opined Cullmann. Thus, Christ underwent death in the fullness its horrors, that is, both in body and soul, descending to nothingness. In other words, what Cullmann inferred from the attitude towards death by Jesus is that since Jesus believed that death is the utter destruction of the soul and the body (that is, nothing survives physical death), then he awaited death amazedly, sorrowfully,

---

5   14. I suppose that Cullmann really means the Orphic [Platonic] Greeks since not all Greeks held this view of death.

6. Ibid., 5.

7. Ibid.

8. It is helpful to remember that Greek concepts of death show great development. What Cullmann is referring to here (although he does not elucidate it), is the later view of death by the Greeks, that the soul was merely imprisoned in the body. Earlier on, Greeks viewed death as descending to nothingness (see Jaeger, "The Greek Ideas," 97–114).

and with strong crying and tears, as opposed to the calm attitude taken by Socrates towards his death, as reported by Plato.⁹

The second view, which has become very dominant, is that early Christians exhibit a completely Hellenized concept of death. As expressed by Jaeger, this view argues that the early Christian concept of death is the final stage in the development of the concept of death that began in the earliest Greek poetic tradition.¹⁰ According to Jaeger, this development, which began during the early poetic tradition when there was a "sharp cleavage between men and gods," reached its climax in the Christian era when Greco-Roman ideas finally merged with the Christian religion.¹¹ During the earliest times, the souls (ψυχαί) of the dead masses descended into what Homer called "idols" that only resemble the former shape of the person after crossing the river Lethe, that is, the river of forgetfulness.¹² However, there was a distinction between the common masses who descended into nothingness and the valiant, the warriors "who had left behind them the glorious memory of their deeds to live in the songs of the ἀοιδοί."¹³

As this development continued, argues Jaeger, the concept of the immortality of the soul was introduced. The idea that the soul is immortal (ἀθάνατος) seems to have first emerged with the Spartan Tyrtaeus who, in the seventh century BC, promised immortality of the soul to his valiant warriors dying for their country. As Jaeger concludes, "Obviously

---

9. It is important to note that Cullmann's view of death here is dictated by his anthropology. According to him, the body (Greek σῶμα), is good in itself. However, the flesh (Greek σάρξ), is the transcendent power of sin and death that entered man after the fall, is evil and man must be delivered from it (see Cullmann, *Immortality of the Soul*, 30–37; Cullmann, *Christ and Time*.). Some scholars see the possibility of an internal inconsistency in Cullmann's anthropology. According to Schep, for example, "Apart from the question of whether Cullmann's conception of the flesh is scriptural, . . . it may be observed here that Cullmann's argumentation seems rather inconsistent. If man was created good in body and soul, then the flesh cannot possibly be evil, for the body Adam received from God was a body of flesh. Accordingly, the 'flesh' which is said to have invaded Adam's body and soul after the Fall as a transcendent evil power cannot have been 'flesh-matter' but some spiritual power—the more so because according to Cullmann the flesh invaded also Adam's *soul*. Consequently this 'invasion' of the 'flesh' cannot be regarded as a ground why the resurrection-body should not consist of flesh" (Schep, *The Nature of the Resurrection Body*, 12–13 n. 5).

10. Jaeger, "The Greek Ideas," 99.

11. Ibid.

12. Ibid.

13. Ibid., 100. I will get back to this Greek concept of death as I discuss fully the Greek concepts of death later in the chapter.

this belief in his [man's] immortality is more than a poetic metaphor, for it assures him of the imperishable value of his immortality."[14] Here is where Jaeger sees the final merger with Christianity taking place. He sees the early church's concept of death as the zenith of the development of the Greek ideas of death. To be fair to Jaeger, however, this Christianization of the concept of death in the church fathers was done with some modifications. "If nevertheless," he writes, "Plato's ideas of the soul and its destiny seem so familiar to us and have kept their distinct appeal, that is, because they have been adopted, with inevitable modifications, by the Fathers of the Church."[15]

Although we will come back to these "modifications," it is important to note that this theory—that is, the early church's concept of death consists of Hellenized ideas of the same—has dominated the scholarship of this topic. Two concepts of the Hellenic understanding of death are seen as dominating second-century Christians' understanding of death in modern scholarship. These are, first, the concept of the noble death and, second, that of the Greek myths of the so-called "false deaths."

The Greek Concepts of the Noble Death and Early Christianity

The first significant enduring Hellenistic understanding of death believed to be evident in early Christianity, especially where death is through martyrdom, is what L. Arik Greenberg and others have called the "Noble Death."[16] Indeed, the concept of the "Noble Death" has been one of the most discussed approaches to understanding death in antiquity.[17] This understanding of death owes its origin to the deaths of some Greek philosophers as well as the Maccabean martyrs. Greg Sterling identifies especially the deaths of the Greek philosophers Zeno of Elea (fifth century BC) and Anaxarchus of Abdera (fourth Century BC) who "were both

---

14. Ibid., 101.
15. Ibid., 112.
16. Greenberg, *My Share of God's Reward*, 1.
17. For many, the idea of the Noble Death, that is, choosing to face death as a sacrifice instead of compromising one's principles or beliefs in the face of persecution, provides the key to interpreting death in antiquity. Some of the key works on the idea of the Noble Death include Seeley, *The Noble Death*; Musurillo, *The Acts of the Pagan Martyrs*; Droge and Tabor, *A Noble Death*; Greenberg, *My Share of God's Reward*; Henten, *The Maccabean Martyrs*, and Henten and Avemarie, *Martyrdom and Noble Death*.

perceived as models of the courageous defiance of tyrants."[18] However, by far, the consensus among scholars is that the protagonist of the Noble Death in Greek tradition is Socrates. Although there are a number of sources for the death of Socrates (that is, the four dialogues of Plato—the *Euthyphro*, the *Crito*, the *Apology* and the *Phaedo* as well as two Xenophon's works, the *Apology* as well as the *Memorabilia* 1.1.1—2.64), it is perhaps in Plato's *Apology* where the basic tenets of the Noble Death are most evident.[19]

For a good number of scholars, the Noble Death has become the only view by which we are to understand Christian death in antiquity. This is especially so whereby death was the result of martyrdom. In other words, according to this paradigm, Christian martyrs saw themselves as participating in a self-sacrificial vicarious death whereby the sufferer dies unjustly and is rewarded with immortality. For example, speaking about the function of Christian martyrdom, Greenberg notes that "the afterlife functions within these as compensation for the loss suffered by the martyr, a feature that becomes inexorably linked to Jewish and Christian valorization of a Noble Death."[20] As he notes, this understanding of death originated within the Deuteronomistic "notion that divine justice will not allow the righteous to suffer unjustly and without compensation."[21] However, by the time Christianity was born, the marriage between the Hellenistic Jewish and Greco-Roman ideas of the Noble Death had already taken place.

According to the proponents of this view, it is within this understanding of the Noble death that Christianity emerged. For some, even the death that Christ died can be aptly understood as "Noble Death." For example, according to Sterling, the third evangelist was clearly acquainted

---

18. Sterling, "*Mors philosophi*," 385.

19. This is how Plato records Socrates' attitude to his own death: "For know well, that if you kill me, I being such a person as I say I am, you will not harm me more than yourselves. Since neither Meletus nor Anytus could ever harm me. That would be impossible. For I believe that it is contrary to divine law that a better person is harmed by somebody worse. He may kill him, yes, or ban him or deprive him of his civil rights, and, perhaps, he and others believe that these. On the contrary, in my view, it is a major evil to do what he is doing now, attempting to kill a man unjustly" (*Apol. 30cd*, quoted in Henten and Avemarie, *Martyrdom and Noble Death*, 13). As Sterling notes, in some occasions, the death of Socrates "became the lens through which the deaths of later philosophers were viewed" (Sterling, "*Mors philosophi*," 387).

20. Greenberg, *My Share of God's Reward*, 1.

21. Ibid., 4.

with Plato's *Apology* and, therefore, crafted the passion of Christ around it. He concludes:

> I suggest that the author of the third gospel used the same procedure [as Plato], but reversed the roles. That is, the evangelist carefully reworked the death of Jesus at critical points to remind the hearer/reader of Socrates, the paradigmatic martyr of his society. Like the author of 2 Maccabees and Tacitus, the evangelist made the comparison implicit rather than explicit.[22]

Donald W. Riddle arrives at the same conclusion as far as the Gospel of Mark is concerned. After arguing that the key to understanding the gospel itself is what he calls the "martyr motif," Riddle concludes that "although there are data which indicate a strong martyr motif in the earliest

---

22. Sterling, "*Mors philosophi*," 401. According to Sterling, the third evangelist could have either learned about the death of Socrates from his basic rhetorical training since "the *chreia* about whether Socrates died justly or unjustly was in the handbooks," or "indirectly through Jewish martyrologies." For more information on how the death of Jesus Christ was understood within the Socratic Noble Death tradition, see Riddle, "The Martyr Motif," 397–410; Harnack, "Sokrates und die alte Kirche," 1:1.29–48; Pfättisch, "Christus und Sokrates bei Justin," 503–23; Benz, "Christus und Sokrates," 195–244; Fascher, "Sokrates und Christus," 1–41; Baumeister, "Anytos und Meletos," 58–63. However, as noted above, an interesting approach in comparing the attitude taken towards death by Socrates and Jesus is that of Oscar Cullman. Instead of seeing a similarity in their attitude towards death, Cullman sees a complete contrast. According to him, this contrast evidences itself in the Greek concept of the immortality of the soul. He writes: "And when the great Socrates traced the arguments for immortality in his address to his disciples on the day of his death, he did not merely *teach* this doctrine: at that moment he lived this doctrine. He showed how we serve the freedom of the soul, even in this present life, when we occupy ourselves with the eternal truths of philosophy. For through philosophy we penetrate into that world of ideas to which the soul belongs, and we free the soul from the prison of the body. Death does no more than complete this liberation. Plato shows how Socrates goes to his death in complete peace and composure. The death of Socrates is a beautiful death. Nothing is seen here of death's terror. Socrates cannot fear death, since indeed it sets us free from the body. Whoever fears death proves that he loves the world of the body, that he is thoroughly entangled in the world of sense. Death is the soul's great friend" (Cullmann, *Immortality of the Soul*, 20–21). Then he makes this contrast as far as Jesus' attitude to His own death is concerned: "In Gethsemane he [Jesus] knows that death stands before him, just as Socrates expected death on his last day. The Synoptics furnish us, by and large, with a unanimous report. Jesus begins 'to tremble and be distressed,' writes Mark (14:33). . . . Jesus is afraid, though not as a coward would be of the men who will kill him, still less of the pain and grief which precede death. He is afraid in the face of death itself. . . . He is afraid of death. It is useless to try to explain away Jesus' fear as reported by the evangelists. . . . He was really afraid. Here is nothing of the composure of Socrates, who met death peacefully as a friend" (Cullmann, "Immortality of the Soul" 14–15).

passion story, and the generalization that the Markan Gospel functioned as a primitive martyrology is supported not merely by the tradition of its rise from the persecution of Nero, but by its internal indicia."[23]

Therefore, according to the proponents of the Nobel Death view, right from her inception, Christianity understood the deaths of her adherents as patterned after the Maccabean and Hellenistic Jewish martyrs. Not only is this so for the founder of the Christian movement, but proponents of this paradigm argue that this is how death was understood and used in early Christianity. But they also see a changing pattern whereby early Christians exhibited a dualistic approach to the world as they faced death. According to Greenberg, for example, "a slightly world-denying attitude is noticeable in much Christian literature that encourages martyrdom, displaying dualistic ideals that treat the present life as paltry compared to the next, an afterlife which is the normal state of the human soul."[24]

Of very special interest to this concept in the second century is the attitude taken towards pain and death by the Antiochene bishop Ignatius of Antioch (d. 108/117 AD?). This paradigm is based on the premise that "the ideal of the Christian martyr was the *imitatio Christi*."[25] Following this concept, some scholars like Preiss have argued that "si sa christologie détermine sa martyrologie, en retour l'immortalité par l'imitation de la passion du Christ détermine profundément sa Christologie. A une mystique de l'imitation correspond tout naturellment une doctrine du Christ-modèle."[26] [if his Christology determines his understanding of martyrdom, in a reciprocal way his consuming desire for immortality through imitating Christ's passion profoundly affects his Christology. A mysticism of imitation corresponds quite naturally to a doctrine of Christ as the model]."[27]

Indeed, the attitude taken by Ignatius of Antioch towards his impending death has been the subject of all kinds of interpretations.[28] On the one extreme is the interpretation of Ignatius' longing for his death as

---

23 Riddle, "The Martyr Motif," 409.

24. Greenberg, *My Share of God's Reward*, 5.

25. Fischel, "Martyr and Prophet," 266.

26. Preiss, "La mystique l'imitation du Christ," 214.

27. Swartley, "The Imitatio Christi," 81.

28. For a thorough discussion of Ignatius's understanding of his impending death, see Mellink, *Death as Eschaton*. See also Morris, "Pure Wheat of God"; Davis, "The Predicament"; Swartley, "The Imitatio Christi."

INTRODUCTION

"neurotic and pathological" disorder.[29] On the other extreme, as Mellink notes, is the social interpretation of Ignatius' attitude towards death. This psychoanalytical approach is based on the assumption that Ignatius saw himself as the cause of the strife in the church in Antioch in some way, and, therefore, his impending death was the only way his damaged image could be restored. Thus, "Ignatius' strong sense of failure caused his anxiety and his desire to be rehabilitated through a glorious death."[30] This is another way of saying that Ignatius' death was a Noble Death.

A subset of the tradition of the Noble Death, a view that presents another Hellenized interpretation of Ignatius' attitude to his impending death, is to understand it within what is known as the "Second Sophistic" phenomenon.[31] Viewed within this paradigm, Ignatius' attitude towards

---

29. Mellink, *Death as Eschaton*, 91. A number of scholars have taken this approach. These include McGinn, *The Foundations of Mysticism*; Gibbon, *The History of the Decline and Fall of the Roman Empire*, 2.111; Croix, "Why Were the Early Christians Persecuted?" 24; Bernard, "The Background," 193; Frend, *Martyrdom and Persecution* 197; Neil and Wright, *The Interpretation of the New Testament*, 55. Others include Streeter, *The Primitive Church*; Laeuchli, "The Drama of Replay," 71–126. Deserving special mention is Walter Rebell's argument that "Ignatius' craving for death can be understood as the desire of the 'Selbst' to sacrifice 'Ich' and thus to become authentic human being," (Quoted in Mellink, *Death as Eschaton*, 94.) See Rebell, "Das Leidensverständnis bei Paulus," 462–63.

30. Mellink, *Death as Eschaton*, 95. Although the traditional understanding of Ignatius' death was that it was a result of Roman persecution during the rulership of Emperor Trajan, this view has in the last few years been highly challenged. The leading proponents of this challenge are: Harrison, *Polycarp's Two Epistles*, 79–106; Bammel, "Ignatian Problems," 66–69; Swartley, "The Imitatio Christi," 98; Schoedel, "Are the Letters of Ignatius of Antioch Authentic?"; Schoedel, *Ignatius of Antioch*, 11–12; Schoedel, "Theological Norms and Social Perspectives," Rius-Camps, *The Four Authentic Letters*, 139–43; Trevett, "Ignatius 'To the Romans,'" Schlatter, "The Restoration of Peace," 469; Corwin, *St. Ignatius and Christianity*, 24–29; Joly, *Le dossier d'Ignace d'Antioch*; Lieu, *Image and Reality*. See also Weiner and Weiner, *The Martyr's Conviction*. For the defense of the traditional understanding of Ignatius' death, see Lightfoot, *S. Ignatius, S. Polycarp Part 2*, 31–37; Zahn, *Ignatius von Antiochien*; Isacson, "Follow Your Bishop!"

31. As Allen Brent notes, the term *Second Sophistic* "is a term originally coined Philostratus [that] has been adopted by modern scholars to describe an extensive historical phenomenon, with implications of the highest importance for our understanding the history of the Greek city states in Asia Minor from the end of the first century after Christ. It describes the emergence, from the time of Domitian onwards (81–96), of a developing narrative of Hellenistic cultural identity that nevertheless drew together and organized, into a new pattern, themes and concepts scattered throughout the history of Greek civilisation from Athens in 404 BC onwards" (Brent, *Ignatius of Antioch and the Second Sophistic*, 1.) See also Kerferd, *The Sophistic Movement*;

his impending death has been understood as a kind of language game. As Brent elucidates, according to this theory:

> Ignatian concepts and vocabulary, as part of an overall vision of social and ecclesial Order, are rooted in the pagan Greco-Roman religious and political culture of Asia Minor characterized as the Second Sophistic, and demonstrable from both literary and epigraphical remains. Ignatius' early Christian world will reflect the world of the city-states of Asia Minor, with the Eucharist, like a procession in a mystery cult, involving a drama of replay.[32]

Indeed, Brent is blunt in his proposal that we no longer need to read Ignatius' understanding of his death in a metaphysical way, noting that "we propose understanding Ignatius, like Wittgenstein's moral rebel, as arising within a form of life, and on the basis of its fundamental, constitutive categories arguing, in a way intelligible to his fellow participants, Pagan and Christian, for a shift in their agreement in opinion."[33] He continues: "We no longer need here the metaphysical notion of a 'collective' as opposed to an 'individual' mind, but a shared discourse rich with both actual and possible meanings."[34]

Although I will come back to Ignatius' concept of death, it is clear from this scholarly emphasis that his death is, for the most part, interpreted in an extremely Hellenized manner. I will seek to demonstrate that although Ignatius utilizes terminology and metaphors that are present in the Greco-Roman culture, he does not employ the same meaning as employed in this milieu. Rather, he adapts and modifies them to emphasize a distinctively Christian view of death as he understands it. Before we explore the Ignatian concept of death, it is necessary to take a look at the other recurrent Hellenized view that has been offered to help us

---

Nasrallah, *Christian Responses to the Roman Art and Architecture*; Braun, *Rhetoric and Reality* and Lotz, *Ignatius and Concord*.

32. Brent, *Ignatius of Antioch and the Second Sophistic*, 7. Brent's entire thesis is that Ignatian *Letters* are very much steeped in the culture of Greek city states of Asia Minor in the *Second Sophistic* culture. In this case, we find in them "the language of ὁμόνοια festivals rivalry between cities, the summoning of assemblies to elect ambassadors (Φεοπρεσβύται), etc. Thus, Ignatius' purpose is understood as functioning in "affirming the identity of Christian communities in terms shared, conceptual structure is both like and unlike the assertion of Hellenic identity in the imperial structures of the Roman power."

33. Ibid.

34. Ibid.

understand the early Christians' concept of death as well as deal with the background issues underlying the concepts of death in the second century.

Greek Concept of False Deaths, False Bodies, and Early Christianity

Another Hellenized paradigm for understanding the meaning of death in the second century has been what Judith Perkins calls "False Deaths and New Bodies" paradigm.[35] According to this paradigm, first clearly articulated by G. W. Bowersock, views of death in early Christianity are patterned after the Greek concept of the "false" or "apparent death."[36] Otherwise known as *Scheintod*, (literally, phony death or death in name only), the "apparent death" literature allows "for all the excitement and tragedy of extinction and resurrection without unduly straining the credulity of the reader."[37]

Although it was Bowersock who argued for the overlap between the rise of Christianity and the "prose fiction," it is, by far, Caroline Bynum and Judith Perkins who closely connect the Greek "false deaths" metaphor with the Christian understanding of death and resurrection in the second century.[38] Both are responding to the connection that Bowersock first made between Christianity and false death fictions when he concluded his discussion by asking whether "from a historical point of view we would be justified in explaining the extraordinary growth in fictional writing, and its characteristic and concomitant fascination with resurrection, as some kind reflection of the remarkable stories that were coming out of Palestine precisely in the middle of the first century AD"[39] Bynum argues that the development of the Christian belief in the resurrection of the flesh is closely patterned after both Greek and Latin prose fictions such as Petronius' *Satyrica* and Apuleius' *Metamorphoses*, believed to have been written in the second century AD, when she observes that:

> By the end of the second century, however, things had changed. "Resurrection" was no longer simply a minor theme of discussion

---

35. Perkins, *Roman Imperial Identities*, 45.

36. Bowersock, *Fiction as History*, 99.

37. Ibid. For an earlier work on this concept, see Rohde, *Der griechische Roman und seine Vorläufer*.

38. Perkins, *Roman Imperial Identities*, 45.

39. Bowersock, *Fiction as History*, 119.

and apologetics; it became a major element of disputes among Christians and in Christian defenses against pagan attacks. Entire treatises were devoted to the topic. Resurrection not of "the dead" or "the body" (*soma* or *corpus*) but of the flesh (*sarx* or *caro*) became a key element in the fight against Docetism (which treated Christ's body as in some sense unreal or metaphorical) and Gnosticism (which carried "realized eschatology" so far as to understand resurrection as spiritual and moral advance in this life and therefore escape from body).[40]

On her part, Judith Perkins argues that these stories are not only traceable to the Jewish martyriological stories, but, also, on a larger scale, to the culture of violent fiction that was characteristic of the Greco-Roman society during period of the rise of early Christianity. According to her, all of the four extant fictive Greek narratives, that is, "those of Chariton, Xenophon of Ephesus, Achilles Tatius and Heliodorus," together with the aforementioned Latin prose of *Metamorphoses*, offer examples of false deaths.[41]

---

40. Bynum, *The Resurrection of the Body*, 26. Although I will explore this development further in chapter 4, it is important to observe here that the more positive view of the body was more of a result of theological understanding than a literary or social explanation. For an explanation that focuses on the function of the literary approach, see Coleman, "Fatal Charades," 45–71.

41. Perkins, *Roman Imperial Identities*, 47. For more information on this Greco-Roman cultural phenomenon of false death literature, see Gleason, "Truth Contests," 287–313; Glancy, "Boastings and Beatings," 99–135; Coleman, "Fatal Charades," 44–73. According to Perkins, one of the best examples of these "false death" romantic stories is that of Clitophon and Leucippe in Achilles Tatius. According to the story, Clitophon and Leucippe are shipwrecked in Egypt where they are separated and seized by bandits and Leucippe is taken away to be a "purificatory sacrifice for the robber band." She notes that this sacrificial ritual involved an elaborate ritual. "Clitophon is rescued by a detachment of soldiers," she writes. "Barred by an impassable trench, the all watch at a distance what they believe is Leucippe's sacrifice. . . . Leucippe is led around an altar to instrumental and vocal music until finally she is tied to stakes in the ground, and the bandits plunge a sword into her stomach, exposing her intestines. The narrative graphically records the rite's finale: 'Tearing them [the intestines] out with his hands and he placed them upon the altar. When they were roasted, each man cut off a portion and ate it'" (Perkins, *Roman Imperial Identities*, 48). The reader continues to be shown the horrors of Leucippe's death through the reaction of Clitophon. "O pitiable Leucippe," he cries, "the unluckiest person in the world . . . your body is laid out there, but where are your innards? If fire had destroyed them, the disaster would be less. Now the burial . . . of your innards has become food for the bandits (νῦν δὲ ἡ τῶν σπλάγχνων σου ταφὴ λῃστῶνε γέγονε τροφή)." He concludes: "I am holding the leftovers of your body, but you yourself I have lost (τὸ μὲν γὰρ λείψανον ἔχω σου τοῦ σώματος, ἀπολώλεκα δὲ σέ) . . . since Fortune denies me the chance to kiss your face,

Thus, although a number of these scholars see a connection between these "false death" fictions and the second-century Christian literature on death, the exact nature of this connection continues to be debated. As noted above, according to Bowersock, much of these fictional stories are themselves patterned after early Christian literature on death. He concludes:

> Already in the days of the emperor Claudius the name of Jesus Christ was known at Rome. The Gospels, as we have them, had not yet been written, but much of the story that they were to contain was obviously already in circulation. By the time of Claudius's successor, the emperor Nero, that great philhellenic patron of the arts, the claims of the Christians were being widely disseminated at Rome as a result of the residence of Paul in the city and the infamous immolation of many Christians in the aftermath of the fire that consumed it in 64. By this time it is possible that the earliest of the extant Gospels was actually being written, If the nature of contemporary fiction [false deaths] helps us, as it does, to explain the interpretation that Celsus brought to the Gospels [that is, "the old heroic stories about the men who descended to Hades and came back or brought women back with them are essentially fantastic tales"], it would be wise next to consider the possibility that the Gospel stories themselves provided the impetus for the emergence of that fiction in the first place.[42]

Thus, according to Bowersock, the Gospel stories predated the false death fiction stories, which were patterned after the death and resurrection stories in the Gospels.

Caroline Bynum sees the opposite as taking place. For her, the martyrdom stories of early Christians reflect an influence of such false death stories. Ignatius of Antioch, writing about AD 110 on his way to execution in accordance with these fictions "sees fragmentation and digestion by the beasts as the ultimate threat and thus as that over which resurrection is the ultimate victory."[43] In other words, just as the false death fictions are just that—false deaths—Ignatius' vision of his anticipated resurrection parallels

---

let me kiss your butchered neck (ἀλλ' ἐπεί μοι τῶν ἐν προσώπω φιλημάτων ἐφθόνησεν ἡ Τύχη, φέρε σου καταφιλήσω τὴν σφαγήν) (Perkins, *Roman Imperial Identities*, 49). Of course, as it is with these kinds of fictions, we later learn that Leucippe is not injured at all! We learn that "Clitophon actually embraces the body of a woman killed by the pirates in Leucippe's clothes in her place" (Perkins, *Roman Imperial Identities*, 53).

42. Bowersock, *Fiction as History*, 119.
43. Bynum, *The Resurrection of the Body*, 27.

the false death fictions since in these fictions, the ending is always a happy one because they are unreal. Therefore, following the lead of Van Eijik, Bynum concludes that Ignatius' "martyrdom *is* resurrection."[44] Therefore, wanting complete destruction "so that his followers will not be endangered by the need to bury his remains, Ignatius nonetheless says he will rise 'with' or 'by' his chains, which are, he says, 'pearls'—an odd phrase, which seems to mean that whatever it is that rises, Ignatius's suffering is never to be lost because it is *who he is*."[45] Thus, this understanding is seen as being very consistent with the false death fictions. But is this really how Ignatius sees his death (that is, a reenactment of these false death stories)? Again, I will address this question as I take an in-depth look into the concept of death in the second-century martyrs.

On a more nuanced note, Bynum also sees the connection between these fictions and early Christian literature on death in terms of the material continuity between both. Speaking of the key metaphor of the seed in the development of the resurrection belief, she notes that this metaphor expresses a "rather crude material continuity."[46] According to her, such continuity is "both defense against and an articulation of the threat of decay, which is understood as an absorption or digestion. Nutrition (eating or being eaten—especially cannibalism) is the basic image of positive change and the basic threat to identity."[47] Thus, according to Bynum, the second-century Christian emphasis on the indestructibility and continuity of the material body clearly corresponds to the false death fictions whereby, in actuality, no death takes place.

Finally, Perkins offers a more complicated analysis of the relationship between these fictions and the second-century Christian views of death. First, in agreement with Bynum, she sees the similarity in both in the fact that no lasting destruction takes place. "In the fictive narratives," she writes, "the elite protagonists escape threats of being eaten alive or killed. In the Christian texts, where such threats are carried out, they have no lasting effect."[48] Thus, according to her, the Christian narratives

---

44. Ibid. See also Eijik, *La résurrection des morts chez les Péres apostoliques*, 122–23.

45. Bynum, *The Resurrection of the Body*, 47.

46. Ibid., 27.

47. Ibid.

48. Perkins, *Roman Imperial Identities*, 54. She quotes the example of the stories of the martyrs of Lyons whereby the treatment of their bodies indicates that the Christians must have boasted of the inviolability of their bodies. According to Henten and Avemarie, the *Martyrdom of Lyons* (177 CE) indicates that even the death of the

assert an equal claim like that of the false death fictions: "Although Christian bodies may appear wounded, mutilated, or even destroyed, they are nevertheless inviolable."[49]

Second, and most significantly, Perkins sees the relationship of both in terms of a "power discourse." In other words, both false death fictions and early Christian views of death "use the language of mutilated body to construct their particular responses to Roman hegemony and to the essential question of power: who counts as fully human."[50] In this case, therefore, the relationship between both kinds of literature is that not of influence per se, but that of response to a common foe: Rome. She concludes:

> Christians trumped this message. They insisted on their bodies' resilience through the doctrine of material resurrection. Their bodies would endure. This was a potent political statement as well as a religious one. The relationship between false deaths and Christian resurrection is likely not one of influence, but rather the responses of two different social constituencies using a closely related register of themes (mutilation, consumption, death, and survival) to address the changing political and social landscape of empire.[51]

Indeed, in the case of the Christians, this message was more powerful than the one communicated by the false death fictions. This is because although the false death fiction involved the elite, in the case of Christians, the "doctrine of material resurrection could offer to these non-elite their own 'apparent deaths.'"[52] Thus, just as it was the case with the false deaths whereby there is always a happy ending and where the "provincial elite asserted their luck and resiliency and their ability to survive Rome's partners in power," the Christians' insistence on the indestructibility of

---

martyrs did not satisfy the mob who had savagely tortured them in the first place. The mob "prevented the burial of the martyrs' bodily remains at the instigation of the devil (5.1.57–63). They burn the bodies and throw the remains into the Rhone, assuming—wrongly, of course, in the view of the author—that they had eliminated every possibility for the martyrs to be resurrected in this way" (Henten and Avemarie, *Martyrdom and Noble Death*, 121).

49. Ibid.

50. Perkins, *Roman Imperial Identities*, 57. For a thorough evaluation of this thesis, see Gleason, "Truth Contests," 287–313.

51. Perkins, *Roman Imperial Identities*, 57.

52. Ibid., 56.

the body because of the belief in the material resurrection made their response to the Roman persecution a political statement.[53]

Conclusion

In summary, therefore, the concept of death in early Christianity has either been understood as a total contrast to the Greco-Roman concepts of death or a total continuation of the same concepts (Hellenization). The latter view has dominated modern scholarship. The possibility that second-century Christians carefully selected, modified, and adapted the existing views on death in order to present a distinctively Christian view of death that reflected their specific circumstances and the level of revelation that they had, although hinted to, has never been fully explored. For example, in his response to Cullmann, Harry Wolfson argued that indeed the Fathers conceived the soul as immortal, just as the Greeks did. The point of departure, according to him, was that the church fathers did not conceive the soul as immortal *by nature*.[54] Rather, they saw immortality as a gift graciously given to individuals by God.[55] However, a thorough exploration of how Christians critically utilized existing ideas of death to present a distinctive Christian view of death is still lacking. The possibility that although second-century Christians used the existing terminology and metaphors to explain their understanding of death, they meant something different from what these cultures meant, needs to be critically examined.[56]

The Need for This Study

The present book seeks to fill this gap. As noted above, this is not a new concern. It has been the concern of a number of scholars over the centuries. Nevertheless, a treatment that seeks to offer a critical analysis of the metaphors and terminology that second-century Christians use to

---

53. Ibid., 57.

54. Wolfson, "Immortality and Resurrection," 56.

55. Ibid., 57.

56. A number of scholars have hinted to this adaptation, albeit with the use of different terminology. For example, Harry A. Wolfson argued that church fathers "recast" certain teachings of both Jewish and Greek philosophy to produce a "Christian version of Greek philosophy" (Wolfson, *The Philosophy of the Church Fathers: Faith, Trinty*, vi).

describe death in relation to the surrounding ideas about death and their varying occasions, is missing. Most scholars have tended to treat each individual Father's view of death, without necessarily making the connection to the entire developing concept of death in the second century.[57] Furthermore, most writers seek to interpret the concept of death in the second century purely within the Greco-Roman metaphors for death, without taking into account the Christian modification of these terms and metaphors. This book will address all of these concerns.

This subject was chosen because of the lack of attention on the subject of death as it relates to the development of a matrix of other pivotal doctrines—especially that of God—in the formative era of the second century.[58] That is, although there are many and useful scholarly works on the subject of death in the Old Testament, the Greco-Roman culture as well as the Middle Ages, the same seems not to be exactly the case with this formative era in the history of Christianity. Obviously, there are significant treatments of some aspects of the understanding of man (such as the soul, body, etc.). Thus, this book seeks to fill this void in the understanding of this aspect of Christianity during this very key era in the history of Christianity.[59]

57. Brian Daley's *The Hope of the Early Church* is an exception here. Indeed, as Daley himself observes, a comprehensive sketch of the eschatological themes in early Christianity is missing. However, his work treats the *entirety* of the eschatological themes of the fathers. Thus, while I certainly share his concerns here, my work deals specifically with the concept of death (Daley, *The Hope of the Early Church*, xi).

58. There are key treatments of some tenets of man in Early Christianity. Most of the literature deals with the issue of the resurrection and how it played into the entire process of the formation of the young Christian community or on some aspect of anthropology (either the soul or the body or both). For the former, please, see Setzer, *Resurrection of the Body*; Setzer, "Resurrection of the Body"; Goldsmith, "The Function of Jesus' Resurrection"; Perkins, *Roman Imperial Identities*. For the latter, see Reeve, "The Theological Anthropology of Theophilus of Antioch"; Gousmett, "Shall the Body Strive and Not be Crowned?"; Tripolitis, "The Doctrine of the Soul." Finally, others focus on the entire concept of martyrdom. See, for example McNamara, *Apocalyptic Eschatological Heritage*; Bakker, "Exemplar domini"; Karin, *Weizen Gottes*; Greenberg, *My Share of God's Reward*; Groh, "Agents of Victory"; McNamara, "Ignatius of Antioch on his Death"; and Mellink, *Death as Eschaton*. A very recent dissertation on the subject is Toews, "Biblical Sources in the Development of the Concept of the Soul."

59. The lack of full-length scholarly treatment of specific aspects of patristic eschatology was noted by Brian Daley in his *The Hope of the Early Church*. For example, on page xi, he helpfully noted: "When, after a long delay due to doctoral studies, I began research on the project in earnest, I discovered that despite the breadth and obvious importance of the subject, and despite the enormous mass of scholarly literature on eschatological themes in various Patristic authors and periods, no single large-scale

The book is divided into two parts in addition to the introduction that traces the concept of death in the Old Testament, the New Testament and the Greco-Roman culture. The first part consists of the writings of the second-century Christians on the concept of death. The second part consists of an evaluation of the concept of death in the second century as expressed through the attitudes towards the dead and the treatment of the remains of the same. In this case, such questions as the attitude and treatment of the material remains of the dead (whether eaten by beasts or buried) will be addressed.

A Note on Methodology

Our methodology in this study will be based on both a selection of the key passages in the writings of second-century Christians on the concept of death and historical and theological analyses of the key terminology and metaphors for death during this time. In other words, after identifying the specific passages in the writings of second-century Christians where the idea of death comes to surface, we will highlight the specific terminology and/or metaphors that the specific works use to express the idea of death. As we will demonstrate, these early Christians spoke about death in images and metaphors. This approach seems to be mostly because of the paradoxical situation that these Christians faced on this difficult subject of death. Living daily in its reality through persecution, these Christians also knew that they were living in the post-resurrection period of Jesus Christ. Thus, although Christians died, they did not explain death as believers had done in the pre-resurrection period. Reflecting this changed attitude towards death, Vassiliades observes:

> Now we do not die the way we died before the resurrection of the Lord; we do not die with the death that was the result of condemnation of Adam and Eve, because condemnation ceased to exist any longer, since with the grace of the resurrection, corruption has ceased and disappeared. Subsequently, only the mortal part of the body will decay and that at a time which the Lord has appointed for each of us. This happens in order that we might be worthy of a better resurrection, because as seed is

---

survey exists of the whole development of ancient Christian eschatological hope." I feel that what Daley says about the lack of the treatment of the development of the eschatological hope in the early church can justifiably be said about the subject of death. This present study will serve a purpose akin to what Daley's book serves.

sown in the earth and does not disappear, so it is with us; when we die, we do not disappear with dissolution but we will rise as if we have been sown, because death has been abolished with the grace of our Savior "to be able to achieve a better resurrection."[60]

As well, recognizing the fact that these terms and metaphors occur within a specific cultural milieu (especially the Greco-Roman culture), for each key term or metaphor, I will offer a brief exegesis of its use and meaning within that cultural milieu.

In summary, we will start by briefly looking at the concept of death within the Old Testament, the late-Second Temple Period and the Intertestamental period, arguing that although there are myriad concepts of death during this time, there is a general agreement the soul survives physical death. Where the soul goes after death remains a matter of debate. Next, we will deal with the concept of death in the Greco-Roman culture. This treatment serves as the basis for the discussion of especially the martyrs' concept of death. Such key concepts of death as sacrifice, discipleship, and imitation, clearly have their origins in the Greco-Roman culture. Depending on which Greek or Roman idea of death one looks at, death was either seen as the flight of the soul from the body (Platonism) or a total annihilation of the individual (Epicureanism). But, as I will demonstrate, second-century Christians adapted and modified these concepts to fit their distinctively Christian concept of death that was commensurate to the level of revelation that they had at the moment since the documents that were to eventually become the New Testament were still being collected. As we will point out, some aspects of the Greek concept of death are evident particularly in Valentinian Gnostic idea of *apolytrosis* (soul-flight). Finally, as far as the necessary background is concerned, I will deal with the concept of death in the New Testament.

With the groundwork for the discussion having been set, I will investigate the concept of death in the thought of second-century Christians. We will start particularly with the Fathers who come immediately after the apostles (the Apostolic Fathers). For the sake of investigation, I have divided these into the non-martyriological and martyriological Apostolic Fathers. This is based on the conviction that the specific occasions of the particular fathers play a significant role in their understanding of death. While the non-martyriological fathers such as *1 Clement* and *The Shepherd of Hermas* use terms and metaphors that signify calmness in death

---

60. Vassiliades, "The Mystery of Death," 278.

such as "sleep," (verb κοιμῶμαι and noun κοίμασις), faced with immediate execution, martyriological fathers use such terms as "sacrifice" and the "attainment" of God that stress what they hope to achieve at death. I will follow this with an investigation of the concept of death in Valentinian Gnosticism, the apologists and the polemicists. Because of her organized nature, Valentinian Gnostic concept of death (*apolytrosis*) offers a good perspective of other concepts of death in the second century to which the apologists respond. This serves as the launching point for my investigation of the apologists' and the polemicists' view of death. With their view of death generally as a temporary and necessary cleansing dissolution of the body in order to be recast, the apologists and the polemicists finally connect death with the grand program of God of getting man back to where he initially was before his disobedience to God. Finally, I hope to demonstrate the change from cremation as the method of the disposal of bodies that was practiced in the Greco-Roman culture to the Christian inhumation is proof of the distinctively Christian concept of death in the second century.

CONCEPTS OF DEATH IN ANTIQUITY

In this section, we will argue that the concepts of death in antiquity played a significant role as conversational partners for the formulation of the concept of death in second-century Christian thought. Evidence throughout the writings of the Fathers of the church during this time reveals awareness, adaptation, modification and utilization of these views in the formulation of their own concept of death.

Biblical Definition of Death

Before talking about the concept of death in the Old Testament, it is needful to define death. Although there is an agreement that each philosophy or theology must confront the significant issue of "what is death," almost everybody acknowledges the difficulty of offering a simple answer to the question. Johnston is surely correct to observe that death "is a profound and complex subject," evoking a wide range of responses by all kinds of human beings irrespective of age, education, culture, ideology or belief.[61] Martin-Achard, quoting Père Féret, justly observes that "from whatever

---

61. Johnston, *Shades of Sheol*, 23.

INTRODUCTION

angle we approach it, and that of the Biblical tradition is no exception, the question of death is not a simple one."[62]

According to the *Theological Dictionary of the Old Testament*, the Hebrew verb, "to die," מות, and its cognates occurs six hundred and thirty times in the qal meaning "die" and polel nine times meaning to "kill off, give the death-blow, slay," as well as the polal participle meaning "those who should be killed" in the Old Testament. In addition, it occurs 138 times in the hiphil meaning to kill someone or have someone executed, as well as sixty-eight times in the hophal meaning to "be killed" or "suffer death."[63] Together with its synonyms like to "lie down to sleep" or to "depart," the term and its cognates means "the departure of the *nepes*."[64]

However, even with the understanding of death as the natural end of life in the Old Testament, there was the agreement that something continued to exist after death. Although I will come back to this in my discussion of the view of death in the Old Testament in the following section, it is clear that "although the departed no longer lives, he nonetheless continues in existence. He does not entirely vanish away, his existence goes on, but under such conditions as do not deserve the name of life.[65]

The two key corresponding Greek words are θάνατος and ἀποκτείνω. Ἀποκτείνω means to kill, and "expresses any kind of violent ending to (someone else's, only later one's own) life. It can thus mean to kill, have put to death, murder, and execute."[66] It is related to the term τελευτάω, which originally meant to come to an end, complete or fulfill.[67] Later, it also came to mean to die or lose one's life. However, by far, the most significant term used to describe death in Greek is θάνατος. As used by Homer, it means "the act of dying or the state of death."[68] As well, it is also used of mortal danger, the manner of death or even death penalty.[69] This

---

62. Féret, "La mort dans la tradition biblique," 16.

63. Illman, "מות," 190.

64. Johnston, *Shades of Sheol*, 25. This understanding is clearly opposed to some who define death as merely the "weakest state of being," in Israel and the ancient Near Eastern religions. For this view, see Greenspoon, "The Origin of the Idea of Resurrection," 247–331. For a response, see England, "An Investigation of Resurrection Language," 27–30.

65. Martin-Achard, *From Death to Life*, 17.

66. Schmithals, "Death, Kill, Sleep," 429.

67. Ibid.

68. Ibid., 430.

69. Ibid.

term in classical Greek usage does not mean the end of human existence. Rather, in classical Greek thought, the dead continue to exist in a shadowy manner in a place called ᾅδης, which, although originally referred to the Greek god of death, came to mean the shadowy place of the dead and translated in Hebrew *Sheol*.[70] But whatever we may say of this continued existence, it certainly cannot be regarded as life, for, according to Greeks, "what is called life is destroyed by death, and none can talk away the terror of death (Hom. *Od.*, 11. 487). Life is the supreme good."[71] It should be pointed out that this was the general understanding death among the Greeks. The three exceptions to this were, first, the understanding that some heroes were translated to the isles of the blessed, second, the Orphic and Pythagorean belief that death is the liberation of the soul that is imprisoned in the body, and, third, the belief in the transmigration of the souls (*metempsychosis*). Otherwise, the general understanding of death among the Greeks was that "death is accepted as the end of life and therefore as something quite terrible."[72] Thus, both in the Old Testament and classical Greek literature, death is seen as an enemy to be dreaded. It is the common destiny of all men. Indeed, its negative side is seen when death is personified in Greek mythology as a demon or monster from the underworld (Eur., *Alcestis* 28ff).[73]

The New Testament's definition of death seems to be clearly in continuity with the Old Testament view. It can be summarized as follows: the mortality of man is taken as a self-evident fact and man lives in the shadow of death (Matt 4:16; Isa 9:1 LXX). In contrast, God is seen as the one to whom immortality belongs (1 Tim 6:16) since he is the source of all life. As in Judaism, "death is always taken as the death of an individual, and the possibility of relativizing death by reference to the continuing life is foreign to the NT thought."[74]

This is how I will be using the term "death" in this book. It is the cessation of the biological function of the individual as a result of the departure of the soul from the body. It is the departure of the "life force." It is the reversal of the act of God of breathing the breath of life into man so that he could become a living being (Gen 2:7). It is the belief that after

---

70. Jeremias, "ᾅδης," 146.
71. Bultmann, "θάνατος, θνήσκω, ἀποθνήσκω, συναποθνήσκω," 8.
72. Ibid.
73. Schmithals, "Death," 431.
74. Ibid., 435.

the end of life as we know it, something continues to live on. Although there are myriad opinions as to what that "thing" is or how it continues to exist, the belief that it continues to exist after death is near unanimous since the time of poetic Greek. It has continued to be the majority view ever since. For believers, this is the immaterial aspect of man, the breath of life: the soul.

The Origin of Death

Before presenting a summary of the book's chapters as well as how each contributes to the development of my overall thesis, a brief answer to the following key question is offered: *what is the origin of death?* In other words, understanding physical death as the cessation of the biological functions of the human person, how did it start in the first place? Was, to use some popular terminology, man created immortal or mortal (that is, was he created never to die or was he created to eventually die)?[75]

Paul deals with this question in his classic comparison of Christ and Adam in Romans 5:12–21. Particularly, he notes in 5:12 that καὶ διὰ τῆς ἁμαρτίας ὁ θάνατος ("and through sin death"). As Cranfield notes, it is clear that Paul has Genesis 2:17 in his mind here.[76] As we recall, the Genesis passage is where God prohibited Adam from eating from the fruit of the tree in the middle of the Garden of Aden. As God declared to Adam, "for in the day you will eat of it, you shall die." As scholars have observed many times, the mood of the verb מות expresses "a strong degree of certainty: *must die, will surely die, yes you will die*, or the like."[77] It is an imperfect with an absolute infinitive, translated; "dying thou shalt die."[78] In other words, it is an issue of certainty. The problem, as commentators have noted, is that man did not die immediately

---

75. The term "immortality" is used here is different from the way it was used in Orphic and Pythagorean circles whereby the soul was seen as eternal (that is, having not originated in the creative act). Rather, I am using it here as it has sometimes been used in Christian circles. Here, it is used to refer to the fact that although man has his origin in the creative act of God, he was created never to die.

76. Cranfield, *The Epistle to the Romans*, 294.

77. Bandstra, *Genesis 1–11*, 145.

78. Leupold, *Exposition of Genesis*, vol. 1, 128. According to Delitzsch, the infinitive intensive before "dying" strengthens the certainty of what is threatened (Delitzsch, *A New Commentary on Genesis*, 138.)

after eating the fruit of the forbidden tree. He, in fact, lived for another 530 years (Gen 5:5)!

In short, therefore, this takes us back to square one: was man created mortal or immortal? Indeed, there have been myriad approaches towards the understanding of the meaning of God's threat, given the fact that man lived all these years after his disobedience.[79] A crosscheck of commentaries on Genesis 2:17 shows that there is no agreement on whether man was created mortal or immortal. Generally, there are three broad approaches towards understanding this passage as it relates to the question of whether man was created to eventually die or never to die unless he transgresses God's commands.

First, there are those who argue that man was created immortal, but became mortal by virtue of eating the prohibited fruit. Thus, had man not eaten this fruit, he and his wife would have lived naturally forever. However, as others have noted, this understanding is somehow contradicted by the existence of the tree of life also (Gen 3:22). In this understanding, "the text regards immortality more as a possibility than an actuality. It hinges on one's partaking of the tree of life, by which Adam could have lived forever even after the fall."[80] Delitzsch sees the tree of life as possessing, in a sacramental manner, the power of immortality just as the tree

---

79. An interesting exchange took place between Barr and Moberly on this subject. The fight was on whether it was the Serpent who got it right since, as he told Eve, she and her husband did not die after eating the fruit from the tree in the middle of the Garden. Barr contended that God's words here appear unreliable in Barr, *The Garden of Eden*, 10–11. This triggered a response by Moberly in his review of the book whereby he noted that Barr had said that God had lied. Barr responded, arguing that Moberly had basically misunderstood his language (see Barr, "Is God a Liar?" 1–22). Rather, he clarified that after Adam and Eve ate the fruit, God simply became interested in other matters and never said anything again about His prior threat. As expected, Moberly responded by arguing that Barr minimized the weight of God's prohibition here ("what the fuss about a mere apple,") arguing that, instead, we should understand the prohibition seriously and treat the death metaphorically in Moberly, "Did the Interpreters Get it Right?" 34. "My thesis," he writes, "*is that the apparent non-realization of God's warning leads the reader to reread and rethink the meaning of the story only thus to construe 'die' metaphorically . . .* this is the writer's explicit purpose ('the writer's concern is with the fact that, in general, disobedience to God does not meet with any such penalty, and that therefore the relationship between human disobedience and divine judgment is to most appearances ambiguous')," ibid., 35–36. Unfortunately, by the time Moberly published this response, Barr was already dead and the fruitful conversation could no longer continue.

80. Pyne, "The Resurrection as Restoration," 165.

of the knowledge of good and evil possessed mortality.[81] Thus, the tree of life seems "redundant had man been created with natural immortality."[82]

The other common interpretation of the passage is that man was created mortal, but with the possibility of immortality. This is what is technically known as "conditional immortality." Clarifying, Cassuto, after assessing other possibilities, concludes:

> The natural meaning of the words requires us to understand them in accordance with what I have stated above: when you eat of the tree of the knowledge it shall be decreed against you never to be able to eat of the tree of life, that is, you will be unable to achieve eternal life and you will be compelled one day to succumb to death; *you shall die*, in actual fact. It was necessary to use simple words like *you shall die*, because prior to his eating of the tree of knowledge man was unsophisticated as a child who knows nothing, and he could not have comprehended a more elaborate warning.[83]

It is important to point out that, according to this view, Adam would eventually have died even if he had not sinned, but need not have.[84] According to John Calvin, man's "earthly life truly would have been temporal; yet he would have passed into heaven without death and without injury."[85] Thus, as Erickson put it, "previously he [man] *could* die; now he *would* die."[86]

Finally, there are those who hold the view that man was created mortal and there is no connection between his inevitable death and Adam's disobedience. While discussing the concept of life in the Bible, for example, von Rad notes regarding Genesis chapter 3:

---

81. Delitzsch, *Genesis*, 139.

82. Pyne, "The Resurrection as Restoration," 165.

83. Cassuto, *A Commentary on the Book of Genesis*, 125. Cassuto offers a number of views on what "you shall die" means. These are, first, that there shall come upon man afflictions cruel as death; second, that man shall fail to attain the full measure of life that was originally allotted him, that is, a thousand years; third, that man shall be deserving death which will overtake him whenever God wills it; four, that death here is an exaggerated statement whose purpose is to restrain man from sinning, and, fifth, that the words were intended literally but God tempered with their severity after man depended (ibid., 124–25).

84. Pyne, "The Resurrection as Restoration," 166.

85. Calvin, *Genesis*, 36. This view is also expressed by Lionel, "The Bible and the People," 105.

86. Erickson, *Christian Theology*, 613.

Something fails in man the further he moves from his creation. J sees in this shortening of life a form of divine punishment (Gn 6:3). It is thus brought into close connection with human sin. The important question arises whether according to this view of J life was given a fixed span at the fall. This must be answered in the negative. No sentence of death is pronounced. The curse is not death, but making of life bitter. Hence the OT does not teach that death is the penalty of sin. Only an early or dishonorable or unusual death is regarded as a punishment.[87]

This is the same view expressed by W. Schmithals when he writes:

Death itself is not a divine punishment, since it was not part of the intention of creation that man should be immortal. Adam was threatened with *early* death as a punishment for a definite act of disobedience; after the fall had taken place he was punished merely by exclusion from the garden of Eden. Even in Ps 90, which refers back to the story of the fall and reflects upon the connection between—sin and death, it is never death, but the fleeting nature of life, which is attributed to human sin (cf. also Ps 51;14:2).[88]

So the question is, where does this leave us? Was man created mortal, irrespective of whether or not he obeyed God? Are these conclusions warranted, in other words?

It seems, however, these conclusions (that man was created mortal and his disobedience had nothing to do with his mortality) are in conflict with the natural reading of the text of Genesis 3. Von Rad, for example, fails to take Genesis 3:19 as part of the God's curse as a consequence of man's disobedience.[89] But as Allen Ross notes, these curses form a package. "The original sin of Adam and Eve," he writes, "brought into the race the conflict between good and evil, with the consequent painful toil, hardship, alienation, and [eventually], death."[90] And, as far as Schmithal's argument is concerned, it seems like he is reading too much of later Old Testament texts into the Genesis account. Although there are many texts that state that man is dust and must return to dust (that is, mortal by nature), it should be understood that all these texts refer to the state of man *after* the fall. As Pyne observes, "Schmithals errs by saying that God never

---

87. Rad, "ζάω," 844.
88. Schmithals, "Death," 433.
89. Pyne, "The Resurrection as Restoration," 167.
90. Ross, *Creation and Blessing*, 148.

intended for man to be immortal."[91] He continues to conjecture that "man was originally intended to eat from the tree of life and live forever."[92]

In conclusion, therefore, although the creation accounts are a bit ambiguous concerning the question of whether man was created mortal or immortal, it seems fair to conclude that man was created mortal with immortality as a possibility. This view is based, as noted above, on the presence of the tree of life which "implies mortality."[93] Further, this view is apparently "confirmed when the death sentence is fulfilled not immediately but by banishment from the tree of life."[94] Thus, man was created mortal but with the opportunity for immortality, which he lost because of his disobedience. Calvin's point that had not man disobeyed, then he would have passed to heaven and eternity without defect, suffering, injury and death, makes sense here.[95]

Finally, as the events of Genesis 2 and 3 come to close, death becomes part of man's life here on earth. All men begin to be referred as "mortals," pointing to their eventual separation of the body and soul at death. Two chapters later in Genesis, we have a list of genealogies whose recurring refrain is "and he died." This state of living with death as the ever present enemy would only be overcome by God, who, according to Deuteronomy 32:39, is the one who is able to kill and make life.

Death in the Old Testament

Our purpose in this section is to show that the second-century views of death are consistent with, but also an advancement of those held by Old Testament believers. In other words, the same pessimism and optimism towards death that we see in early Christianity is what we see in the Old Testament and the ancient Near East. As Illman and Ringgren summarize, in the ancient Near East, "the attitude toward death vacillates between pessimism and optimism. Generations pass away . . . . They build buildings, their places are no more . . . . No one returns from

---

91. Pyne, "The Resurrection as Restoration," 167.
92. Ibid.
93. Johnston, "Death and Resurrection," 443.
94. Ibid.
95. Calvin, *Genesis*, 36.

over (there).''[96] But, as I will demonstrate, second-century Christians will stress the optimistic aspect more than the pessimistic aspect.

As noted above, the Hebrew term for death, מות, together with its cognates, occurs more than one thousand times in the Old Testament. With its noun *môt* being found in many ancient Near Eastern communities like Egypt, the term means the loss of life, "be dead, die."[97] That is, its "semantic field emerges quite naturally from circumstances. The antithesis to 'to live' ... occurs frequently, and combinations such as 'as a dead person or as a living person ('dead or alive'), 'not to die, but rather to live,' 'to love life and to hate death' are all frequently attested" in the ancient Near East.[98] As such, therefore, in the ancient Near East, death was understood to be something natural, part of the cosmic order and something inescapable. When it comes, it steals away "the infant which is on its mother's lap like him who has reached old age."[99]

Before offering a summary of the views of death in the Old Testament, it is necessary to emphasize what death was not. This necessity has been created by some ongoing attempts to redefine death in the Old Testament and ancient Near East in terms of merely the weakest state of being. Greenspoon, for example, citing such passages as Psalms 31:12; 88:4–6; 143:3; and Lamentations 3:6, concluded that anyone suffering from grave illness or any other serious distress is "already experiencing life draining death."[100] As England notes, the existence of elaborate funerary rites for the dead in these cultures indicates that they understood death as bodily and actual.[101] In short, we do not have elaborate funerary rites for the living however weak they may be.

According to the Old Testament, death is universal and natural. It is the departure of the *nepeš*, that is, the departure of life from the body. In death, "a person lies down (to sleep, *šākab*) or departs (*hlk*)."[102] That

---

96. Illman, "מות," 187–88.
97. Ibid., 187.
98. Ibid.
99. Ibid.
100. Greenspoon, "The Origin of the Idea of Resurrection," 257.
101. England, "An Investigation of Resurrection Language," 31.
102. Illman, "מות," 191. The concept of death as "sleep" plays a significant role in the New Testament and Early Christianity's view of death. But, as I will demonstrate, the metaphor undergoes modification to grasp an understanding of death that reflects further revelation and changing occasions as evidenced by these writings. This understanding necessitates an elaborate study of this metaphor in Early Christianity.

is, for the Israelites, when a person dies, his breath, *ruah*, is withdrawn. Indeed, the Old Testament clearly explains that the breath, that is, the spirit of man, is not originally from man. It came from God. According to Ecclesiastes 12:7, the dust (flesh) returns to the dust while the spirit goes back to God who gave it.

The Old Testament also makes it clear that upon death, a person does not completely vanish. His existence goes on, but "under such conditions as do not deserve the name of life."[103] In this case, death is not seen as the antithesis of life. It is, rather, "conceived as a state in which the powers of life are at their lowest ebb, as a shade remains, some undefinable and insubstantial vestige of the individual formerly full of force and activity in the land of the living."[104] As such, therefore, death is seen not only as natural, but as an enemy. It is seen as the bitter enemy of life, often personified as "a hunter with traps and snares, a marauding shepherd, as an insatiable glutton" (Ps 55:4; Ecc 7:26; Pss 18:4; 49:14).[105]

In summary, according to the Old Testament, death is understood as something that affects the whole person. However, something that is difficult to define (spirit, soul, etc.) escapes the dissolution of the corpse at death. That is, rather than descent to nothingness, the Old Testament understands the dead as continuing in some hard to define sort of existence. The dead are seen as existing in two paradoxical states. On the one hand, they are seen as mere shadows or vestiges of the individuals that they formerly were. In this case, they deserve the pity and support of the living. On the other hand, they are seen as possessing power akin to that of the divines (or even demons). In this case, the living must reckon with their power which can either be used for good or evil.[106] These two conceptions of the dead determined the treatment of the dead in the Old Testament. Chapter 4 of this work deals with how the dead were treated in Israel, the Greco-Roman world and early Christianity.

---

103. Martin-Achard, *From Death to Life*, 17. In addition, the Old Testament also uses such sweet phrases like "passed away," "passed on," "gone to heaven," or is "no longer with us". Even more curious is the phrase "gathered to his people." However, this last phrase most probably refers to the fact that the departed was buried in the family tomb, as was the custom in the Old Testament (see Hallote, *Death, Burial, and the Afterlife*, 43).

104. Ibid.

105. Johnston, *Shades of Sheol*, 28. Thus, although there are a few passages that talk about death as a friend, the general consensus of the Old Testament testimony is that death is a bitter enemy (see Job 3:13; 17).

106. Martin-Achard, *From Death to Life*, 16–18.

Concerning the destiny of the departed in the Old Testament, Routledge notes that "what is less clear is what the Old Testament has to say about life beyond the grave."[107] Although it was generally agreed that the dead went to Sheol, what that meant has been the subject of much discussion. A term used sixty-six times and whose meaning continues to be debated, Sheol is variously described as a "shadowy place" (Job 10:21–22; Ps 143:3), a place of ancestral re-union (Gen 15:15; 25:8; 35:29; 37:35; 49:33; Num 20:24; 28; 31:2; Deut 32:50; 2 Sam 12:23), a place that is "down" or "beneath the earth" (Job 11:8; Isa 44:23; 57:9; Ezek 26:20; Amos 9:2).[108]

However, recently, the understanding of Sheol as a monolithic place has been questioned.[109] As Merrill and Heidel argue, it is futile to attempt to recover the etymology of the Hebrew שְׁאוֹל.[110] My tentative inclination is to agree with Levenson that the experience of the dead in Sheol depended on their spiritual state at the time of death. "Sheol is best conceived," he writes, "as a kind of continuation of the end of the deceased's life. If the deceased has died prematurely, violently, bereft of children, rejected by God, or brokenhearted, he faces Sheol."[111] Thus, although Sheol is pestilential, not all who die experience its sufferings in the same manner or degree. Rather, in a summary statement that encapsulates the entire view of death in the Old Testament, Levenson notes that "the pattern predominant in the Hebrew Bible is the duality of the death that closes a fortunate life, one blessed by God, and the death that prolongs an unfortunate life, one lived, for whatever reason, outside the blessing of God."[112] In other words, although all the dead in the Old Testament go to Sheol, the righteous go there to await resurrection to everlasting blessedness while the others go there to await resurrection to everlasting damnation.

This view of Sheol as a double-leveled place (one level for the wicked and the other for the righteous), seems to be the result of an internal development of the Jewish view of death. In the pre-exilic period, death was seen as the end of everything human. In other words, death was "the end of the individual from the practical point of view. There was little thought of full personal survival. The dead are in the grave. To die is to go

---

107. Routledge, "Death and Afterlife," 22.
108. Morey, *Death and the Afterlife*, 78.
109. See for example Johnston, *Shades of Sheol*.
110. See Merrill, "שְׁאוֹל," 6; Heidel, *The Gilgamesh Epic*, 173.
111. Levenson, *Resurrection and the Restoration of Israel*, 77.
112. Ibid., 81.

down to the grave (Pss 15:10; 30:9; 55:23)."[113] However, as the Old Testament progresses, it also makes it clear that God, who created everything in the first place, will ultimately overthrow death. From the famous song of Moses to the effect that God is the only One powerful enough to kill and make alive (Deut 32:39) to Isaiah's declaration that God will swallow up death forever (Isa 25:8), the Old Testament clearly teaches that God's power will ultimately overcome death.[114]

In conclusion, the Old Testament concept of death is a muddled one. Of all the terms and metaphors used in the Old Testament to define and describe death, it is the metaphor of death as "sleep" that dominates the understanding of the concept of death in the second-century Christian thought. In his significant exploration of the meaning of the term šākhābh, Ogle noted that the metaphor first appears in Kings and Chronicles in the traditional phrase: "he sleeps with his fathers."[115] Specifically, the term occurs in such passages as 1 Kings 1:21; 2:10; 2 Kings 4:32; 1 Chronicles 17:11; 2 Chronicles 16:13; Ezekiel 31:18; 32:20–32; Job 3:11–14; 14:12; 21:26; Psalms 3:6; 4:9; 87:6; Jeremiah 2:33 and 28:39.[116] Although there is a mixture of literal and metaphorical usage of the term "sleep" in these passages, when the Fathers use them, the passages "received an anagogical or metaphorical interpretation."[117] I will explore these further as I take a deeper look at the usage of the term κοιμῶμαι ("sleep") in second-century Christian thought here below.

---

113. Hurst, "The Destiny of the Individual," 300.

114. See also 1 Sam 2:6 and 2 Kgs 5:7. Indeed, the Isaiah passage is seen as the basis for Paul's declaration that "when this perishable will have put on the imperishable, and this mortal will have put on immortality, then will come about the saying that is written, "Death is swallowed up in victory" (1 Cor 15:54). There have been a number of suggestions concerning the origins of a positive view of death in the Old Testament. The earliest suggestions pointed to a Jewish' borrowing of the views from their neighbors some of whom believed in the concept of the death and resurrection of their gods (see Birkeland, "The Belief in the Resurrection" 60–78. However, many scholars are on the opinion that these views developed internally within Judaism, the question of whether they were a result of evolution or revelation notwithstanding (see Spronk, *Beatific Afterlife in Ancient*, 65–66).

115. Ogle, "The Sleep of Death," 90.

116. Ibid., 91.

117. Ibid., 90.

Death in Greco-Roman Culture

It is impossible to talk about a single concept of death in Greek philosophy. This is because, as scholars have noted, there are a number of threads in Greek philosophy. At least, five threads of Greek philosophy have been noted. There were the Epicureans, Aristotelians, the Stoics, the Pythagoreans, and the Platonists. Later, Neoplatonism emerged as another key thread of Greek philosophy. However, as far as the question of what happens to the individual after death is concerned, it is the last two that had significant correspondence with early Christianity. The Stoics, for example, were agnostic and indifferent to the question of individual immortality.[118] "In the normal Stoic view," write Armstrong and Markus, "the destiny of the soul, either at death or at the conflagration which closed the Great Year, when the divine fire took all things back into itself, was absorption into the divine substance."[119] In other words, the Stoics were convinced that "both body and mind dissolved at death," urging people to make sure that they detach themselves from life, material possessions, their spouses in order to be able to bid farewell easily when it comes time to die (Epictetus, *Enchiridion* 7).[120] Thus, according to the Stoics, death is a pantheistic re-absorption of the individual into the divine.

The basis for this conception of death in Stoicism was its view of man. In Stoic anthropology, man was made up of the body and the soul. However, according to them, the soul was of "ether, a divine fragment."[121] At face value, this conception of man as having some part of the divine within itself can be read in terms of the biblical concept of the "image of God" in man. However, according to the first-century Hellenistic biblical exegete, Philo, this is not the case. He complained of some who "by asserting that our mind is a portion of the ethereal nature, have claimed for man a kinship with ether."[122] According to Philo, this is not what Moses meant by likening "the species of the rational soul to any created thing, but averred it to be a genuine coinage of that divine and invisible breath."[123] Indeed, what Philo illustrates here is essentially what I hope to demonstrate in this work, that is, although there is clear correspondence

---

118. Armstrong and Markus, *Christian Faith*, 43.
119. Ibid.
120. Bolt, "Life, Death, and the Afterlife," 68.
121. Wolfson, *Philo*, 394.
122. Philo, *Plant.* 5.18.
123. Ibid.

in terminology between Christianity and its cultural milieu, there is also a clear departure in the meaning. Wolfson's comment that "here as elsewhere, use is made by Philo of the Stoic vocabulary, but there is a departure from the Stoic doctrine," is applicable to many aspects of early Christian doctrinal thought.[124]

The Epicureans' view of death, on the other hand, which goes all the way back to Democritus (ca. 460–370 BC), is that at death both the body and the soul perish completely. Epictetus himself taught that the human body "dissolved into its component parts and disintegrated at death, so that in the end death does not affect a person (*Ad Menoeceum* 124; cf. Plutarch, *Moralia* 1103D, 1105A; Diogenes *Laertius* 10.139)."[125] In other words, both Stoicism and Epicureanism saw death as the disintegration of the person into nothingness. In a very similar manner, Aristotelians believed that after death, an individual is survived by the "impersonal 'active intellect,' the eternal principle which sets our thinking going ... which is identified by the greatest of Aristotelian commentators, Alexander of Aphrodisias ... with God, the first cause."[126] In Aristotelianism, however, this principle was not considered as part of the individual.[127] Thus, all of these three philosophical threads saw death as descend to nothingness. Since Christianity (and Judaism) has insisted from her inception that death is not descend to nothingness, we do not see a lot of interaction as far as the concept of death is concerned between these philosophies and Christianity. Rather, it is with Platonism that Christianity interacts. As Armstrong and Markus observe:

> Only in the dialogues of Plato and the contemporary teachings of Platonists, and of the adherents of a revived Pythagoreanism much influenced by Plato and hardly distinguishable from Platonism, could Christians find a doctrine of the survival of man's self, of his intellectual and moral personality, of judgment and rewards and punishments in the hereafter. And though ... there are serious differences between Christianity and Platonism, the Christians recognized the kinship of their teaching with

---

124. Wolfson, *Philo*, 395.
125. Bolt, "Life, Death, and the Afterlife," 67.
126. Armstrong and Markus, *Christian Faith*, 43–44.
127. Ibid., 44. Aristocles, the teacher of Alexander of Aphrodisias, is believed to have held the same view of death.

Platonism on these very important points by the Platonic view of the nature of man.[128]

This "kinship," we will argue, in second-century Christianity, manifested itself in the form of a critical adaptation in order to present a distinctively Christian view of death. But what was the Platonic concept of death?

Death in Platonism

Platonic concept of death underwent development over the centuries prior to its interaction with Christianity. Although, as Sonnemans has observed, it is impossible to reconstruct the individual stages of this development, some general observations in this process are possible.[129] According to Werner Jaeger, the earliest stage in this development was the poetic stage.[130] During this stage, emphasis was placed in the great cleavage between men and gods. While gods were understood as immortal, man (ἄνθρωπος/ἀνήρ) was mortal. "Indeed," writes Jaeger, "we look in vain in the Homeric epics, the *Iliad* and the *Odyssey*, for the view that men survive their bodies."[131] According to Homer, there is a difference between the person when he is alive (referred to as *autos* or himself) and when he is dead (referred to as *psychê*) or "that portion of man's being which departs to the world below."[132] Burkett clarifies that according to Homer, at death, "something, the psyche, leaves man . . . and enters the house of *Ais*, also known as *Aides*, *Aidoneus* and in Attic as *Hades*."[133] This *psychê*, which is not the soul, continues to exist as "*eidôlon*, a phantom image, like the image reflected in a mirror which can be seen, though not

---

128. Ibid.

129. Sonnemans, "Soul, Afterlife, Salvation," 250.

130. Jaeger, "The Greek Ideas," 99.

131. Ibid.

132. Garland, *The Greek Way of Death*, 1. This concept of man in Homer needs further elucidation. As Sonnemans clarifies, "Homer is familiar with the concepts *psychê* and *sôma* only for the deceased man; for the living man there are different expressions, particularly *thymós*, all of which signify his "life." The *thymós* is also separated from the living man (and animal) in death. But the *psyche*, the image of the entire man, is separated only from man. It must go to Hades, as must all *psychai*. The *sôma* the corpse, remains behind. For Homer the *psyche* is an eschatological concept and scientific a specific element of man" (Sonnemans, "Soul, Afterlife, Salvation," 250).

133. Burkert, *Greek Religion*, 195.

always clearly, but cannot be grasped; the dream image and the ghostly image, the forms in which the dead man can still appear."[134] Thus, the dead in this very ancient stage in the development of the concept of death in Greek thought were thought to exist in some form of shadowy state. However, in some cases, it was thought that the dead "could be a positive force for those who are still alive if they [the dead] were kept happy by offerings—or, if not, they could be an unhappy and malevolent force, being outraged and angry ghosts."[135]

There are differing opinions among scholars as to how Homer understood the state of the dead to be after crossing the river or lake Acherousian that "forms the boundary" between the dead and the living.[136] While some, like Jaeger, argue that the souls (ψυχαί) that cross this river/lake and enter into the house of Hades (εἰν'Αἴδαο δόμοισι) exist as "mere shadows without conscious life or mental activity," others see it otherwise.[137] For example, Burkert, while arguing that *psyche* became an unconscious shadowy image at death, also observes that the dead have so much power that they need to be constantly appeased and "kept in good spirits by continual offerings: *meilissien, hilaskesthai*."[138] Garland seems to oscillate between death as an unconscious existence and the power of the dead. In a summary of his understanding of the concept of death among the Greeks, he, after dealing with the difficulties involved in answering such a question, answers the question of the meaning of death according to the Greeks this way: death means loss of strength and power (the dead cannot control the living), lack of full command of one's faculties, loss of personality (according to *Iliad*), ignorance, as well as being defenseless and ineffective.[139] On a more positive note, he also sees the Greek dead as being divided into heroes and the ordinary, signifying that they also continue to have influence on the living.[140] One such influence involves their continued property rights. In other words, although, on the one hand, the dead are seen as unconscious and powerless, on the other hand, they are seen as active and powerful!

---

134. Ibid.
135. Bolt, "Life, Death, and the Afterlife," 66.
136. Burkert, *Greek Religion*, 197.
137. Jaeger, "The Greek Ideas," 99.
138. Burkert, *Greek Religion*, 195.
139. Garland, *The Greek Way of Death*, 2–7.
140. Ibid., 3.

Homer understood Hades (Ἀΐδης), to be a being (a god), whose realm of activity is the underworld (*Il.* 5.395).[141] Here, he is described as the "lord from below," a "brother of Zeus and Poseidon."[142] He is further described as a monster, who suffered under the son of Zeus, who "smote him in Pylos amid the dead, and gave him over to pains."[143] Thus, as Garland summarizes, as we continue to read about this Greek god, Homer tells us that he is implacable, relentless, most hated by the mortals and all the other gods, monstrous and strong. He concludes that "probably as god rather than as place he is on several occasions described as 'famous for his deeds.'"[144]

Even more elaborate, notes Garland, is the Homeric *Hymn to Demeter*. In this Hymn, Hades is presented in very graphic details as a god who is "dark-haired, a characteristic that he shares with his brother Poseidon."[145] As the hymn opens, we are introduced into the myth of the abduction of Demeter's daughter, Persephone, by Hades (here, the term Ἀιδωνεὺς, is used for Hades), a god who possesses "many names."[146] He transports her to the underworld, intending for her to be his queen. This raptures the great bond that exists between Demeter and her daughter, a bond that is "reestablished when Demeter's mourning forces the gods to return her daughter."[147] Hence, in all these presentations, Hades is presented as a person (that is, a god and not a realm). As Garland concludes, "In the Classical period, 'Hades' always refers to the god, never to his realm, descent to which [that is, to Hades] is described as '*es Haidou*' ('to the House of Hades)."[148] The same sentiment is expressed by Burkert who notes that "For the [Greek] poets, Aides/Hades is a personal god, brother of Zeus—hence known also as the other Zeus, the subterranean Zeus—and husband of Persephone whose mysterious name may point

---

141. See *Homer The Illiad*, 223.
142. Garland, *The Greek Way of Death*, 52.
143. *Homer The Illiad*, 225.
144. Garland, *The Greek Way of Death*, 52.
145. Ibid.
146. *Hesiod*, 289.
147. Lincoln, "The Rape of Persephone," 223.
148. Garland, *The Greek Way of Death*, 53. This is the same conclusion reached by Shipp, who writes that "In Hesiod, Ἀΐδης is, it seems, always god." However, he adds that in Θ 16, it is used to refer to the underworld (see Shipp, *Studies in the Language of Homer*, 265).

to a formerly independent, uncanny Great Goddess."[149] However, it was during the second stage of the development of the Greek concept of death that a clear concept of Hades as a place emerged.

The confusion exhibited by scholars concerning the state of the dead in Greek thought seems to be a result of mixing this earliest stage of the development of the Greek concept of death with the second stage. It was during the second, rightly known as the "Heroic age," that the idea of death as descend into a collective dwelling place known as Hades, emerged.[150] A term originally used to refer to the personal god of death in Homeric times, as noted above, Hades came to be known as the realm of the dead.[151] Its entrance was now seen as being "marked by a confluence of rivers; the river of fire, *Pyriphlegethon*, and the river of wailing, *Kokytos*."[152] It is said to be guarded by the "three-headed hound Cerberus" who guards its gateway.[153] It is during this time, also, that the consciousness and classification of the inhabitants of Hades becomes clear. While, on the one side, there are those sinners whose punishment Homer had described as "pushing a stone uphill which forever rolls back down again" as well as "striving to grasp the fruit and to drink the water without ever reaching it," a different class of inhabitants, the heroes, is introduced.[154]

Sometimes referred to as "demi-gods," the heroes were "valiant and noble warriors who left behind them the glorious memory of their deeds to live on in the songs of the ἀοιδοί."[155] Rather than existing in the glorious memory of these songs, during this stage of the development of the Greek concept of death, these men were now expected to enjoy blessedness in Hades.[156] Epithets that were originally used exclusively for gods now began to be used to refer to these men. Garland summarizes"

> In early Greek *makarios* is an epithet which properly describes the condition of the gods in distinction to that of mortal man. It was Hesiod who extended the meaning to include those who were exempted from the normal dreary existence of the dead in Hades, by referring to the men of the silver generation who live

149. Burkert, *Greek Religion*, 196.
150. Bolt, "Life, Death, and the Afterlife," 66.
151. Bass, "The Battle for the Keys," 29.
152. Burkert, *Greek Religion*, 196.
153. Ibid. See also *Il.* 7.368; Hes. *Theog.* 311.
154. Ibid., 198. See *Od.* 11.576–600.
155. Jaeger, "The Greek Ideas," 100.
156. Bolt, "Life, Death, and the Afterlife," 66.

underground as *hypochthonioi makares* (blessed beneath the earth). In the fifth century *makarios* seems to have been used especially of the heroised dead.[157]

The existence of these heroes led to what has come to be known as a "hero" cult. This cult "involves setting apart one particular grave, known as a *heroon*, from other burials by marking off a special precinct, by bringing sacrifices and votive gifts, and occasionally by building a special grave monument."[158] The growth of this hero cult was directly related to Greek wars and the rise of the *polis*. Thus, those who came to be understood as "heroes" included the great defenders of the city. A Greek hero, in other words, was "a person whose virtue, influence, or personality was so powerful in his lifetime or through peculiar circumstances of his death that his spirit after death is regarded as a supernormal power, claiming to be reverenced and propitiated."[159] Indeed, in addition to being worshipped, for the first time in Greek thought, the attribute of "immortality" (ἀθάνατος) is applied to them. But the term is applied in a somewhat paradoxical way. That is, the concept of immortality applies to the almost immortal memory of the hero in the society.[160]

It is this stage of the development of the Greek concept of death that most scholars see as the origin of the idea of "Noble Death." In this case, the definition of what constituted a "hero" was expanded to include not only those who died valiantly serving their country, but those who obeyed their moral code or laws of their religious obligations to the point of death. Later to be known as a martyr, a person in this category "chooses death rather than compromising his integrity, focusing on his volitional act of sacrifice for the sake of Truth, Justice, and the Athenian way."[161] As I observed above, the "Hero death" or the "Noble Death" eventually became a very significant paradigm for understanding the concept of death especially in the martyriological literature of the second century. While some scholars like Droge, Henten, and Avemarie understand second-century martyrs as using the Greek concept of the Noble Death as their only source of paradigm to understand and explain their view of death, others like Greenberg enlarge the field from which these martyrs are

157. Garland, *The Greek Way of Death*, 9–10.
158. Burkert, *Greek Religion*, 203.
159. Garland, *The Greek Way of Death*, 88.
160. Jaeger, "The Greek Ideas," 101–2.
161. Greenberg, *My Share of God's Reward*, 2. See also Plato *Phaedo* 117b–118.

borrowing to include the Intertestamental Maccabean martyrs as well.[162] However, I believe that trying to establish a chronological connection here as far as the borrowing of this concept is concerned, is like chasing the proverbial labyrinth. For our purposes here, the more significant question is that of semantic and functional connection. In other words, although there is clearly a correspondence of terminology between the Hellenistic concept of the Hero death and the stories of the martyrs, it seems clear that both groups don't necessarily mean the same thing albeit using similar terminology.

Although the question of the adaptation and modification of this concept of the "Hero death" in the development of a distinctively Christian view of death is the subject of the next chapter, one example is in order here. While, for example, the martyrs of 2 and 4 Maccabees are understood to have seen their death as "expiatory sacrifice," it is clearly a stretch to argue that such second-century believers like Ignatius of Antioch understood their deaths as having any salvific value.[163] This proposition will become clear as I explore meaning of the term περίψημα in Ignatius' thought in chapter 2.

The third and final phase of the development of the Platonic-Orphic concept of death involves a fully developed Platonic anthropology and a complete idea of the afterlife for all individuals. Influenced particularly by Orphism, Platonism understood man as having a soul, "which is of divine origin and immortal."[164] Specifically, Orphism moved Platonism

---

162. See Henten, *The Maccabean Martyrs*; Henten and Avemarie, *Martyrdom and Noble Death*; Greenberg, *My Share of God's Reward*. The concept of the Noble Death among the Greeks and the Maccabean martyrs was predicated upon the belief that, since these individuals received no recompense for their good actions and virtue on earth, this must, somehow, be granted elsewhere. "The deaths of the Maccabean martyrs," writes Greenberg, "exemplify these features, embodying this operative definition of martyrdom, and, as such, enable Jewish theology to incorporate Greco-Roman valorization of the Noble Death into its renovation of Deuteronomistic theodicy, thus, paving the way for Christian martyrdom to do the same. The stipulation of a post-mortem compensation is a natural outgrowth of this phenomenon of theological assimilation, adaptation, and experimentation" (Greenberg, *My Share of God's Reward*, 2).

163. Henten, *The Maccabean Martyrs*, 184.

164. Sonnemans, "Soul, Afterlife, Salvation," 250. For a brief introduction to the ancient religious movement known as Orphism, see Mourelatos, "Orphism." According to him, although we do not have direct information on this movement, there is enough to make this conclusion: the movement's central tenet was "a theogonic-cosmogonic narrative that posits Night as the primal entity—ostensibly a revision of the account offered by Hesiod—and gives major emphasis to the birth, death through dismemberment, and rebirth of the god Dionysius" (ibid). According to Bolt, Orphism

beyond ascribing the immortal soul to only a certain group of people, the heroes, to ascribing it to everyone. As Jaeger explains, after its interaction with Orphism, in Platonism, we notice a character change: "the warrior is no longer the only one who is entitled to this immortality. Other men of fame share his honor."[165] Indeed, the key achievement of the Orphics "consists in having made immortality not only the privilege of a few favorites of the gods and [also] in having transferred the idea of indestructibility of the living ... to the immortality of the soul."[166]

What Orphic Platonism meant by the terms "body" and "soul" has been a bone of contention amongst scholars. Owing especially to the Platonic dictum, "σῶμα σῆμα"—that is, "the body is the tomb of the soul," some have concluded that while at death the soul is released from the body since the body is really not part of the individual, others see more value to the material composition of the individual.[167] According to the latter, although Orphic Platonism did not believe in the resurrection (actually, it clearly spurned it), it did not believe in an inherent rejection of the body as the source of evil. Rather, according to them, "the body is not the origin of evil; rather, the spiritual soul brings a previous guilt with itself which it now atones in the body in earthly existence."[168] And, therefore, as we will see in chapter 3, while other systems like Valentinian Gnosticism agreed with Orphic Platonism in defining death as the flight of the soul (*apolytrosis*) from the body, both differed when it came to the value of the body. According to Orphic Platonism, the body, though being a prison for the soul, was not the source of evil. According Valentinian Gnosticism, the body (and all matter, for that case), was evil. Finally, in contradistinction with Catholic Christianity, both rejected the doctrine of the resurrection. Armstrong and Markus offer an elaborate summary of this contrast:

---

was invented by the legendary poet Thracian and musician Orpheus, both of whom offered a greater explanation of the afterlife (Bolt, "Life, Death, and the Afterlife," 66). For skepticism concerning the influence of Orphism on Platonism, see Wilamowitz-Moellendorff, *Der Glaube der Hellenen*, 1931–32.

165. Jaeger, "The Greek Ideas," 102.

166. Sonnemans, "Soul, Afterlife, Salvation," 251–52.

167. For the former view, see Armstrong and Markus, *Christian Faith*, 46. According to this view, in Orphic Platonism, the body is seen as more of a hindrance to the soul's attainment of virtue and wisdom.

168. Sonnemans, "Soul, Afterlife, Salvation," 251. See also Ricoeur, *Symbolik des Bösen*, 15.

In Jewish-Christian tradition, man is a single whole of which body is just as much a part as a soul; and for this way of thinking the resurrection of the body is a natural and inevitable part of any doctrine of the future life. And the evils and impediments to the spiritual life which our present life in the body brings are explained not as natural and inevitable consequences of earthly embodiment but as the result of the Fall of Man, which leaves open the possibility that the Redemption from that fall may bring us to a perfect and glorious life in a spiritualized earthly (in the cosmological sense) body and not require our transference to a body actually placed in the heavens and made celestial material. The contrast with the Platonic view, it would seem, could hardly be sharper.[169]

To be fair to Platonism, however, the immortal soul now exists in a much better shape than it did in the body. There is expected in the future in Orphic Platonism an apotheosis, that is, a "divinization (*theòs egenou ex anthrôpou*)."[170] In this future existence, later understood as "astral immortality," the soul will transcend all of human contingency, that is, the "subjection to becoming and passing away." In this case, therefore, death becomes the "condition of possibility for a new mode of existence."[171] Although slightly beyond our scope here, these "astral bodies" ultimately become the picture of the resurrected bodies in Neoplatonism. Even in the case of Neoplatonism, these "astral bodies" do not correspond perfectly to how Christianity has envisioned the resurrected bodies. As Christian theologians have insisted, the resurrection bodies "will be real human bodies, however spiritualized and transformed, and not properly astral or celestial bodies."[172] In this case, Christianity has managed to avoid a "complete slipping back into the spatial other-worldliness of the cosmic religion."[173] As I will demonstrate in the succeeding chapters, entrusted with the seminal development of Christian belief, second-century believers offered a clear navigation of this tricky path.

Finally, as far as the Romans' view of death is concerned, there is a significant similarity with the Greeks. Davis is correct when he observes

---

169. Armstrong and Markus, *Christian Faith*, 47. For a discussion of the contrast between the unitary and the dualistic views of man's nature, see Zaehner, *At Sundry Times*, 173; Gousmett, "Shall the Body Strive and Not be Crowned?" 22.

170. Armstrong and Markus, *Christian Faith*, 253.

171. Ibid., 255.

172. Ibid., 49.

173. Ibid.

that "in a variety of forms these ancient [Greek] stories were reinvented and reinvigorated in the Roman Empire which subsumed both Classical and Hellenistic Greece, and added its own traditions to them."[174] But, as research in the Roman concept of death has been handicapped by a number of methodological problems. First, according to Keith Hopkins, there is the problem of evidence. This is because there are no "general ancient descriptions of Roman funerary practices or beliefs in life after death."[175] Second, we are handicapped as far as the emotions of the Romans that were aroused by death are concerned. This is because the Romans tended to record events and not necessarily graceful epitaphs.[176]

However, we can make these observations concerning the Roman views of death in general. Since the Romans' views of the afterlife were influenced by such philosophies and religions as Stoicism, Mithraism, Judaism and Christianity, they were quite varied. There was a general belief in the afterlife of some sort. As Hopkins notes, the souls of the dead were thought to exist in a "ghostly existence," an existence whereby they would sometimes be subject to purgatorial moral judgment.[177] Later in Roman history, we see a much more developed view of the individual's existence after death. Hopkins comically remarks that for Romans, philosophical skepticism "sometimes crumbled in the face of an unexpected death" in that mourners found some consolation in the belief that there might be, after all, some life after death.[178]

In conclusion, I believe that Hopkins offers a fine summation of the intricate details of the interaction of the ideas about the meaning of death from various religions as expressed through each religion's funerary rites:

> At this stage, we should distinguish between *(a)* rites which dramatized the life-cycle, *(b)* belief in the immortality and resurrection of the Godhead, and *(c)* belief in the immortality and redemption of all believers. The first two, *(a)* and *(b)*, are both found in "Oriental" religions. But Christianity put more stress than any ancient religion on the possible salvation of its followers.[179]

---

174. Davies, *Death, Burial and Rebirth*, 128.
175. Hopkins, *Death and Renewal*, 203.
176. Ibid., 204.
177. Ibid., 226.
178. Ibid., 230.
179. Ibid., 231.

This similarity and difference, I believe, is best elucidated in the writings of second-century Christians. It is a major aspect of this book.

In summary, therefore, although many recognize the fact that Greek philosophy and its concepts of death is a major conversation partner of believers in the second century, the corollary fact that this philosophy is not monolithic, needs to be taken into account. Not only are there many tenets interwoven in the Greek concept of death, but, more significant, there is an internal development of the concept. Thus, although it is beyond the scope of this study to fully explore this development, the recognition of its existence provides a helpful background towards understanding second-century Christians' adaptation and modification of these views in order to provide a distinctively Christian concept of death. Before doing this, however, it is imperative to offer a brief overview of the other key conversational partner for these Christians, viz., documents that were to eventually become the New Testament.

Death in the New Testament

The connection between second-century Christianity and the New Testament cannot be overstated. Since I have offered an analysis of the principal terms for death in Greek, I will not repeat them here. It seems like there is continuity between the Old Testament understanding of the meaning of death and the New Testament views of the same. In other words, there does not seem to be much influence from Hellenism and the Intertestamental period as far as the understanding of death is concerned. As noted above, when the term *thnetos* (mortal) occurs in the New Testament, it is taken as a natural condition under which man lives. Man lives under the constant fear of death (Heb 2:15).[180]

The general understanding of death in the New Testament can be summarized in a number of ways. First, a clear connection between physical death and sin is established. That is, death is now clearly understood to be the consequence of sin. As Bultmann explains, "the question of the origin of death is thus the question of the origin of sin, and, as in the corresponding understanding of—ἁμαρτία, the question is not treated speculatively."[181] Thus, even Bultmann, who sees Paul as having adopted some Gnostic speculative language in his *anthropos* myth, nevertheless,

---

180. Schmithals, "Θάνατος," 435.
181. Bultmann, "θάνατος," 15.

has no option but to conclude that "the speculative conception is diverted to a different end in R[om]. 5:12ff., [sic] for sin is consistently regarded as a responsible act and death as a consequence."[182] Even the skeptical Schmithals, who had earlier on declared that "death itself is not a divine punishment," has to grudgingly grant that, in the New Testament, there is a clear focus on what causes death. As he grants, according to Romans 6:23, the answer to the question of what causes death is clear. It is sin.[183]

Second, there is no effort whatsoever to treat death as a natural process, thus neutralizing it. Rather, it holds its destructive power over all human life, robbing it of its quality. It holds life in φόβος (Heb 2:15; Rom 8:15).[184] Thus, death is seen as the power that enslaves all humanity. As far as the New Testament is concerned, "the possibility of removing the horror of death by means of intellectual insight concerning its inevitability, or through a heroic act of dying, is therefore excluded in the NT thought."[185] Elsewhere, Jesus is said to have been sent to those who are καθήμενος ἐν σκότει ("those living in darkness") (Matt 4:16, cf. Luke 1:79), that is, those living in continued fear of death.

Third, of all the passages dealing with death in the New Testament, perhaps none has generated more discussion than Paul's words in 2 Corinthians 5:1–10. Paul's words in this pericope have been the center of an extraordinarily great controversy in New Testament in the last few decades beginning from the nineteenth century, a controversy that focuses on the question of whether or not Paul's eschatology underwent internal development.[186] Of interest here have been the key terms and phrases that

---

182. Ibid.

183. Schmithals, "Θάνατος," 436.

184. Bultmann, "θάνατος," 17. As noted above, the concept of a hero's death (Noble Death) was significant in some Greek circles, especially Socratic tradition.

185. Ibid., 15.

186. It is beyond the scope of this study to explore at length this discussion at length. For some helpful discussions, see Harris, "The Interpretation of 2 Cor 5:1–10"; Harris, "Resurrection and Immortality"; Harris, "2 Corinthians 5:1–10?" 32–57; Osei-Bonsu, "Does 2 Cor 5:1–10 Teach the Reception of the Resurrection Body," 81–101; Metts, "Death, Discipleship and Discourse Strategies," 57–76. For the theory that Paul's eschatology undergoes development over the decades of writing his epistles, see Longenecker, "Is There Development?" 171–202. Longenecker argues that the theory of development in Pauline thought itself developed in two phases. Phase one was from 1832 to 1870. This phase was characterized by such works as Newman, *An Essay on the Development*; Rainy, *The Delivery and Development*; Orr, *The Progress of Dogma*; Harnack, *The History of Dogma*; Sabatier, *The Apostle Paul*; Lüdemann, *Die Anthropologie des Apostels Paulus*; Pfleiderer, *Der Paulismus*; Weiss, *Lehrbuch Der*

Paul uses to refer to his impending death. For example, in 2 Corinthians 5:1, Paul notes that Οἴδαμεν γὰρ ὅτι ἐὰν ἡ ἐπίγειος ἡμῶν οἰκία τοῦ σκήνους καταλυθῇ, οἰκοδομὴν ἐκ θεοῦ ἔχομεν, οἰκίαν ἀχειροποίητον αἰώνιον ἐν τοῖς οὐρανοῖς ("For we know that if our earthly house, the tent we live in, is dismantled, we have a building from God, a house not built by human hands, that is eternal in the heavens").

Interpreters have wrestled with these key phrases and terms: ἡμῶν οἰκία τοῦ σκήνους, καταλυθῇ, οἰκοδομὴν ἐκ θεοῦ ἔχομεν, οἰκίαν ἀχειροποίητον and αἰώνιον ἐν τοῖς οὐρανοῖς. While there is general agreement on the fact that the phrase ἡμῶν οἰκία τοῦ σκήνους ("our earthly house") refers to our physical bodies, and, that the term καταλυθῇ ("dismantled") is a metaphor for physical death, the meanings of both οἰκοδομὴν ἐκ θεοῦ ἔχομεν ("we have a building from God") and οἰκίαν ἀχειροποίητον ("a house not built by human hands"), have been the source of much disagreement.[187] On the one hand, there are those who have con-

---

Biblischen Theologie; Teichmann, *Die paulinischen Vorstellungen*; Lightfoot and Hort, "The Chronology of St. Paul's Life"; Matheson, *The Spiritual Development*; Holtzmann, *Lehrbuch der neutestamentlichen* and Charles, *Eschatology*, 450, 453, and 459. During this phase, Paul's theology was understood to have undergone development in a number of areas. For our purposes here, it was argued that his eschatology both from focusing on Christ's coming (Parousia) to focusing on his own death and from expecting himself to be alive at the time of Parousia and so be involved in the resurrection without dying to a consciousness that he would probably die before the Parousia. The second phase, argues Longenecker, runs from 1932 to the present. The most influential work during this time is Dodd, "The Mind of St. Paul," 3–17. The emphasis during this phase has been the argument that, faced with his own "spiritual crisis," Paul changed from a world-renouncing attitude whereby he saw the state of being united "with Christ" as reserved for the future to a world-affirming attitude whereby salvific fulfillment is here and now. This is what has come to be known as "Realized Eschatology." For a critique of the concept of development in Pauline thought (eschatology), see Schweitzer, *Paul and His Interpreters*; Weiss, *The History of Primitive Christianity* and Loewe, "An Examination of Attempts," 129–42. Any attempt to argue for shifts and contours in Paul's eschatological thought, however, must carefully take into account the apostle's own and his addressees changing situations. Longenecker is correct in observing that "nonetheless, whatever shifts of thought, mood, or personal expectation might be postulated, it needs to be emphasized and enunciated clearly that the focus of Paul's teaching regarding the resurrection of believers was always on Christ's Parousia and the resurrection of believers that would then take place. And it is this resurrection message that remains constant in his teaching" (Longenecker, "Is There Development," 201).

187. For the view that Paul is here referring to his prospect of death before the Parousia, see Schmiedel, *Die Briefe an die Thessalonicher*, 238; Windisch, *Der zweite Korinther-Brief*, 158, and Lincoln, *Paradise Now and Not Yet*, 62. There is a lot in terms of background material for the use of σκῆνος as a metaphor for the body in Greek

tended that Paul's use of the verb ἔχομεν indicates that the believer will receive the resurrection body (what he calls the "spiritual body"— σῶμα πνευματικόν) immediately after death.[188] The most recent proponent of the view is the New Testament scholar, Murray J. Harris. According to him, from the time Paul wrote 2 Corinthains 5:1–10, he believed that "believers would receive the resurrection body immediately after death."[189] He builds his case on the verbs ἔχομεν ("we have") in v. 1, ἐπενδύσασθαι ("to put on over") as well as the phrases ἐνδημοῦντες ἐν τῷ σώματι ("being absent from the body") and ἐνδημῆσαι πρὸς τὸν κύριον ("being present with the Lord").

Having argued for this thesis in his dissertation in 1970, Harris returned to it in a lecture in Tydale House the same year. The most important part of this lecture is when Harris addresses the question of when Paul expected to receive the resurrected body. He writes:

> If, then, the ἔχομεν of 2 Corinthians 5:1 alludes to a future acquisition of the spiritual body, does this occur at the Parousia or at death? Not a few commentators interpret the verb as a futuristic present: what is, in fact, to be obtained only at the Advent has become, to faith, an assured possession of the present, this sure conviction arising from the apostle's knowledge of the character of God whose word was his deed and from the pledge of the resurrection-transformation God had already given in the Spirit (2 Cor 5:5). But, apart from the fact that the futuristic present is usually found with verbs of motion, what consolation would be offered Paul in the present event of his *death* (ἐὰν ... καταλυθῇ) by the knowledge that at the *Parousia* is [when] he would receive a spiritual body? The moment when the consolation is needed must be the moment when the consolation is given; and the consolation received at death cannot simply be identical with that assurance of the future acquisition of the resurrection body which is already possessed during life.[190]

---

literature. According to BDAG, the term here means "a temporary abode as opposed to a permanent structure, tent, lodging," (BDAG, s.v. σκῆνος). See also Wis 9.15.

188. See, for example, Volz, *Die Eschatologie der jüdischen Gemeinde*, 156–71; Charles, *Eschatology*, 453, 457–79; Teichmann, *Die paulinischen Vorstellungen*, 62, 66, and Robinson, *The Christian Doctrine*, 130.

189. Osei-Bonsu, "Does 2 Cor 5:1–10 Teach the Reception of the Resurrection," 81.

190. Harris, "2 Corinthians 5:1–10," 41. See also Harris, "Resurrection and Immortality," 168.

Thus, according to Harris, if Paul had envisaged the reception of the resurrection body at the Parousia, it would be impossible for him to find any consolation in the face of his impending death. Furthermore, identifying the οἰκοδομὴν ἐκ θεοῦ ("house/building from God") with the heavenly spiritual bodies, Harris argues that Paul envisaged the punctiliar dismantling (καταλυθῇ) of this earthly tent (ἡμῶν οἰκία τοῦ σκήνους) to be immediately followed by the reception of the heavenly bodies. In other words, according to Paul, "there was no interval homelessness. The moment one residence [earthly dwelling/body] was destroyed, another [heavenly dwelling/spiritual body] was received."[191]

On the other hand, there are many who maintain that although the phrase οἰκοδομὴν ἐκ θεοῦ refers to the resurrection body, the time of its reception is not at death but during the Parousia. Agreeing that the phrase οἰκία τοῦ σκήνους ("earthly bodily dwelling") refers to the physical death whose prospect of dissolution is nearing for Paul, Thrall argues that the view that the reception of the resurrection body at death creates a problem. This is because "according to 1 Cor 15:52, this reception takes place at the Parousia itself, not before."[192] In other words, if this phrase is read as Harris reads it, then it would seem that Paul is not consistent in his understanding of death and resurrection in terms of the chronology of the events. Likewise, Osei-Bonsu argues that although the verb ἔχομεν is in the present tense, it refers to the future reception of the resurrection body because "the possession of the 'building from God' comes only after the dissolution of

---

191. Harris, "2 Corinthians 5:1–10," 42–43. For the many possible meanings of the phrase οἰκοδομὴν ἐκ θεοῦ, see Thrall, *A Critical and Exegetical Commentary on The Second Epistle to the Corinthians*, 363–67. According to her, there are at least nine possible referents of this phrase. These are (i) the phrase refers to the resurrection body, the σῶμα πνευματικόν, (ii) it refers to the heavenly habitation just like the dwellings mentioned in John 14:2 and not the bodies, (iii) it refers to the interim heavenly body that is received immediately after death and will be eventually united with the σῶμα πνευματικόν, (iv) it refers to a kind of spiritual garment (the ἔσω ἄνθρωπος of 4:16), a kind of "garment" received at baptism and preserved beyond the grave, but distinct from the σῶμα πνευματικόν received at the resurrection, (v) that the phrase refers to the body of Christ, the church, (vi) that the οἰκοδομὴν refers to the heavenly temple, (vii) that the οἰκοδομή refers to the resurrection body of Christ, (viii) that the οἰκοδομή refers to an image of the glory of the eschatological age, and, (ix) that the οἰκοδομή signifies the heavenly dimension of the present existence. I certainly agree with her that, of all these possibilities, the first view is most probable (i.e., the phrase refers to the resurrection body, the time when it is achieved notwithstanding).

192. Thrall, *The Second Epistle to the Corinthians*, 362.

the tent."[193] The present nature of the verb "points to a future possession which is so real and assured in the apostle's perspective that it is appropriately spoken of in the present tense."[194] Furthermore, it is argued that Paul gives us a clue as to when believers will receive the resurrection body in 2 Corinthians 5:4. This will take place at the Parousia. Indeed, Paul's message here is the same as what we see in 1 Corinthians 15:54, where, with the Parousia in mind, he talks about the mortal as being swallowed up by life.[195]

A somehow more idiosyncratic mediating view is that Paul, borrowing from Hellenistic anthropology, "develops a view of intermediate state wherein a believer's 'self' acquires immortality at death and so gains at that time conscious fellowship with Christ."[196] This is what Ratzinger calls "incipient resurrection."[197] According to him, "the existence with Christ inaugurated by faith is the start of resurrected life and therefore outlasts death (see Phil 1:23; 2 Cor 5:8; 1 Thess 5:10)."[198] In other words, according to this view, in death, the whole person is resurrected albeit still awaiting his perfection in the Parousia.[199]

A definitive conclusion of the matter is elusive especially because of the force of the verb ἔχομεν (present indicative active, third person plural, "we have"). As noted above, there are those who take it as a futuristic present and read it as implying that the reception of the resurrection bodies is at the Parousia.[200] On the other hand, there are those who maintain that the force of this verb clearly demands the reception of the resurrection body immediately after the dissolution of this physical body. Harris is blunt: "ἔχομεν would then point to an immediate succession between two forms of embodiment," he writes, "without implying a long-standing or even momentary coexistence of two bodies. As soon as our earthly tent-dwelling is taken down, we are recipients of a building from God."[201]

---

193. Osei-Bonsu, "Does 2 Cor 5:1–10 Teach the Reception of the Resurrection Body," 86.

194. Ibid. See also Gundry, *Sōma in Biblical Theology*, 150.

195. Osei-Bonsu, "Does 2 Cor 5:1–10 Teach the Reception of the Resurrection," 86.

196. Longenecker, "Is There Development," 194.

197. Sonnemans, "Soul, Afterlife, Salvation," 260.

198. Ratzinger, *Introduction to Christianity*, 352–53.

199. Sonnemans, "Soul, Afterlife, Salvation," 260.

200. Osei-Bonsu, "Does 2 Cor 5:1–10 Teach the Reception of the Resurrection," 81.

201. Harris, "2 Corinthians 5:1–10," 43.

Likewise, Thrall, after discussing all the possible interpretations of the verb ἔχομεν, concludes:

> We may provisionally conclude that in [2 Cor] 5:1 Paul may express his confidence that, should a believer die before the Parousia, he will at that moment come into possession of a permanent αἰώνιος), spiritual (ἀχειροποίητος), and heavenly (ἐν τοῖς οὐρανοῖς) form of existence. In view of the explicit contrast with the οἰκία τοῦ σκήνους, this must be seen as somatic existence, and hence as the σῶμα πνευματικόν.[202]

When we take into consideration the fact that Paul wrote these words while undergoing tough experiences in the province of Asia, it seems that here he is becoming more reflective of his own mortality and what it means. Thus, although we cannot reach a definitive conclusion on whether Paul understands death as resurrection here, his general understanding of the chronology of personal eschatology seems clear. That is, "the sequence of events . . . continues to be: (1) death, (2) resurrection, (3) transformation, and then (4) immortality."[203]

It is very probable that such second-century Fathers as Ignatius of Antioch have Paul's idea of death as resurrection when they write about their own deaths. Although I will discuss the concept of death as resurrection in the second century in chapter 2, it is worth mentioning here that Ignatius of Antioch describes his own death as resurrection in such passages as *Mag* 9.2, *Eph* 11.2 and *Rm* 4.3. As expected, what Ignatius means by describing his death as resurrection (ἀνίσταμαι) is the subject of much contention among scholars.[204] But I will get back to this. Suffice it to make the point here that there seems to be a conceptual relationship

---

202. Thrall, *The Second Epistle to the Corinthians*, 370. According to her, there are at least four possible ways that the present ἔχομεν can be read. These are, (i) That believers already have the spiritual body already as an idea in the mind of God, (ii) that believers will have the spiritual body at the Parousia, (iii) that the resurrection body is received immediately after death, and, (iv), that ἔχομεν has no temporal force. Rather, it is a general statement showing the relationship between the protasis with the apodosis (Ibid., 368–69).

203. Longenecker, "Is There Development," 196.

204. For a recent discussion of the concept of death as resurrection, see Bryan Louis Kromholtz, "Resurrection in Death in the Theology of Rahner and Balthasar." Some current proponents of the concept of death as resurrection include Sonnemans, "Soul, Afterlife, Salvation," 248–61; Ratzinger, *Eschatology*, 181–94; Prusak, "Bodily Resurrection," 82–84, 99–105 and Greshake and Lohfink, *Naherwartung-Auferstehung-Unsterblichkeit*, 156–92.

between Paul's description of his death as the attainment of a heavenly house and Ignatius' description of his death as resurrection.

The Abode of the Dead in the New Testament

Concerning the place of the dead in the New Testament, there are two clearly established places. The story that Jesus gives in Luke 16:19–31 perhaps gives us a glimpse in to the present dwelling places of the dead. In this story, the nameless rich man is said to be in Hades while Lazarus was at Abraham's side. As the story is told, upon the deaths of both men, Lazarus, the poor man, is carried by angels to Abraham's side while the rich man, presumably an unbeliever, died and was buried. The next phrase (v. 23) is intriguing: καί ἐν τῷ ᾅδῃ ἐπάρας τοὺς ὀφθαλμοὺς αὐτοῦ ("And in Hades, as he was in torment . . ."). Thus, we are introduced to the concept of Hades now being a place of torment for some! And, consequently, now there is a clear contrast between the places where the departed dead go. As Liefeld notes, "'Abraham's side,' may picture reclining at a banquet, like the 'feast in the kingdom of God' at which Abraham will be present. . . . Otherwise it might be a symbol of reunion with Abraham and the other patriarchs at death."[205] Either way, the point is the same: now there are two distinct places for the departed.

The place for the dead believers is clearly identified by Christ on the cross later as "Paradise." The term Paradise, as is used here, is a reminder of the Garden of Eden. However, specifically, here it is used to refer to "a transcendent place of blessedness, *paradise*."[206] In addition, the term also occurs in 2 Corinthians 12:14 where Paul describes his assumed extra-terrestrial tour of the heavens. He points out that he was caught up into Paradise. Although there are some differences as to what this place exactly is (whether it is the Genesis Paradise reserved for the enjoyment of God's people or it is a synonym for heaven), there is a general agreement that "Luke 23:43 should be understood as a way of describing Jesus 'entrance into his glory' after death, implying a heavenly existence. . . . In either case, the adverb today suggests that Jesus' and the thief's enjoyment of heaven would begin immediately subsequent to death."[207] Obviously, therefore, this can be said to be true of every believer today. Some

---

205. Liefeld, *Luke*, The Expositor's Bible Commentary, 992.
206. Bauer, *A Greek-English Lexicon of the New Testament*, 761.
207. Lunde, "Heaven and Hell," 309.

scholars have, however argued that this story simply reflects "one strand of current Jewish belief, with the dead already experiencing torment or bliss."[208] However, when it is coupled with other texts that make a mention to Paradise, two clear intermediate places for the dead for the period between death and resurrection are evident. According to Luke 23:43, Paradise is the "abode of the souls of the redeemed in the intermediate state between death and resurrection."[209] Other corresponding phrases for Paradise in the New Testament are "being with the Lord" (2 Cor 5:8) and the "heavenly Jerusalem" (Heb 12:22).[210] But, as Paul describes it, existence in Paradise, even for believers, feels like being "naked" (2 Cor 5:1–4). According to him, the existence in a disembodied intermediate state feels like nakedness. Finally, in some other texts, Paul refers to the state of being dead for believers as "falling asleep" as well as being translated into the presence of the Lord (Phil 1:23).[211] The emphasis is here on the restful nature of believers as they await the resurrection from the dead. This concept resurfaces in the thought of the Apostolic Fathers here below.

By contrast, the ungodly dead are said to be presently somewhere, awaiting judgment (2 Pet 3:7; Jude 6–7).[212] This "somewhere" corresponds to the Old Testament "Sheol/Hades." In the New Testament, Hades is fully associated with a realm. In its first appearance in the New Testament in Matthew 11:23, Jesus, while condemning Capernaum for her unbelief, declares to her that she will not be exalted to heaven, but will descend to Hades (ᾅδου καταβήσῃ). This is clearly a reference to a realm and not a Greek god as the term had been used earlier on in Greek thought. Second, the term occurs in Matthew 16:18, where Jesus promises Peter that he (Jesus) will build his church and the gates of Hades will not overcome it (πύλαι ᾅδου οὐ κατισχύσουσιν). Again, this is also a reference to a realm/place and not a person in the name of a Greek god. The same is true of

---

208. Johnston, "Death and Resurrection," 445.

209. Jeremias, "Παράδεισος," 769.

210. Ibid.

211. The phrase "falling asleep" occurs nine times in 1 Corinthians and 1 Thess 4. In most of these usages, the term "asleep" is used to imply "a future awakening" during the resurrection. (See Robertson and Plummer, *A Critical and Exegetical Commentary on the First Epistle*, 337.)

212. Peter even says that Christ "proclaimed" [judgment] to the spirits in prison (1 Pet 3:19), a phrase that some have taken to refer to the souls of the ungodly dead and/or some fallen angels.

all other New Testament references to Hades. Finally, as the term occurs in the pivotal Revelation of St. John, it is first pictured as a realm whose keys Jesus Christ holds (1:18); second, in 20:13 where, together with the sea, this realm gave up its dead for judgment, and, third, in 20:14 where, together with Death, this realm was thrown into the lake of fire.[213] Thus, these two clear destinations of the dead are delineated in the New Testament: Paradise for the believing dead and Hades for the unbelieving dead.

Very significantly, therefore, the New Testament's understanding of death also focuses on the theological rather than the biological meaning of death. The concept of God as the giver of life to the dead that is first introduced in the Old Testament is brought to its fullest meaning in the New Testament. Not only is God the one who gives life to the dead and calls to existence things that do not exist (Rom 4:17), but He has ultimately destroyed death and its power through the work of His Son (2 Tim 1:10). In the death and resurrection of Jesus Christ, sin, the cause of death, and death, the consequence of sin, have been defeated. In other words, meaning of death for a believer is clearly tied to the death and resurrection of Jesus Christ. The New Testament emphasis is that Christ died for our sins, was buried, and was raised on the third day in accordance with the Scriptures (1 Cor 15:3–4).[214] This theological interpretation of death will play a significant role in the works of second-century Christian apologists.

However, as we have argued, God's (that is, Jesus') victory over death is very qualified in the New Testament. It still retains the paradox that is evidenced from the Old Testament. For those who are in Christ, death has been defeated. Indeed, that person can join Paul in scorning death, as he does in 1 Corinthians 15:55. In this pivotal verse, after declaring that death has been swallowed up in victory, Paul asks, perhaps sarcastically: ποῦ σου, θάνατε, τὸ νῖκος; ποῦ σου, θάνατε, τὸ κέντρο ("Where, O death, is your victory? Where O death, is your sting?"). However, this song of victory can be sung by those who believe in the death and resurrection of the Son of God. For the rest, Paul has a rather different song! In other words, where there is no hope grounded in Christ, the slogan is: φάγωμεν καὶ πίωμεν, αὔριον γὰρ ἀποθνῄσκομεν ("let us eat and drink, for tomorrow we die"). Thus, death (and life), in this case, is pretty pessimistic. However, the controlling thought of the New Testament is that "God deals with the world through Christ (2 Cor 5:19), and that inasmuch as in this action

---

213. Hastie, "The Doctrine of Hades," 58. For a recent treatment of the pivotal passage of Rev 1:18, see Bass, "The Battle for the Keys."

214. This formula is perhaps the earliest form of the gospel message.

God took death to Himself in Christ it lost its destructive character and became a creative divine act."[215] Therefore, although it remains truly an enemy, it is an enemy that has been judged and will ultimately be thrown in the Lake of Fire (Rev 20:14).

Conclusion

After surveying the various concepts of death in the Old Testament, the Greco-Roman culture and the materials that later came to be known as the New Testament, the context has now been set for the study of the concept of death in the thought of second-century Christians. With this background, we are now prepared to demonstrate that second-century Christians critically adapt, modify, and utilize existing views of death to offer a distinctively Christian view of death that is both occasional as well as commensurate with the degree of revelation that they have. Although there is correspondence of terminology between second-century Christians and their conversation partners, this does not guarantee the same meaning in their usage. A study of select writings of key thinkers on the subject of death, their differing occasions as well as that of the key terms that they use to define and describe death will serve to reinforce this conclusion.

We now move to the study of the earliest time of the second century; the Apostolic Fathers. How do these Christians understand death? What terms and metaphors do they use to define and describe death? How do their differing situations affect their understanding of death? These and related matters form the content of the next chapter.

---

215. Bultmann, "θάνατος," 18.

CHAPTER 2

The Concept of Death in the Apostolic Fathers

This chapter examines the concept of death in the Apostolic Fathers. The term "Apostolic Fathers" has traditionally been used to designate what we know as the earliest Christian writings that stand outside the New Testament.[1] These writings are believed to cover the time period between AD 70 and 150, otherwise known as the "post-apostolic" period.[2] Many of the writers of these documents remain anonymous. But they are quite engaging in their thought. Jefford remarks that although these texts never made it to the New Testament canon, "the collection of the Apostolic Fathers are considered to be consistent with the general principles and theologies of an apostolic tradition," a tradition that "circulated among the churches from the end of the first century into the middle of the second century."[3] That is, although the writings of these Fathers are not part of the New Testament, their teachings are consistent with those of the New Testament itself. They are, in other words, "small yet precious gems that glitter with the features of Christianity immediately after the

---

1. Holmes, *The Apostolic Fathers*, 3.

2. Some of the key texts and translations of the writings of the Apostolic Fathers include Bihlmeyer, *Die apostolischen Väter*; Lightfoot and Harmer, *The Apostolic Fathers*; Lightfoot, *S. Ignatius, S. Polycarp Part 2*; Ehrman, *The Apostolic Fathers*; Kirsopp, *The Apostolic Fathers*; Goodspeed, *The Apostolic Fathers*; Glimm et al., *The Apostolic Fathers* and Grant, *The Apostolic Fathers*.

3. Jefford, *The Apostolic Fathers*, 8–9.

New Testament from the close of the first century to the latter part of the second."[4] While some scholars, like Schoedel, do not see any significant theological concerns emerging in these writings, many see these documents as pivotal towards our understanding of the theological concerns of the earliest Christians.[5] Holmes, for example, observes that these writers are "real people struggling to deal with various opportunities, problems, and crises as best as they can."[6] Because a number of them face death through martyrdom, a key crisis becomes the question of the definition and understanding of death.

Recognizing the fact that these Christians wrote in response to differing occasions, it seems necessary to come up with some kind of organizational structure that can help us synthesize their views on death. In the first part of the chapter, we will examine the non-martyriological Apostolic Fathers' concept of death. With such writings as *1 Clement* and the *Shepherd of Hermas*, the term "sleep" is mostly used to explain the concept of death. In the second part of the chapter, we examine the concept of death as far as the second-century martyrs are concerned. With such fathers as Ignatius of Antioch, Polycarp, as well as the writings known as *The Acts of the Christian Martyrs*, such terms as discipleship, sacrifice, imitation, and witness are used to define and describe death.

DEATH IN EARLY APOSTOLIC FATHERS

In this section, we will argue that the writings of the early Apostolic Fathers on the subject of death reveal a consistent definition of death geared towards exhorting the living towards virtuous living. For them, the subject of death is part of broader exhortations towards other aspects of Christian life such as church unity and holiness. The restful state of those who are dead (mostly described as "sleep") is presented as the incentive for these exhortations in these writings.

---

4. Bingham, *Pocket History of the Church*, 20.

5. Schoedel, *Polycarp, Martyrdom of Polycarp*, v.

6. Holmes, *The Apostolic Fathers*, 4. These documents include the writings of Barnabas, Clement of Rome, Hermas, Ignatius of Antioch, and Polycarp of Smyrna. In addition, this list has been expanded to include *The Epistle to Diognetus*, the fragments of Papias, and Quadratus as well as *The Didache*.

1 Clement: Death As Sleep

1 Clement is understood to have been written in Rome, most probably in late nineties A.D. The writer is identified in Christian tradition as "Clement," perhaps a key leader of the church in Corinth.[7] It seems to have been occasioned by divisions in the Corinthian church. In it, the writer addresses the same factions that Paul had addressed in his Corinthian letters. It "appears that some of the younger men in the congregation had provoked a revolt . . . and succeeded in deposing the established leadership of the church (3.3; 44.6; 47.6)."[8] Therefore, since this was the occasion for the writing, treatment of the concept of death, as noted above, is within the aspect of church unity.

Clement treats the concept of death specifically in 24.1–5. In these verses, he ties the death of Christians to that of Christ. After exhorting his readers to consider (κατανοήσωμεν) how the Master continually points out the resurrection of which he made the Lord Jesus Christ to be the first fruit when he raised him from the dead, the writer proceeds to compare death with falling asleep as night does, awaiting the arising of the day when the resurrection takes place.[9] He then compares death with the planting of seeds. "Let us take as an example the crops: how and in what manner does the sowing take place?" He then quotes from the parable of the sower as told in Mark 4:3 to argue that the seeds which are sown to the earth "dry and bare," decay. However, out of their decay, the majesty of the Master's providence then raises them up.[10] They then go on to bear more fruit.

Finally, the author connects his understanding of death with the exhortation to holiness. In chapter 26.1–2, the writer tells the factitious Corinthians that the Lord will resurrect those who "have served him

---

7. Eusebius *Ecclesiastical History* 4.23.11. I am using Eusebius, Cruse, *Eusebius' Ecclesiastical History*.

8. Holmes, ed. *The Apostolic Fathers*, 34. Unless otherwise stated, all the quotations of First Clement are from this text. Based on the classic work of Joseph Barber Lightfoot (1828–89), the translation of the Apostolic Fathers by Homes has only minor changes of Lightfoot's work that are geared towards readability and corrections of misprints as well as a revision of the introductions to the *Letters of Ignatius*, the *Shepherd of Hermas*, and the *Epistle to Diognetus* to accommodate for text critical apparatus. See Lightfoot and Harmer, *The Apostolic Fathers: Revised Greek Texts*; Lightfoot, *S. Ignatius, S. Polycarp*.

9. *1 Clem.* 24. 2.

10. *1 Clem.* 24.4–5.

in holiness."[11] Then, he quotes Job 26:3 to the effect that when we die, we lay down and sleep, waiting to be raised again in the same flesh that has endured all these things, namely, the atrocities of physical death. He concludes his understanding of death by suggesting that those who are perfected in love have already entered their glorious places in Christ's kingdom. He writes:

> All these generations from Adam to this day have passed away, but those who by God's grace were perfected in love have a place among the godly, who will be revealed when the kingdom of Christ visits us. For it is written: "Enter into the innermost rooms for a very little while, until my anger and wrath shall pass away, and I will remember a good day and will raise you from your graves."[12]

In other words, not only does the writer of *1 Clement* understand death in terms of sleep, but he also, within the tradition of the Old Testament, affirms the survival of the soul beyond the physical death. As Dewart observes, "it is interesting to note that the letter contains one of the passages in the Apostolic Fathers which seems to affirm the survival of the soul independently of the body" after death.[13]

The Shepherd of Hermas: Death As Sleep

Hailed as one of the most enigmatic documents to have survived from the postapostolic period, the *Shepherd of Hermas* was written to deal with a varied number of questions and issues including "postbaptismal sin and repentance, and the behavior of the rich and their relationship to the poor within the church."[14] The style of *The Shepherd* is a narration of the revelations of visions (as well as explanations of the meanings of these visions) purported to have been given to Hermas by the Shepherd, an angelic figure from whom the book derives its name.[15]

11. *1 Clem.* 26.1.
12. *1 Clem.* 50.3–4.
13. Dewart, *Death and Resurrection*, 42.
14. Holmes, *The Apostolic Fathers*, 442.
15. Ibid. The authorship and dating of *The Shepherd of Hermas* has been the subject of much discussion. An early suggestion was that the book was written by Paul on the basis of Acts 14:12 where Paul Hermes is mentioned as a name that was given to Paul for raising a man from the dead in Lystra, therefore equating him with one of the gods of Lystra. Certainly, this is not true. Also, according to Origen, the book was written by

The first cursory treatment of the subject of death in *The Shepherd* occurs in *Vis*. 3. 5.2. In the entirety of this vision, *The Shepherd* presents the Lady's explanation to Hermas of the vision that he had seen of the Tower.[16] The Tower is understood to be a reference to the church, a metaphor reminiscent of the mountain in *Sim*. 9. Particularly, in *Vis*. 3.5–7, the Lady explains the different groupings of the stones that Hermas saw either building the Tower or being rejected by the builder of the Tower.[17] Of interest here are those stones that the Lady says fit easily into the Tower. These stones the Lady identifies as the apostles, bishops, teachers, and deacons who have walked in holiness and of whom some *have fallen asleep* (ἀπόστολοι καὶ ἐπίσκοποι καὶ διδάσκαλοι καὶ διάκονοι οἱ πορευθέντες κατὰ τὴν σεμνότητα τοῦ θεοῦ . . . οἱ μὲν κεκοιμημένοιμέν). The phrase οἱ μὲν κεκοιμημένοι ("have fallen asleep"), which will be repeated in *Sim*. 9, is used in the New Testament and early Christianity as a figure of speech meaning to "be dead, sleep." In the substantive, it means one who has fallen asleep. It appeared in Hebrew graves as inscription for the state of sleeping or lying down to sleep.[18] The emphasis, therefore, is on the fact that these dead Christians are now in a peaceful rest, compared to merely falling asleep.

The Shepherd comes back to the subject of death in *Sim*. 9. In a vision similar to the one in *Vis*. 3, Hermas is shown twelve mountains (9.1), a revisitation of the vision of the Tower (9.2–9), the young women/virtues (9.10–11), the explanation of the tower and the young women (9.12–16), and, an explanation of the twelve mountains (9.17–29).[19] Specifically, while explaining the meaning of the twelve mountains to Hermas, the Shepherd turns his attention to those who have fallen asleep in 9.15–16. A key difference, however, occurs between the ones who are identified as asleep here and the ones who are identified as such in *Vis* 3.5.1–5.

---

the Hermes mentioned in Rom 16:14, one of the members of the church of Rome that Paul sends his greetings. According to some, most probably, it seems more likely that the suggestion by the Muratorian Canon (ca. AD 180–200?) that this is the work of the brother of Pius, the bishop of Rome (ca. 140–154) was the author. But this is at best uncertain. For further discussion on this subject, see Snyder, *The Shepherd of Hermas*, 1–3; Osiek, *The Shepherd of Hermas*.

16. *Herm. Vis.* 3.3–7

17. For a full structural analysis of the groupings of these stones, see Osiek, *The Shepherd of Hermas*, 70.

18. Bauer et al., eds., *A Greek-English Lexicon of the New Testament*, s.v. κοίμησις.

19. For a discussion of the place of this Similitude in *The Shepherd of Hermas*, see Osiek, *The Shepherd of Hermas*, 211.

Whereas in the Vision the ones who are asleep were identified as apostles, overseers, teachers, ministers, and those who have suffered for the name of the Lord, here, it seems like the phrase "ones asleep" goes deeper than the Christian times. As Osiek notes, "verse 16.5 will make it clear that the intended people except for the forty are pre-Christian."[20]

In a very complicated argument that involves the meaning of baptism as well as the symbolic meaning of death and the activity of the dead, the author, perhaps appealing to some local folk traditions, lays bare his views of the existence and some activities associated with the dead.[21] First of all, according to the Shepherd, it is necessary for everybody to "come out through water" in order to be made alive so that they can enter the kingdom of God.[22] Without doubt, the reference here is to baptism, without which everybody is considered to be "in their deadness." Thus, death here is understood metaphorically, as a reference to the pre-baptismal state, with baptism being the only way out of this kind of death.[23] However, the situation becomes even more interesting when the Shepherd tells Hermas that as far as the pre-Christians are concerned, the apostles and the prophets preached to them in their dead state and even "gave them the seal of the preaching."[24] Since the "seal" is understood here as a reference to baptism, the argument expressed here is that the apostles and the prophets baptized these pre-Christian dead in their place of the dead.

The belief that indeed Christ also preached to the dead sometime between His death and resurrection is well-attested in the early church.[25] Most probably, the concept here is based on that belief. However, it seems like *The Shepherd* sees more than preaching taking place here: the

---

20. Ibid., 237.

21. Ibid. See also Dibelius, *Der Hirt des Hermas*, 624–25.

22. *Herm. Sim.* 9.16.2.

23. According to Osiek, "the association of passing through water with entering the kingdom of God (v. 2) and receiving the seal (σφαγίς) is unmistakably a reference to baptism, more explicit than the original allusion in Vis. 3.3.5. The language of death and life is similar to Pauline language [see Rom 6:1–11] but not exactly the same: here, death is the pre-baptismal state, not the dying process that is symbolically enacted in the course of baptism (Osiek, *Hermas*, 238).

24. *Herm. Sim.* 9. 16.5.

25. See especially 1 Pet 3:19–20; 4:6; *Ep. Apost.* 27; *Apoc. Pet.* 14; *Odes Sol.* 42:11–20; Irenaeus *Haer.* 1.27.3 ; Tertullian *Adv. Marc.* 4.24 ; Hippolytus *Antichr.* 45. For further discussion, see Hill, *Regnum Caelorum*, 86. For a current discussion, see Bass, "The Battle for the Keys."

baptism of the dead by the apostles and prophets who have themselves also fallen asleep.

In conclusion, therefore, the concept of death in these earlier sub-apostolic writings is subsumed under such other concerns as the unity of the church and the holiness of believers. The views are held as an encouragement for the unity of believers as well as for virtuous living.[26]

The Meaning of κοιμᾶσθαι

In Judaism and Christianity, the metaphor of the "sleep of death" has been largely employed to describe and perhaps define death.[27] Because of the centrality of this metaphor in understanding the concept of death since antiquity, there has not been a small scholarly controversy as far as its meaning is concerned. On the one side, there have been scholars like Oscar Cullmann who, because of what has been expressed as "more than a little distaste for Greek notion of disembodied soul" on their part, understand the term quite literally.[28] According to Cullmann, since death is both the last enemy and the wages of sin, it results in the possible annihilation of both the body and the soul. Cullmann starts by proposing an anthropology which states that man was created originally good both in body and soul. However, according to him, after the fall of Adam, the "flesh," the "power of sin or the power of death," entered man, the inner

---

26. In its teaching on the belief of the resurrection, the Christian homily known as 2 *Clement*, written perhaps at the same time as 1 *Clement*, also emphasizes reward after death as an encouragement for a holy life of a believer (see 2 *Clem.* 5.5). Similar teaching is also found in the *Didache*. Talking about the second coming of the Lord, the document stresses the expected behavior appropriate for those who are waiting for his coming and the accompanying rewards in *Did.* 16.6–8. Thus since these are not lengthy treatments of the concept of death, I don't feel that they need much treatment. Furthermore, their themes are quite similar to those of 1 *Clement* and *The Shepherd of Hermas* when it comes to the concept of death.

27. For some examples where the "sleeping" and "awaking" metaphor occurs, see 1 Kgs 1:21; 2 Kgs 4:32; 1 Chr 17:11; 2 Chr 16:13; Ezk 31:18; 32:20–32; Dan 12:2; Job 3:11–14; 14:12; Pss 3:6; 4:9; 87:6; Jer 2:33; Isa 57:2; 59:3–4; Sir 46:20; 2 Macc 12:43–45; Mark 5:39; Luke 8:52; Matt 28:52; Acts 7:60; 1 Cor 7:39; 15:6, 51; 1 Thess 4:13–15; Eph 5:14; Justin *Dial.* 72.4; 97; 1 *Apol.* 38.3; 1 *Clem* 24–26; Irenaeus *adv. haer* 5.13.4, etc. For an excellent study of the use of the metaphor of the sleep of death in antiquity, see Ogle, "The Sleep of Death," 81–117. See also Miguel, "Zur Lehre vom Todesschlaf," 285–90.

28. Peters, "Resurrection," 69.

man and the outer man.²⁹ The existence of this power, argues Cullmann, necessitates that death be understood as the annihilation of both the inner man and the outer man in order to eradicate this power permanently. Thus, according to him, the metaphor of the "sleep of death" means something akin to "repose." Rejecting Karl Barth's assertion that this term implies "a peaceful going to sleep which those surviving have," Cullman notes that "the expression [sleeping] in the New Testament signifies more, and like the repose in Apocalypse 14:13 refers to the *condition* of the dead before the Parousia."³⁰

Cullmann seems to move back and forth between what has come to be known as "soul sleep" and what he calls being "with Christ" to describe the interim state of the dead believers. By the expression "with Christ," he means the continued existence of the inner man (soul) through the power of the Holy Spirit that has renewed him.³¹ This oscillation has earned him the support of some proponents of soul sleep, such as Reichenbach. Arguing that Cullmann is inconsistent, he observes that "yet in arguing that an essential part of man can continue to exist subsequent to death he [Cullmann] is adopting a Greek Dualistic position."³² Thus, Reichenbach sees Cullmann as an inadvertent proponent of the very thing that he (Cullmann) has vehemently rejected: that is, the concept of Greek philosophical influence in early Christianity's idea of death.

Even before Cullmann came in the picture, the idea that both the body and the soul go to "sleep" at death, was prevalent. Scholars point out that this concept started in the second century as believers struggled with the concept of rewards and judgment especially at the wake of persecution and martyrdom. According to Gavin, the idea of "soul sleep"

---

29. Cullmann, *Immortality of the Soul*, 34. For a critique of this anthropology, see Schep, *The Nature of the Resurrection Body*, 12 n. 5.

30. Cullmann, *Immortality of the Soul*, 51 n. 6. To be fair to Cullmann, he understands those who are in Christ to have already started being "resurrected" through the presence of the Holy Spirit. But he does not know how to deal with the statement of Jesus to the thief on the cross that, "today, you will be with me in Paradise." After a lengthy discussion of this passage, he concludes: "The thief asks Jesus to remember him when he 'comes into His kingdom,' which according to Jewish view of the Messiah can only refer to the time when the Messiah *will come* and erect the kingdom. Jesus does not grant the request, but instead gives more than he asked for: he will be united *with Jesus* even before the coming of the kingdom" (ibid., 50 n. 5). What kind of form this union takes place, Cullmann does not define.

31. Ibid., 52.

32 Reichenbach, "Resurrection of the Body," 39. See also Bailey, "Is Sleep the Proper Biblical Term," 161–67.

started with Tatian and has been common in the Syrian church theology ever since.[33] Since such apologists as Tatian emphasized what has come to be known as the "unitary anthropology" (that is, the body and the soul are so united that neither could experience either judgment or rewards without the other), it was believed that during the time between death and resurrection, nothing happens in terms of the soul's consciousness.[34] And, as noted above, in contrast to the Greek and Latin fathers, the Syrian church has continued to hold on to this position concerning the state of the dead during the intermediate period. A key proponent of this view today is A. C. Rush, who, according to Gousmett, argues that the belief in "soul-sleep" on the part of the early Christians was in stark contrast to the existing pessimistic pagan view of death as an eternal sleep from which there was no awakening.[35]

However, a majority of scholars understand the expression κοιμᾶσθαι ("fallen asleep") as a metaphor for the infinitive "to die." Indeed, this metaphorical understanding is consistent with the usage of the term in Greek since the time of Homer. The expression appears for the first time in *Il.* 11.241 and 14.482–3. It occurs again in the Homeric poetry in *Odyss.* 13.79–80. In these occurrences, the expression is used as a simple comparison between natural sleep and death.[36] As time progressed, the expression was softened to a simile, being used to refer to the "peaceful end of men in the Golden Age."[37] As Ogle explains, the tradition of comparing death with sleep continued throughout the Platonic Age. During this time, the expression was used as an argument to combat the fear of death.[38] While the usage of this metaphor somehow diminished in the Poetic period, it is widely used in the Hellenistic period.

In regard to the use of this expression to refer to death in the second century, it seems like the immediate context is the Old Testament and Hellenism (especially after Alexander the Great) and the New Testament. Ogle summarizes:

---

33. Gavin, "The Sleep of the Soul," 107–8.

34. Gousmett, "Shall the Body Strive and Not be Crowned?" 42.

35. Rush, *Death and Burial*, 8–9, 12–13. See also Gousmett, "Shall the Body Strive and Not be Crowned?"; Rush, "Death as a Spiritual Marriage," 81–101.

36. Ogle, "The Sleep of Death," 81. The expression also occurs in Sophocles *Electra* 509.

37. Ibid.

38. Ibid.

That it was the influence of the Hebrew conception of death as sleep, whether working through the Bible or through later Jewish documents of an apocalyptic character, which led to the same metaphorical use of words for sleep by the early Fathers, both Greek and Latin, is proved, if proof is needed, by the fact that the Fathers, in their discussion of death and resurrection of the dead, invariably quote in support of their arguments the passages from the Old Testament, the Apocrypha and the New Testament.[39]

In other words, the Fathers' usage and interpretation of the metaphor of the sleep of death is in continuity with the earlier occurrences of this metaphor in the literature mentioned above. For example, when the writer of *1 Clement* talks about death as night that falls asleep and day arises (κοιμᾶται ἡ . . . ἀνίσταται ἡ ἡμέρα), he clearly has in his mind such Old Testament passages as Psalm 3:6.[40] And, as we noted above, with his concern being focused on Christian interaction with Judaism, the author of *The Shepherd of Hermas* applies the term metaphorically as well. But instead of the verb, the author uses the noun (κοίμησιν αὐτῶν) "their falling asleep."[41] Although there are questions as to whether the author is taking the expression from *Sirach* or some other passage(s) in the Old Testament, what is clear is that he is taking the expression metaphorically.[42]

When we come to the New Testament, we find multiple references to death as "sleep." Key examples include Matthew 27:52; John 11:11; Acts 7:60; 13:36; 1 Corinthians 7:39; 15:20, 22; 11:30; 1 Thessalonians 4:13–14; 2 Peter 3:4. In most of these occurrences, the passive κοιμᾶσθαι is used. Again, in continuity with the usage of the expression in the Old Testament, the term is used metaphorically to refer to death. However, the term is used mostly to refer to the death of believers.[43] Indeed, in some cases, it seems to refer to the manner of death (thus, Stephen was stoned, but "fell asleep"). He, in other words, dies peacefully as though going to a sleep, albeit being killed violently.

In conclusion, with this background, one is hard pressed to reach the conclusion of Cullmann and others that, according to early Christians, death means literal sleep. While Cullmann and others are correct in

39. Ibid., 95.
40. *1 Clem.* 24.3.
41. *Vis.* 3.11.3.
42. Ogle, "The Sleep of Death," 99.
43. Bailey, "Is 'Sleep' the Proper Biblical Term," 164.

noting that this is the term used for death in the New Testament, what the term means needs careful qualification. Bailey is correct in noting that the emphasis of the term is theological and eschatological and not anthropological.[44] In other words, this term is used as an euphemism for death and not a reference to "soul-sleep." I agree with Bailey's conclusion that:

> The state of the dead ... is not a sort of "soul-sleep." Rather, the term is an euphemism for death—a euphemism which indicates the manner of dying to some extent (as in e.g., Acts 7:60) and also the meaning of the death for the Christian. The Christian stands under the promise of the resurrection and death has for him lost its power, its sting. Those who die in Christ (I Thess 4:16) have the terror of death behind them—they are at rest (Rev 14:13). Because the dead are in Christ they may be said to be "asleep", though outwardly death retains its character as the enemy. Because Christ is risen, the dead in Christ do not perish in death (I Cor 15:17ff.). The eschatological factor is Christ.[45]

I contend that this aspect of being at rest in death is what these Fathers have in mind when they speak of death as sleep. This is consistent with the majority of thought in Hellenism, the Old Testament, and the New Testament. But, as noted above, with the onset of martyrdom and a growing need for an apologetic response to the critics of the Christian faith, the view of death as an unconscious sleep of the soul gained momentum especially with the Syrian church.[46] However, this exploration is beyond the scope of this study.

MARTYRS' CONCEPT OF DEATH

It is impossible to overemphasize the value of the writings of Ignatius, bishop of Antioch, on his way to martyrdom on the concept of death in second-century Christianity. Studies on Ignatius' view of death in view of his very own impending martyrdom as expressed in his seven letters considered authentic are multiple.[47] His views on death, I believe, give us

44. Ibid.
45. Ibid., 165.
46. Examples here include Aphrahat, Ephrem of Edessa, and Isaac of Syria.
47. These studies include but are not limited to McNamara, "Ignatius of Antioch on his Death"; Mellink, *Death as Eschaton*; and Bommes, *Weizen Gottes*. Mellink's analysis of these studies is helpful. He notes that first, there were the representatives of the so-called religion-historical school who argued that "Ignatius envisaged his road

insight to the concept of death from the perspective of those who literally stared death on its face in the second century. Four words (and their related derivatives and variations) come up in the discussion of the concept of death in the lives and works of Christian martyrs in the second century: discipleship, sacrifice, imitation, and resurrection. This is particularly the case with the Letters of Ignatius and the *Martyrdom of Polycarp*.

Ignatian Letters

A number of terms (or their variations) have been used to describe Ignatius' concept of death in lieu of his own impending martyrdom. These include μαθητής ("discipleship"), ἀνίσταμαι ("to rise"), θυσία/περίψημα ("sacrifice/dedication"), and μιμητήν ("imitator/imitation"). We will deal with these terms in the same order here. We will conclude by offering a summary of Ignatius' concept of death.

Death As True Discipleship

The term μαθητής or its equivalents in Ignatian usage occurs in these passages in the letters of Ignatius of Antioch: *Mag.* 9.1; *Rm.* 3.2; 4.2; *Eph.* 1.2; 3.1–2 and *Pol.* 7.1. In *Mag.* 9.1, Ignatius is interested in showing that if his readers patiently endure in Christ, then they will be found to be disciples of Jesus Christ (ἵνα εὑρεθῶμεν μαθεταὶ).[48] Similarly, in *Rm.* 3.2, talking about his attitude towards his martyrdom, Ignatius tells the Christian believers that he prays to have strength to not only talk about being a Christian, but to prove to be one. Once he proves to be a Christian, then he will have become "faithful when he is no longer visible to the world." It seems that the term μαθητής has been substituted with one of its Ignatian

---

unto death as a celestial journey like that of a Gnostic, or as a reenactment of the death of his Lord like that experienced by the initiate of certain mystery cults," (Mellink, *Death as Eschaton*, 52). Secondly, he notes that there were those who noticed that Ignatius rarely mentioned Christ. According to these, "Ignatius understood himself rather as an *alter Christus* than as a follower or imitator of Christ, and that he perceived his death rather as a second passion than an imitation of the passion of Christ" (ibid). In short, therefore, the emphasis of Ignatius' understanding of death has been either sociological or psychological. In some case, the focus is to situate "Ignatius' reflection of his violent death within the context of certain cultural and ideological trends at the time of the early Roman empire, such as the widespread fascination with death, and the rise of an imperial cult" (ibid).

48. Ign. *Mag.* 9.1.

equivalents, πιστός, here.⁴⁹ In a similar manner, Ignatius declares in *Rm.* 4.2 that after the beasts have completely consumed his body, leaving him not a burden to anyone, after he has fallen asleep, then he will "truly be a disciple of Jesus Christ" (τότε ἔσομαι μαθητὴς ἀληθῶς Ἰησοῦ Χριστοῦ).⁵⁰

In *Eph.* 1.2, Ignatius is thanking the Ephesian church that had hurried to visit him when they heard that he was in chains on his way from Syria to Rome. He thanks them for their prayers, by which he hoped to succeed in fighting with the wild beats and, succeeding, he "might be able to be a disciple" (ἵνα διὰ τοῦ ἐπιτυχεῖν δυνηθῶ μαθητὴς εἶναι).⁵¹ While "succeeding" here might mean overcoming the beasts, other contexts suggest that Ignatius is thinking about succeeding in dying at the hands of the beasts. In *Eph.* 3.1–2, Ignatius informs the Ephesian believers that he is not qualified to command them because he is yet to be perfected in Christ. In other words, he sees himself as "only beginning to be a disciple" (γὰρ ἀρχὴν ἔχω τοῦ μαθητεύεσθαι).⁵² He, therefore, only succeeds in encouraging them to be in harmony with the mind of Christ. In these verses, therefore, it has been proposed that "Ignatius understood suffering to be the beginning, and martyrdom the completion, of discipleship."⁵³ I will come back to this as I evaluate Ignatius' understanding of death as it relates to his discipleship. Finally, the term appears in *Pol.* 7.1. While reporting his encouragement because of the peace that the church at Antioch in Syria had finally achieved, thanks to Polycarp's prayers, Ignatius tells Polycarp that he has himself also received freedom from anxiety from God. However, he adds the remark that this freedom is only possible if he, through suffering, reaches God and proves to be a disciple (εὑρεθῆναί με ἐν τῇ αἰτήσει μαθητήν).⁵⁴

The question that scholars have struggled with is what exactly Ignatius means by the term μαθητής as it relates to his view of death. In

---

49. Ign. *Rom.* 3.2. It was Lightfoot who first observed correctly that the terms μαθητής and πιστός are actually equivalents, (*S. Ignatius, S. Polycarp*, 204). He noted that "his martyrdom alone will make him πιστός a believer, as it alone will make him truly a μαθητής." However, as McNamara perceptively notes, "what is unclear is the cause and effect relationship between martyrdom and being a μαθητής" (McNamara, *Ignatius of Antioch*, 24).

50. Ign. *Rm.* 4.2.

51. Ign. *Eph.* 1.2.

52. Ign. *Eph.* 3.1.

53. McNamara, "Ignatius of Antioch," 31.

54. Ign. *Pol.* 7.1.

THE CONCEPT OF DEATH IN THE APOSTOLIC FATHERS 67

other words, is there a causal relationship between discipleship and martyrdom? As McNamara observed, for over a good number of years, two theses proposed by Lightfoot and Bauer have dominated the discussion as far as the meaning of μαθητής in relation to Ignatius' view of death is concerned. First, "it is proposed that martyrdom would actually make him a disciple. Second, it is proposed that Ignatius understood suffering to be the beginning of discipleship, and martyrdom its completion."[55] Thus, based on these two theses, scholarly analyses of Ignatius' view of death "have concluded that Ignatius saw martyrdom to be an important and necessary part of the life of all true followers of Christ."[56] William Schoedel makes the same equation without qualification when he writes "Ignatius' discipleship has only begun and depends on a successfully completed martyrdom for its perfection."[57] Schoedel, however, does not see this attitude as a reflection of all the martyrs in the second century. Rather, he sees this conditional discipleship as expressed by Ignatius here as reflective of his own personal "self-doubt and self-effacement . . . ."[58]

However, there has been serious questioning of these theses. For example, in his lengthy study on the subject, McNamara concluded that the Lightfoot-Bauer theses misunderstood the meaning of the term μαθητής as it pertains to Ignatius' view of death. On the contrary, according to him, these texts really bear on "how he [Ignatius] will face his death."[59] Thus, the discipleship texts really are referring to the *manner* in which Ignatius desires to face his death; that is, as a disciple, and not the *cause* or *result*. This makes sense if we recall the continued concern by believers from the earliest times for the possibility of failing in their Christianity. In this case, therefore, Ignatius sees martyrdom as the chronological

---

55. McNamara, "Ignatius of Antioch," 22. See Bauer, *Die Briefe des Ignatius von Antiochia*, 198.

56 Ibid. Bauer went to the extent of equating martyrdom with discipleship, writing "gleichwertig mit mätyrer" (equivalent to martyr). (Bauer, *Die Briefe*, 198).

57. Schoedel, *Ignatius of Antioch*, 28–29.

58. Ibid., 29. Schoedel is among scholars who interpret Ignatius' attitude towards his impending death as a response to his failure as the bishop of Antioch. He, therefore, interprets the letters of Ignatius within this theory. Setting his thesis, he writes: "We shall argue that the bishop's reactions to his situation reveal a person whose self-understanding had been threatened and who was seeking to reaffirm the value of his ministry by what he did and said as he was taken to Rome" (ibid, 10). For similar views, see also Corwin, *St. Ignatius and Christianity* and Trevett, "Ignatius and His Opponents."

59. McNamara, "Ignatius of Antioch," 24.

limit of his discipleship and not a proof of it. In other words, before his martyrdom, there is still the possibility of failure and falling back, a concern that colors his writings.

Likewise, in his careful study of the discipleship passages of Ignatius as they pertain to his concept of death, Osger Mellink concluded that Ignatius does not see his death as what *causes* him to be a true disciple. Death, rather, according to Ignatius, is the final point of the completion of his discipleship, beyond which there is no questioning of his position in Christ. "Ignatius will have completed his task," he writes commenting on *Rm.* 4.2 that "beyond any doubt when the beasts have not left even the tiniest bit of his body. When the earthly Ignatius has ceased to exist . . . his life is fulfilled and his discipleship is perfected."[60] Most importantly, as he concludes, it is also important to note that "the use of the adverb ἀληθῶς, which suggests that Ignatius did see himself as a disciple, but only thought to become a *true* disciple in death."[61] Clearly, this conclusion challenges the Lightfoot-Bauer theses.

Indeed, the twin phrase that Ignatius uses in reference to his death sheds more light here. In a number of places, he equates his impending death with "attaining God" (θεοῦ τυγχάνειν).[62] Ignatius sees his death as the method through which he attains God, begging the Roman Christians not to do anything to impede this process from taking place in *Rom.* 2.1.[63] Appearing twenty times in Ignatian letters, the verb ἐπιτυγάχνω is certainly an important one for Ignatius. While some like Swartley and Schoedel hold to the position that this phrase means that Ignatius sees the "achievement of unity in his own church and its realization in the churches of Asia as a certification of his ministry and a sign that there is no further question about his worthiness to attain God and become a disciple," this interpretation seems like a bit of a stretch.[64] In all the

---

60. Mellink, *Death as Eschaton*, 187.

61. Ibid.

62. See, for example, Ign. *Eph.* 10.1; Ign. *Mag.* 1.2; Ign. *Sm.* 9.2; cf. Ign. *Pol.* 4.3. An alternative phrase occurs in Ign. *Rom.* 1.2: "to reach God" (θεοῦ ἐπιτυχεῖν). See also Ign. *Pol.* 2.3. For a complete study of the meaning of the term τυγχάνειν in Ignatian corpus, see Bower, "The Meaning of ΕΠΙΤΥΓΧΑΝΩ," 1–14. In total, the verb ἐπιτυγχάνω occurs twenty times in the letters of Ignatius, certainly not a small count by any standard.

63. Apparently, Ignatius saw the Roman church as being in a position to influence the political leaders at Rome, and, perhaps, block his impending execution. This, in his opinion, would rob him of his only opportunity to attain God.

64. Schoedel, *Ignatius of Antioch*, 29. See also Swartley, "The Imitatio Christi,"

eighteen times that Ignatius uses the phrase θεοῦ ἐπιτυχεῖν to refer to his journey towards his martyrdom, it seems clear that he is using it as a reference to his trajectory which he sees as ending with his death, and, thus, attainment of God. Thus,

> In sum, no less than twelve times Ignatius speaks about his imminent death as a possibility to attain God or Christ. We do not get much information about what Ignatius understood by this notion in itself. Yet the framework seems clear. On the road to attainment Ignatius is supported by some and opposed by others. The grace of God and the prayer of the local communities stand over against the envy of things visible and invisible. His death is the last stage on the road to the final goal: the attainment of God and Christ.[65]

Again, it seems that Ignatius' concern with both the terms μαθητής and τυγχάνειν is the chronological outcome of being a disciple of Christ and not a cause and effect relationship. Therefore, it will be an unnecessary stretch for anyone to "infer that Ignatius understood that death itself would transform him to a μαθητής."[66] In other words, the argument that death, according to Ignatius means discipleship needs to be carefully defined.

Death As Resurrection

The other contentious phrase that Ignatius uses to describe his own death is the infinitive ἀνίσταμαι ("to rise"). Ignatius either uses this term or its conceptual synonyms in at least three key passages. These are *Eph* 11:2, *Mag* 9.2 and *Rm* 4.3. In his letter to the *Eph* 11.2, Ignatius writes: χωρὶς τούτου μηδὲν ὑμῖν πρεπέτω, ἐν ᾧ τὰ δεσμὰ περιφέρω, τοὺς πνευματικοὺς μαργαρίτας, ἐν οἷς γένοιτό μοι ἀνατῆναι τῇ προσευχῇ ὑμῶν, ἧς γένοιτό μοι ἀεὶ μέταχον εἶναι, ἵνα ἐν κλήρῳ Ἐφεσίων εὑρεθῶ τῶν Χριστιανῶν, οἳ καὶ τοῖς ἀποστόλοις πάντοτε συνῄνεσαν ἐν δυνάμει Ἰησοῦ Χριστοῦ ("Let nothing appeal to you apart from him, in whom I carry around these chains (my spiritual pearls!), by which I hope, through your prayers, to rise again. May I always share in them, in order that I may be found in the

---

81–103.

65. Mellink, *Death as Eschaton*, 214.

66. McNamara, "Ignatius of Antioch," 26. It helps to remember that Ignatius' concern in these letters was pastoral. Rather, he was concerned that believers in Asia would not turn back on Christ when faced with persecution which many times resulted in martyrdom.

company of the Christians of Ephesus, who have always been in agreement with the apostles by the power of Jesus Christ)."[67]

Scholars have wrestled with the question of the meaning of Ignatius' difficult phrase here: "to rise again." In his monograph on the concept of the resurrection of the dead in the Apostolic Fathers, van Eijik argues that for Ignatius, martyrdom is resurrection in the sense that both are two aspects of the same event.[68] Likewise, Schoedel, agreeing with Eijik that Ignatius sees his death as resurrection, commenting on this verse, writes:

> Especially in light of *Mag.* 9.2 and *Rom.* 2.2 (4.3) Ignatius probably thinks of resurrection as a state immediately after death. In any event, his talk of rising in his bonds is not intended to clarify the state of human beings in the other world but to express his hope of seeing his martyrdom through. Hence also his reference to the prayer of the Ephesians on his behalf.[69]

Thus, according to Schoedel, Ignatius sees his resurrection as taking place immediately after death. However, he does not deal specifically with the question of the nature of this resurrection.[70] The question, hence, is this; does Ignatius see his resurrection taking place immediately after death or at the Parousia, according to this verse? It would help to, before making any conclusion, look at the other key passage (*Rm* 4.3).

In his letter to the church in Rome, Ignatius famously wrote in 4.3: οὐχ ὡς Πέτρος καὶ Παῦλος διατάσσομαι ὑμῖν. ἐκεῖνοι ἀπόστολοι, ἐγὼ κατάκριτος· ἐκεῖνοι ἐλεύθεροι, ἐγὼ δὲ μέχρι νῦν δοῦλος. ἀλλ' ἐὰν πάθω, ἀπελεύθερος γενήσομαι Ἰησοῦ Χριστοῦ καὶ ἀναστήσομαι ἐν αὐτῷ ἐλεύθερος. νῦν μανθάνω δεδεμένος μηδὲν ἐπιθυμεῖν ("I do not command you as Peter and Paul. They were apostles, I am a condemned man; they are free, I am still a slave. But if I suffer, I shall be a freedman of Jesus Christ, and I shall arise free in him").[71] My concern is the last part of the passage.

Scholars are divided on what exactly Ignatius means by the phrase ἀναστήσομαι ἐν αὐτῷ ἐλεύθερος ("I shall rise in him free.") Taking the preposition ἐν spatially, Eijik argues that Ignatius is here thinking

---

67. Ign. *Eph* 11.2.

68. Van Eijik, *La résurrection des morts*, 119–20. However, Eijik also understands Ignatius as seeing his own resurrection as ascension unto God in heaven (ibid., 121–24).

69. Schoedel, *Ignatius of Antioch*, 72 n. 2. See also Bynum, *The Resurrection of the Body*, 171–72.

70. Mellink, *Death as Eschaton*, 253.

71. Ign. *Rom* 4.3.

resurrection as another aspect of his suffering (πάθος).[72] Mellink, on the other hand, insists that there is no proper justification to take this preposition as spatial. Rather, according to him, "it appears more probable that the preposition ἐν should be taken in an instrumental sense, just as in Eph 11:2."[73] Taken this way, therefore, Ignatius is understood to be saying that he will rise in Christ after his suffering. This understanding seems consistent with his understanding of the role of Christ in the ultimate resurrection of all believers at the Parousia.[74] Indeed, Ignatius' language here is reminiscent of Paul's in reference to the union of believers with Christ both in his death and resurrection.[75]

Most probably, Ignatius here is thinking of the hope that he has of resurrection after having suffered persecution (hence the conditional ἐὰν πάθω). He is thinking of the chronology and not necessarily the nature and time of the resurrection here. Bearing in mind how Ignatius sees believers' resurrection as taking place in the future, I concur with Mellink, that "Ignatius perceived his violent death as a condition to participate in the resurrection at the end of time and not as a gateway to a heavenly existence with God."[76]

To be fair, however, it is also significant to note that there is a significant amount of literature that talks about the immediate resurrection of the martyr. This literature includes both Jewish and Hellenistic corpus. These texts use the specific verbs ἀνίστημι/ἐγείρω or the noun ἀνάστασις to refer to the martyrs' death.[77] Specifically, in the Intertestamental document known as 2 Maccabees, resurrection is mentioned in a number of places as in connection with violent death. In many of these passages, it seems like death is understood as resurrection. One key passage serves to illustrate this.

---

72. Eijik, *La résurrection des morts*, 120.

73. Ibid.

74. See, for example, Ign. *Sm* 1–2 and Ign. *Tral* 9.1–2.

75. See Rom 8:11; 1 Cor 6:14; 15:12–5; 2 Cor 4:14; 1 Thess 4:14; Rom 6:5. Notice the similarity of the language especially in Rom 6:5: "Εἰ γὰρ σύμφυτοι γεγόναμεν τῷ ὁμοιώματι τοῦ θανάτου αὐτοῦ, ἀλλὰ καὶ τῆς ἀναστάσεως ἐσόμεθα" ("For if we have been united in a death like his, we will certainly be united with him in a resurrection like his.")

76. Mellink, *Death as Eschaton*, 257.

77. According to BDAG, the term ἀνάστασις means "a change for the better in status, rising up, rise," as well as "resurrection from the dead" (BDAG, s.v. ἀνάστασις).

Chapter 7 of this document records the execution of the seven brothers and their mother during the reign of Antiochus Epiphanes.[78] In 2 Maccabees 7, we see the record of the final moments of one of the seven brothers who are the subjects of the document. All are put to death on account of the Torah:

> Each brother is brought forward, refuses to obey the king's command, is tortured, and makes a speech before he dies. The mother makes two speeches, which are placed between the speeches of the sixth and the seventh brothers. The subject matter of the speeches is twofold: a) the mother and the second, third, and fourth brothers speak of dying for the Torah and the hope of the resurrection; b) the fifth, sixth, and seventh brothers discuss the suffering of the nation and the punishment that awaits Antiochus.[79]

Particularly, when the second brother addresses the king, he declares in 7.9: σὺ μὲν ἀλάστωρ ἐκ τοῦ παρόντος ἡμᾶς ζῆν ἀπολύεις, ὁ δὲ τοῦ κόσμου βασιλεὺς ἀποθανόντας ἡμᾶς ὑπὲρ τῶν αὐτοῦ νόμων εἰς αἰώνιον ἀναβίωσιν ζωῆς ἡμᾶς ἀναστήσει ("Thou like a fury takest us out of this present life, but the King of the world shall raise us up, who have died for his laws, unto everlasting life").[80] Although there is agreement that this and similar texts speak of the ultimate vindication of the Jewish nation, what has concerned many interpreters here is the timing of the resurrection of these brothers. According to Kellermann, 2 Maccabees is really a text about the immediate resurrection of the martyr in heaven after death, which is in contrast to the eschatological resurrection at the end of time.[81] Further, with other passages like 2 Maccabees 7:36 whereby a comparison between the brother's brevity of suffering and the reception of the rewards ("διαθήκην Θεοῦ—the covenant of God") is made, the conclusion has been made by some that "the termination of the suffering" is the beginning of eternal life. In other words, the brothers are raised immediately after death.[82] Death, accordingly, is seen as resurrection. And, consequently, these and similar passages in Hellenism and Judaism are

---

78. For some key studies of 2 Maccabees, see Kellermann, *Auferstanden in den Himmel*. For a helpful discussion of the authorship of 2 Maccabees, see Cavalin, *Life After Death*, 111.

79. Nickelsburg, *Resurrection, Immortality, and Eternal Life*, 119.

80. 2 Macc 7.9. See also 2 Macc 12:43–44.

81. Kellermann, *Auferstanden in den Himmel*, 64–65.

82. Mellink, *Death as Eschaton*, 271.

seen as the precursors of passages like the ones we have come across in Ignatius of Antioch.[83]

However, a careful reading of the passage shows that it is neither concerned with the time nor the place where the martyrs will be raised. In other words, the view that they have been raised immediately in heaven after death cannot be textually substantiated. Rather, "the main point seems to be the opposition between the reward of the faithful Jewish martyrs (οἱ μέν) and the punishment of the lawless Antiochus (σὺ δέ)."[84] But, "when and where this settlement—may it be vindication or damnation—will take place is left unsaid."[85] Nickelsburg's observation seems in order, that this story preserved that hope that God would avenge the unjust deaths of these sons and their mother "by means of an apocalyptic catastrophe" in the eschaton.[86]

In summary, therefore, although Ignatius uses language that suggests that he understands his death as resurrection, there is no clear indication in the relevant texts that he sees this resurrection taking place immediately after death. Also, neither is this clear in the literature that Ignatius may be alluding to, that is, 2 Corinthians 5:1–10 and 2 Maccabees 7 as discussed above. Rather, what seems clear is the continued hope of resurrection, reward and vindication in spite of the impending suffering and death.

Death As Sacrifice

The other key expression that Ignatius uses to describe his death is περίψημα ("sacrifice") and its related terms.[87] Although the idea of sacrifice as the guiding theme of Ignatius' view of death was hinted at by Zahn, Lightfoot, and Walter Bauer, it was Hans von Campenhausen who explored it to the fullest.[88] Since the term "sacrifice" implies giving one's

---

83. Kellermann, *Auferstanden in den Himmel*, 131. For the possible utility of this Maccabean passage in the New Testament book of Hebrews, see Lane, "Living a Life of Faith," 247–69.

84. Mellink, *Death as Eschaton*, 271.

85. Ibid.

86. Nickelsburg, *Resurrection, Immortality, and Eternal Life*, 137.

87. Ign. *Rom.* 2.2; 4.2b; Ign. *Eph.* 8.1; 18.1; 21.1; Ign. *Tral* 13.3; Ign. *Smyr.* 10.2; Pol. 2.3; 6.1. The other key substitute term is θυσία.

88. Zahn, *Ignatius von Antiochien*, 420; Bauer, *Die Briefe*; Campenhausen, *Ignace d'Antioche*, 51.

life for someone or something else, the focus of the discussion has been on these key questions: Did Ignatius himself understand his death as a sacrifice in a technical manner? Did Ignatius believe that there would be some people who would benefit from his death? If so, who are these people and what kind of "benefit" did he believe his death would bring?[89] As we look into these questions, it is important to look more keenly at the key passages where Ignatius uses the term περίψημα or its equivalents.

One of the key passages in understanding Ignatius' conception of death as sacrifice is *Rom.* 2.2. In this passage, Ignatius appeals to the Roman Christians to grant him nothing short of being "poured as an offering to God" (σπονδισθῆναι θεῷ, ὡς ἔτι θυσιαστήριον).[90] As noted above, in his plea to the Roman church, Ignatius asks them not to use their presumed political power in order to influence the outcome of his anticipated martyrdom there since he is on his way to be poured as an offering/sacrifice to God. Since Ignatius mentions this "offering" as taking place in the altar at Rome (ἕτοιμόν), the meaning of the term has been associated with the Lord's Supper. For example, Gilles P. Wetter saw Ignatius as understanding his death as participation in a cultic event.[91] In this case, "Ignatius pictures the Roman Christians as gathered around him in the arena, just as they normally are gathered around the eucharistic altar in the church."[92] Wetter saw Ignatius as understanding his death as a representation of Christ and his passion, "but then in a more realistic way," going as far as speaking of Ignatius' death as *ein blutiges Abendmahl* (a bloody Lord's Supper).[93]

The other set of passages are those whereby the term περίψημα occurs. In the passages where the term "sacrifice" occurs, Ignatius uses the combination of the terms περίψημα ὑμῶν ("I am dedicated to you.")[94] On his part, Frend, commenting on *Rom.* 4, notes that "primarily, therefore, Ignatius regarded martyrdom as a sacrifice."[95] But he locates the benefits of Ignatius' sacrifice in something else: the defeat of Satan. He concludes: "Ignatius takes up the theme of innocent, expiatory suffering as the means

---

89. McNamara, "Ignatius of Antioch," 43.

90. Ign. *Rom.* 2.2.

91. Wetter, *Altchristliche Liturgion I*, 134–38.

92. Mellink, *Death as Eschaton*, 84.

93. Ibid.

94. See especially Ign. *Eph.* 8.1; 18.1; 21.1; Ign. *Trall.* 13.3; Ign. *Smyr.* 10.2; *Pol.* 2.3; 6.1.

95. Frend, *Martyrdom and Persecution*, 199.

THE CONCEPT OF DEATH IN THE APOSTOLIC FATHERS

of overthrowing Satan in the Last Times," adding that the "imitation of the Passion thus becomes the imitation of Jesus' own sacrifice on the model of that performed for Israel by the Maccabean martyrs."[96] Thus, although Frend sees Ignatius as understanding his death as sacrificial, the benefit of that sacrifice is that of the final defeat of Satan. However, Frend does not explain how this defeat of Satan is related to Ignatius' sacrifice.

The question is whether these two sets of passages are enough to support the conclusion that Ignatius saw his death as a sacrifice with salvific benefits, or even with an atonement value similar to that of Christ. As noted above, this has been the conclusion of some scholars like Wetter who based his conclusions on the mention of Ignatius in the subsequent *Acts of the Martyrs*.[97] This definitely creates a theological concern of seismic proportions. Winslow correctly elucidates the nature of the problem:

> The apparent contradiction, then, is this. On the one hand, it is Christ that ταῦτα πάντα ἔπαθεν δι' ἡμᾶς, ἵνα σωθῶμεν ["suffered all things for our sakes, in order that we might be saved"] (Smyr. 2.1); yet, on the other hand, Ignatius claims that it is only through his *own* [Ignatius'] suffering and death that he can receive the ἀμοιβή ["reward"] of God (Smyr. 9.2). Ignatius proclaims salvation through Christ, yet, in these Epistles, it is only his own death which he describes in "sacrificial" terms (Rom. 2.2., 4; Smyr. 10.2), even referring to himself as an ἀντίψυχον ὑμῶν ["my spirit be a ransom on your behalf"] (Eph. 21.2; Smyr. 10.2).[98]

For many, therefore, in contrast to the finished work of Christ of salvation, Ignatius sees his work as that which ensures his (and possibly others') salvation. T. F. Torrance drew the same conclusion in his Basel dissertation.[99] Indeed, according to McNamara, this has been the consensus since the time of Theodore Zahn. "The merit of that death [of Ignatius]," he writes, "moreover, is almost universally acknowledged to be either an atonement or even salvific sacrifice similar to that attributed to Christ."[100]

Although I will explore this idea further as I evaluate Ignatius' use of the term περίψημα below, a couple remarks are in order. It seems like there are enough reasons to cast doubt on the conclusion that Ignatius understood his death to be similar to that of Christ as far as securing

---

96. Ibid.
97. Mellink, *Death as Eschaton*, 84.
98. Winslow, "The Idea of Redemption," 125.
99. Torrance, *The Doctrine of Grace*.
100. McNamara, "Ignatius of Antioch," 44.

salvific benefits is concerned. Although these interpretations sound attractive, the main problem is that it is quite doubtful that the terminology of *Rom.* 2.2 really points to a Eucharistic service. First, although the term σπονδίζω and other comparable terms were used in the pagan cultic practices, it was never used either in the New Testament or the Apostolic Fathers in a Eucharistic context. Indeed, the verb σπονδίζω is a *hapax* within the New Testament and the Apostolic Fathers.[101] Second, in another context, Ignatius clearly differentiates his looking forward to celebrate the Eucharistic elements but not becoming the elements himself.[102] It seems, therefore, that Ignatius is not merely expressing his longing for a regular earthly Eucharistic service. But he "envisages his death as the beginning of a new, incorruptible, life."[103] Thus, since elsewhere Ignatius sees the Eucharistic elements as "symbols of immortality" (see Ign. *Eph.* 20.2), he sees participation in them as participation in the eternal life, a life in Christ that is "adumbrated in the eucharist," and a life that "will be realized in the future."[104]

In sum, therefore, there is no support for the conclusion that Ignatius saw his death as a sacrifice in the same way as that of Christ was. Although Ignatius uses the terms θυσία (sacrifice) and τοῦ σπονδισθῆναι (a libation) to refer to his death, it is hardly possible to demonstrate that, by the mere use of these terms, Ignatius saw his death as meritorious. In other words, Ignatius seems to be using the Eucharistic language in these passages to refer his death as "an image selected from the realm of baking to express the transformation that . . . [he] looked for as the result of his martyrdom."[105] The transformation is from the body characterized by sin and disobedience of God to an incorruptible state, a transformation he cannot wait for.

---

101. Mellink, *Death as Eschaton*, 85.

102. In Ign. *Rom.* 7.3, he writes: "I take the bread of God, which is the flesh of Christ who is of the seed of David; and for drink I want his blood, which is incorruptible love."

103. Mellink, *Death as Eschaton*, 86.

104. Ibid.

105. Schoedel, *Ignatius of Antioch*, 176.

Death As Imitatio Christi

Related to both discipleship and sacrifice, the other key term that Ignatius uses to explain his concept of death is μιμητής and/or its cognates.[106] Of all the occurrences of this term in Ignatian letters, it seems like it is only in Ign. *Rom.* 6.3 where Ignatius applies it directly to his own death.[107] In this passage, Ignatius urges the Romans not to impede his martyrdom. Instead, he urges them to allow him to "be an imitator of the suffering of my God." (ἐπιτρέψατέ μοι μιμητὴν εἶναι τοῦ παθους τοῦ θεοῦ). This passage has created a number of problems for interpreters. As McNamara observes, "here (and here alone) we have the grounds for relating the theme of imitation with Ignatius' understanding of his death."[108] In this understanding, Ignatius is seen as conceiving his death as patterned after the "Hellenistic mystery religions and/or Gnosticism."[109] Based on the *religionsgeschichtliche* model (school of comparative religion), "imitation was understood as a type of repetitive divinization oriented consciously toward attainment of the salvation of the devotee."[110]

There have been variations of this view as far as Ignatius' concept of death is concerned. Four names have come up as proponents of this view. These are Heinrich Schlier, Campenhausen, Théo Preiss, and E. J. Tinsley. According to Schlier, Ignatius saw himself as a Gnostic, "battling against satanic powers while attempting to flee from the cosmos and matter in order to complete his journey to God in the heavens."[111] In other words, Schlier saw Ignatius as understanding his death as ascension that is formulated after the widespread myth of *salvator salvandus*, that is, an unredeemed redeemer.[112] However, Schlier also saw a difference between Ignatius and the Gnostics in that while the latter reaches his goal

---

106. The term μιμητής occurs in Ign. *Rm.* 6.3; *Eph.* 1.1; 10.3; Ign. *Trall.* 1.2; Ign. *Phld.* 7.2.

107. In *Eph.* 1.1, Ignatius is talking about the Ephesians as "being imitators of God . . ." (μιμηταὶ ὄντες θεοῦ). Again, in *Ph.* 7.2, Ignatius urges the Philadelphians to "become imitators of Jesus Christ, just as he is of his father" (μιμηταὶ γίνεσθε Ἰησοῦ Χριστοῦ, ὡς καὶ αὐτὸς τοῦ πατρὸς αὐτοῦ).

108. McNamara, "Ignatius of Antioch," 57.

109. Ibid.

110. Ibid., 86. For the support of this theory, see Campenhausen, *Die Idee des Martyriums* and Preiss, "La mystique l'imitation du Christ."

111. McNamara, "Ignatius of Antioch," 60. See Schlier, *Religionsgeschichtliche Untersuchungen*, 132–75.

112. Mellink, *Death as Eschaton*, 58.

through asceticism, Ignatius "accepts a gruesome death" in order to reach his goal.[113] Schlier emphasized these two terms as the key to understanding Ignatius' concept of death as related to that of the Gnostic redeemer: "bond" (δεσμός) and "suffering" (πάθος). He wrote:

> In them [the Gnostic texts] the thought of Ignatius is clarified. In them and in Ignatius' suffering is a partaking in the sufferings of the Lord. Ignatius "imitates" the "pathos" of his God as the Gnostic expresses that of the fallen "Primal Man" or of Sophia or as the mystic "suffers anew" in his dance that of the Saviour. Ignatius calls the faithful to suffer with him as the Apostle Andrew calls Maximilla. The sufferings of both are identical since both are those of the Lord.[114]

It is the theme of πάθος that Campenhausen picked on. However, in a further expansion of Schlier's thought, Campenhausen saw Ignatius' understanding of his death even in more radical terms. According to him, Ignatius' understood his death as soteriologically rivaling that of Christ. Rather, instead of seeing Ignatius understanding of his πάθος as an imitation of Christ, he saw it as standing side by side to that of Christ.[115]

The question that we are faced with here is whether Ignatius really understood his imitation of Christ in the terms that have been set by these scholars. In other words, does Ignatius' concept of death show similarity with that of Hellenistic mystic's repetition that results in his divinization? Do we have to conclude with Preiss that "martyrdom in imitation of the πάθος of Christ was considered normative in Ignatian Christianity?"[116], In other words, was death, according to Ignatius, salvific?

It seems that Ignatius' concern in talking about imitating Christ and/or God is different from that of the Hellenistic mystics. Schoedel, while discussing *Rm.* 6.3, offers the helpful caution that "it is to be noted, however, that this is the only passage in which Ignatius connects the theme of imitation with his own suffering and death," observing that this "suggests

---

113. Ibid.

114. Schlier, *Religionsgeschichtliche*, 163.

115. Campenhausen, *Die Idee des Martyriums*, 64. Apparently, this idea of πάθος as a soteriological aspect in Ignatius' concept of death proved to be a significant contribution of Campenhausen. Since I have discussed it under "sacrifice" above, it does not bear repeating here. For a complete discussion of the usage of the term in Ignatian corpus, see Mellink, *Death as Eschaton*, 132–47.

116. McNamara, "Ignatius of Antioch," 69.

how questionable it is to take the imitation theme in the letters as indicative of an unqualified preoccupation of the bishop with personal salvation."[117]

It seems most probable to understand Ignatius' imitation language, therefore, within the precincts of the New Testament usage of the same.[118] In these usages, the emphasis is on the ethical imitation of Christ. But even more significant, it seems like Ignatius saw a parallel between his death and the Passion of Christ. However, this parallel needs to be nuanced carefully. Rather, it seems that Ignatius' concern here is that, in accordance with his other ideas about his own death, in the face of his death, he be found as faithful as Christ was in his own death. As Mellink observes, Ignatius is actually speaking of similarity in terms of "motivation." Thus, "probably the passage could be paraphrased. . . . Allow me to be an imitator of Christ, which means—at least for me, Ignatius, in my particular situation—to suffer like Christ suffered, i.e. to endure like Christ did, to remain faithful like Christ did, and to die free-willed for God like Christ did."[119] I will come back to the theme of imitation as I discuss Polycarp's view of death as expressed in the *Martyrdom of Polycarp*.

Conclusion: Ignatius' Use of περίψημα

Of all the terms that Ignatius uses to describe his concept of death, the term περίψημα has been the most problematic. This is because of its origin and usage in Greek culture. According to the entry in BDAG, the term περίψημα comes from the root word περιψάω, which means "wipe out or wipe around," and is used to refer to "that which is removed by the process of cleansing; dirt, off-scouring."[120] In addition, and even more relevant to our consideration here, BDAG adds the aspect of "ransom, scapegoat, [and] sacrifice."[121] It quotes the presbyter Photius, who seemed to have relied on Hesychius of Jerusalem (fifth century AD), and who noted that the term also referred to "the custom of making a human sacrifice every

---

117. Schoedel, *Ignatius of Antioch*, 183.

118. See, for example, Paul's language in Phil 1:29 and 3:8. It is important to note that Paul never speaks of "dying for Christ or God." In any case, even in Peter's answer to Christ that he (Peter) is ready to lay his own life down for the sake of Christ in John 13:37, the reference seems to be that of suffering and persecution. See also Jenks, "Paul and His Mortality," 171–83.

119. Mellink, *Death as Eschaton*, 198.

120. BDAG, 808.

121. Ibid.

year for the benefit of the rest of the people."[122] Even more relevant, in his discussion of the meaning of the term περίψημα in the Post-Apostolic Fathers, Stählin argues that Ignatius sees his death as a "ransom . . . for his fellow-believers, and he does so, indeed, in the sense that he goes to death vicariously for the many others who are spared in the persecution."[123] In other words, he sees Ignatius as seeing his death as having some meritorious value. However, he is quick to offer the caveat that Ignatius "certainly does not wish to deny the uniqueness of the death of Jesus."[124] BDAG's note that the term had "become more and more a term of polite self-depreciation, common in everyday speech," comes closest to describing how the Antiochene bishop is using the term in his letters.[125]

Any reasonable attempt to understand Ignatius' conception of his death as a sacrifice must take seriously into consideration a number of factors. First, we must recall the circumstances within which Ignatius is writing his epistles. These were hurriedly written letters as Ignatius was led towards his place of execution by guards who he referred to as the "ten leopards."[126] He was, in other words, not offering a systematic treatment of the subjects at hand. Thus, instead of judging him from a position of fully developed doctrine of death, we must recall that for Ignatius, death is not a matter of speculation. Rather, he is faced with the real threat of execution.[127] Second, it must be recalled that Ignatius' view of imitation is much more elaborate than mere following after. It involves "participation." This participation, Ignatius argues, involves suffering. For him, although Christ has indeed made the one perfect sacrifice for all humanity, "Christian discipleship necessitates sacrifice on our part as well."[128] But this is "not because it *adds* to what Christ has already done, but because it serves to *reflect* Christ's finished work."[129] Thus, for Ignatius, true discipleship involves sacrificial suffering for Christ if need be. But this sacrifice is just a reflection of what Christ has done than an addition to it. It has, in other words, no salvific value either for himself or anyone else.

---

122. Ibid.
123. Stählin, "περίψημα," 92.
124. Ibid.
125. BDAG, 808.
126. Ign. *Rom.* 5.1.
127. Winslow, "The Idea of Redemption," 127.
128. Ibid.
129. Ibid., 128.

In summary, Ignatius, bishop of Antioch, presents us with one of the most elaborate concepts of death in second-century Christianity. Among others, he uses these key terms to describe his own death: discipleship, resurrection, sacrifice, and imitation. Although the meanings of these terms have been debated over the years, it seems that it is fair to conclude that, for Ignatius, death is an immediate attainment of God (that is, completion and success of his journey of discipleship), reception of the lot as well as the resurrection and life. For Ignatius, death must be understood within the premise of sanctification. Suffering for him is not inconsistent with the Christian life.[130] Thus, it is an unjustified stretch to interpret his views of death in terms of any kind of psychological delusion. Most importantly, although Ignatius uses terms familiar in his milieu to describe his death, he gives them a distinctive Christian meaning. Finally, for Ignatius, there is no conception of a time period between death and resurrection (a time that later came to be known as the intermediate state). As noted above, this will come later as the concept of death continues to develop. But we must now turn to Ignatius' friend and bishop of Smyrna, Polycarp.

Death in Polycarp of Smyrna

Two documents come to mind when we think of Polycarp, the renowned bishop of Smyrna and a great friend of Ignatius, bishop of Antioch. These are his personal letter to the church at Philippi known as *Philippians* and the letter that was written to the church at Philomelium known as *The Martyrdom of Polycarp*, documenting the death of the bishop of Smyrna. Polycarp was one of the most notable leaders in Asia Minor in the post apostolic period.[131] Ignatius addressed one of his letters to him (*To Polycarp*). Polycarp had a successful ministry that spanned between "the end

---

130. See Matt 16:24; Luke 9:23. It can justifiably be argued that in his use of the concept of death as sacrifice, Ignatius has modified the meaning for the term περίψημα from a soteriological emphasis to sanctification one. This provides the reader with a clear example where a term's meaning has been modified to help express a distinctively Christian concept of death. And, since this meaning is applied within the precincts of the New Testament idea of following Christ even if it means participating in suffering for Christ's sake, it is commensurate with the level of revelation that Ignatius had at the time. To demand a thoroughgoing theological interpretation of the term at this stage of doctrinal development seems a bit anachronistic. In any case, Ignatius' use of the term here is the precursor to countless similar uses of the idea of suffering for Christ.

131. Holmes, *The Apostolic Fathers*, 272.

of the apostolic era and the emergence of catholic Christianity."[132] His place as one of the most significant church leaders in the early Smyrnaean Christianity cannot be overestimated. He is known to have concerned himself with the key issues during this formative time of Christianity like:

> The growing threat of persecution by the state, the emerging gnostic movement (he is particularly known for his opposition to Marcion, one of the movement's most charismatic and theologically innovative teachers), the development of the monepiscopal form of ecclesiastical organization, and the formation of the canon of the New Testament.[133]

His only surviving work is the *Letter to the Philippians*. But the most elaborate discussion of his life comes from the work known as *The Martyrdom of Polycarp*, a document of unknown authorship that is the earliest work on the subject of Christian martyrdom outside the documents of the New Testament.

To the Philippians: Death As imitatio Christi

Bishop Polycarp of Smyrna (d. 155–160) wrote a letter to the church in Philippi known as *To the Philippians*.[134] This letter is a complex hortatory speech that "(1) combines elements of at least three common letter types (encouragement, advice, and admonition), and (2) employs in portions of the letter a sermonic or homiletic style of discourse."[135] In the letter, Polycarp addresses the Philippians' request for a discussion on the topic of righteousness (3.1–10.3) as well as the problem of Valens (11.1–4), an "avaricious elder."[136] Polycarp's main concern in the letter, in other words, is to preserve church integrity whereby orthodoxy is matched by orthopraxy. "Polycarp's key goal was to maintain and protect the integrity of the community in terms of both its beliefs and its behaviors."[137] Thus, he

---

132. Ibid.

133. Ibid.

134. A suggestion was made by Campenhausen to the effect that Polycarp was the author of the Pastoral Epistles. As Holmes observes, however, this suggestion has been met with little acceptance (Holmes, *The Apostolic Fathers*, 273 n. 1).

135. Holmes, *The Apostolic Fathers*, 273.

136. Ibid., 274.

137. Ibid.

believed that wrong beliefs were actually characteristics of outsiders and not members of the Christian community.

Polycarp's discussion of the concept of death should be understood within this occasion of the letter. Although the subject of death comes up in 9.1-2, Polycarp prepares his readers in the preceding chapters. He starts the discussion in chapter 6. After exhorting the elders of the church to be compassionate, merciful to all, and turning back those who have gone astray, Polycarp reminds the Philippian Christians that all of us will stand before the judgment seat of Christ.[138] He then proceeds to exhort them to δουλεύσωμεν αὐτῷ μετὰ φόβου καὶ πάσης εὐλαβείας καθὼς αὐτὸς ἐνετείλατο καὶ οἱ εὐαγγελισάμενοι καὶ ἡμᾶς ἀπόστολοι καὶ οἱ προκηρύξαντες τὴν ἔλευσιν τοῦ κυρίου ἡμῶν ("serve Him [Christ] with fear and all reverence, just as he himself has commanded, as did the apostles who preached the gospel to us, and the prophets who announced in advance the coming of our Lord.")[139]

In chapter 8, he proceeds to exhort his readers to be imitators of Christ. In language reminiscent of what we have seen with his friend, Ignatius, Polycarp proceeds to specifically exhort his readers that μιμηταὶ οὖν γενώμεθα τῆς ὑπομονῆς αὐτῶ ἐὰν πάσχομεν διὰ τὸ ὄνομα αὐτοῦ, δοξάζωμεν αὐτόν ("Let us, therefore, become imitators of his [Christ's] patient endurance, and if we should suffer for the sake of his name, let us glorify him.")[140] Polycarp here combines two of the most significant terms in reference to the concept of death in this time of the development of Christianity. These are imitation (μιμηταί) and suffer (πάσχομεν). Because of the close connection in the life and thought of Ignatius and Polycarp, it is hard to avoid the conclusion that both are using these terms in the same manner in these texts. In other words, Polycarp here is not thinking of his death or that of any other Christian as exactly the same in terms of its sacrificial value as that of Christ. Rather, he is exhorting his readers to, if need be, accept suffering for their faith just as Christ suffered. As in Ignatius' thought, Polycarp sees an imitator as one who "strives to conform to another person's general stand."[141] Thus, "in general, the notion of imitating Christ is linked to the concepts of love, humility, endurance,

---

138. Pol. *Phil.* 6.1-2.
139. Ibid., 6.3.
140. Ibid., 8.2.
141. Mellink, *Death as Eschaton*, 67.

and peaceful union within the community."¹⁴² Again, we can justifiably make the same conclusion as far as the term "suffer" is concerned. Polycarp sees his suffering (and that of other Christians) for the sake of Christ not as exactly the same as that of Christ, but as hopeful because Christ Himself overcame death. In other words, the suffering of Christians in death is not a reenactment of the suffering and death of Christ, but a following of it.

Polycarp now makes his exhortation in view of his concept of death in chapter 9.1–2. He encourages the Philippian believers to exercise unlimited endurance (πᾶσαν ὑπομονήν) like the one that they saw with their own eyes not only in the blessed Ignatius and Zosimus and Rufus, but also from others from the congregation in Philippi as well as the rest of the apostles.¹⁴³ He then urges them to remember that the faithfulness of all these martyrs is not in vain. In verse 2, he explains that all these are now in the "place due them with the Lord, with whom they also suffered."¹⁴⁴ The phrase "place due them in the Lord" (ὀφειλόμενον αὐτοῖς τόπον εἰσί) is similar to Ignatius' idea of the "attainment of the lot."¹⁴⁵ Although I will come back to this phrase as I discuss the *Mart. Pol.*, it seems like Polycarp sees the departed believers as having been rewarded and already enjoying the benefits of their faithfulness in the Lord. Again, the concept of death here is consistent with the idea combining all the eschatological expectations together: attainment of God, reception of the lot (rewards), and participation in the resurrection. We have already seen these three notions with Ignatius. And, as it is presented, the concept of death here is to "instill courage at the prospect of martyrdom" in lieu of the expected rewards immediately after death, just as the departed martyrs experienced.¹⁴⁶

---

142. Ibid., 69.
143. Pol. *Phil.* 9.1.
144. Ibid., 9.2.
145. See Ign. *Ph.* 5.1; Ign. *Rm.* 1.2; 9.2; Ign. *Eph.*12.1; Ign. *Trall.* 12.3; *Mart. Pol.* 14.2.
146. Dewart, *Death and Resurrection*, 51.

The Martyrdom of Polycarp: Death As Imitatio Christi

The work we know as *The Martyrdom of Polycarp* is the oldest written account of martyrdom outside the New Testament.[147] This letter was written from the church of Smyrna to the church at Philomelium.[148] The work documents the trial and execution of Polycarp, bishop of Smyrna at the age of eighty-six years. It was apparently written by an eyewitness (see 15.1), and was aimed at setting forth what martyrdom in accord with the gospel means.[149] As the work progresses, a clear distinction is made between Quintus who volunteered himself for martyrdom, "forced others to go forward, and then turned coward" and Polycarp whose behavior is presented as exemplary and worthy of imitation.[150] It is this exemplary behavior that helps us understand Polycarp's concept of death.[151]

In the *Mart. Pol.*, Polycarp's trial and execution is presented as an imitation of the passion of Christ. However, as I hope to demonstrate, the emphasis in Polycarp is on death as obedience and faithfulness to Jesus Christ rather than dying for the same reason and with the same benefits as Christ did. As Holmes notes, "the concept of imitation [in Polycarp's thought], which could lead to a focus on the martyr, is subordinated to the idea of following after, which emphasizes more the concept of faithfulness and obedience to God's will, in whatever form it may take."[152]

---

147. Holmes, *The Apostolic Fathers*, 298.

148. For a full discussion of the transmission of the text of the *Martyrdom of Polycarp*, see Khomych, "A Forgoten Witness," and Lightfoot, *S. Ignatius, S. Polycarp*.

149. Holmes, *The Apostolic Fathers*, 299.

150. Ibid.

151. For a detailed explanation of the death of Polycarp and other martyrs in the Roman games, see Thompson, "The Martyrdom of Polycarp," 27–52. Thompson dates the execution of Polycarp on February 23, 155 or thereof at about noon. According to him, the Roman execution games consisted of three phases in the Roman amphitheaters. With the grandest amphitheater being the Flavian Colosseum at Rome, there were others all over the kingdom. Obviously, Polycarp was executed at the one in Smyrna. The first phase was in the morning when "animals [that] appeared in the wild but, contained in the arena, displayed the power of the empire" (ibid., 32). This took place in the morning. Later on in the afternoon, gladiators took the stage. However, according to him, it was the midday executions that were most brutal. "During those executions," he writes, "many spectators left the stadium to lunch on the grounds . . . but the remaining hardcore [ones] were vicious." It was during this time that Polycarp was executed, according to the Mart. Pol.

152. Holmes, ed. *The Apostolic Fathers*, 299.

Before looking at specific texts, a few comments are in order concerning this pivotal text on death in early Christianity. Because of the nuanced prescription of exactly what martyrdom is, the *Martyrdom of Polycarp* has been understood by some scholars as the first instance whereby the term μάρτυς is used in its technical sense, meaning "a Christian who bears witness unto death for his or her faith."[153] This conclusion is, however, debated. But, as Greenberg notes, "regardless of the term's earlier history, the significance of the term's current application is clear, providing at least a *terminus post quem* for such contextualized usage of the term."[154]

The author starts by declaring clearly that his aim is to offer an account of those who were martyred, "especially the blessed Polycarp, who put an end to persecution as though he were setting his seal upon it by his martyrdom."[155] This sets the stage for the comparison between the exemplary Polycarp who "waited to be betrayed as the Lord did," and the cowardly Quintus who forced himself and others to come forward, only to retreat afterwards.[156] The author then moves forward to describe how Polycarp prophesied his own death whereby, in a trance, he had seen his pillow being consumed by fire. According to the author, Polycarp understood this as a message from God that it was necessary for him to eventually be burned alive.[157] Of course, this is understood to be reminiscent of Jesus' prophecy of His own death.

In chapters 6 and 7, the author discusses the search and the arrest of Polycarp. Not surprising, the report of the search is also patterned after that of Jesus Christ. After reportedly pursuing him and tracing him in a country house, they found him and seized him together with two young slaves. He was reportedly betrayed by those closest to him (members

---

153. Greenberg, *My Share of God's Reward*, 151. According to Greenberg, there are two scholarly theories concerning the origin of the term "martyr." The first, which was advanced Bowersock, saw the concept of martyrdom as originating purely in the Greco-Roman concept of the Noble Death. The second theory was that of Rajak. Borrowing from Frend, Rajak saw martyrdom as a Judeo-Christian concept, having its origin in the Maccabean tradition of suffering death for one's beliefs (Greenberg, *My Share of God's Reward*, 45–60). For more discussion, see also Bowersock, *Martyrdom and Rome*, 5; Rajak, "Dying for the Law." For a discussion of the Noble Death, see Droge and Tabor, *A Noble Death*; Henten and Avemarie, *Martyrdom and Noble Death* and Henten, *The Maccabean Martyrs*.

154. Greenberg, *My Share of God's Reward*, 151.

155. *Mart. Pol.* 1.1.

156. *Mart. Pol.* 1.2; 4.1.

157. *Mart. Pol.* 5.2.

THE CONCEPT OF DEATH IN THE APOSTOLIC FATHERS

of his own family), just as Christ was betrayed by one of his disciples. Again, the captain of the police who arrested him is said to have been named Herod![158] In chapters 9-12, the author presents us with a detailed report of Polycarp's trial in the Arena by the Proconsul (he was accused of being an atheist), attempts to threaten him in to recanting Christ, his refusal to do so as well as the verdict and sentence. It is, however, in Polycarp's personal prayer and the final comments by the author that the concept of death is clearly elucidated (chapters 14-22). I will deal with the relevant texts here.

The author prepares the readers for Polycarp's prayer by telling us that he was tied with his hands behind himself, ὥσπερ κριὸς ἐπίσημος ἐκ μεγάλου ποιμνίου εἰς προσφοράν, ὁλοκαύτωμα δεκτὸν τῷ θεῷ ἡτοιμασμένον ("like a splendid ram chosen from a great flock for a sacrifice, a burnt offering prepared and acceptable to God").[159] Polycarp's death is, therefore, presented as a sacrifice to God. Although the reader cannot decipher much here as far as the meaning of the phrase "a burnt offering prepared and acceptable to God," is concerned, it seems like the phrase anticipates the author's presentation of what is purported to have happened at the actual execution of Polycarp. This is the subject of chapter 15, which I will discuss below.

In 14.1-3, the writer presents us with a scenario whereby, instead of cursing his circumstances, Polycarp offers a prayer of praises to God. Some scholars like Jefford have argued that it "is quite possible that this particular text was inserted into the Martyrdom as an endorsement of contemporary church traditions associated with the eucharist since the prayer mentions the sharing of the cup and a sacrifice which is acceptable to God."[160] However, there is nothing in the text to suggest that. Although the prayer contains significant Eucharistic language, Schoedel is correct in noting that this kind of language is not unlikely during this period of the history of the church. "There seems to be no evidence," he writes, "that the elements in the prayer are beyond the range of the possibilities in the middle of the second century."[161] In this prayer, Polycarp thanks God for having considered him εὐλογῶ σε, ὅτι ἠξίωσάς με τῆς ἡμέρας καὶ ὥρας ταύτης, τοῦ λαβεῖν με μέρος ἐν ἀριθμῷ τῶν μαρτύρων ἐν τῷ ποτηρίῳ

---

158. *Mart. Pol.* 6.1-2.
159. *Mart. Pol.* 14.1.
160. Jefford, *Reading the Apostolic Fathers*, 92.
161. Schoedel, *Polycarp, Martyrdom of Polycarp*, 70-71 n. 14:1-3.

τοῦ Χριστοῦ σου εἰς ἀνάστασιν ζωῆς αἰωνίου ψυχῆς τε καὶ σώματος ἐν ἀφθαρσίᾳ πνεύματος ἁγίου ("worthy of this day and hour, so that I might receive a place among the number of the martyrs in the cup of your Christ, to the resurrection to eternal life, both of soul and body, in the incorruptibility of the Holy Spirit"[162]). Without doubt, this is a significant summary of Polycarp's concept of death.

The adjective "worthy" is a dominant concept in the thought of many Christians during this time. Indeed, in Polycarp's contemporary and fellow martyr, Ignatius of Antioch, the adjective ἄξιος and its compounds such as ἀξιόθεος, ἀξιομακάριστος, and ἀξιόπιστος occurs thirty-seven times.[163] As well, the verbs ἀξιόω and καταξιόω occur fourteen times in Ignatian corpus.[164] In an in-depth summary of how the term and its variants are used in the New Testament and early Christianity, Mellink points out that these terms are fairly frequent. For example, Paul uses the ἄξιο-terminology in two instances. These are, first, Philippians 2:27 where he exhorts the Christians in Philippi to live a life worthy of the gospel, and, second, in 1 Thessalonians 2:12 where he pleads with the Thessalonians to lead a life worthy of God.[165] In addition to Paul's language, there are other stories in the Gospels that emphasize the unworthiness of humans in the sight of God.[166] However, in contrast to both Ignatius and Polycarp, in these New Testament passages seldom is the ἄξιο-terminology used in the context of suffering. But it seems like starting from Ignatius and Polycarp an emphasis arose whereby persecution and death for being a Christian is considered an honor because the martyr has been considered worthy to partake in God's judgment.

But there is a clear connection between Ignatius' and Polycarp's view of death with the use of the ἄξιο-terminology in some other New Testament passages. The connection seems to be in the tension that both Ignatius and Polycarp create here: although they are counted worthy to participate in God's judgment through martyrdom, they must *prove* worthy. This "proving" to be worthy is possibly a reference to such passages like 2 Thessalonians 1:5 whereby the persecutions that the Thessalonians are enduring are said to be "evidence of the righteous judgment of God,

---

162. Mart. Pol. 14.2.
163. Mellink, *Death as Eschaton*, 154.
164. Ibid.
165. Ibid., 160–61.
166. See, for example, the instance of the prodigal son in Luke 15:19–21.

that you may be found worthy of the kingdom of God" (ἔνδειγμα τῆς δικαίας κρίσεως τοῦ Θεοῦ, εἰς τὸ καταξιωθῆναι ὑμᾶς τῆς βασιλείας τοῦ Θεοῦ, ὑπὲρ ἧς καὶ πάσχετε), and Matthew 10:38 whereby Christ points out that "whoever does not take up the cross and follow me is not worthy of me" (καὶ ὃς οὐ λαμβάνει τὸν σταυρὸν αὐτοῦ καὶ ἀκολουθεῖ ὀπίσω μου, οὐκ ἔστι μου ἄξιος). As Mellink points out, in both texts, "the implication seems to be that only by accepting sufferings and hardships a Christian can (eventually) be found worthy of God."[167] Polycarp, therefore, sees his death as a badge of honor to be worn with dignity and pride.

Polycarp uses other key terms to describe his concept of death in this prayer. He praises God for having seen him worthy of being counted among the number of the martyrs in God's Christ. The phrase "receive a place among the number of the martyrs" (τοῦ λαβεῖν με μέρος ἐν ἀριθμῷ τῶν μαρτύρων ἐν τῷ ποτηρίῳ τοῦ Χριστοῦ σου) seems to be a reference to Polycarp's concept of death as the gateway to the presence of God where all the other martyrs are already present.[168] Thus, according to him, death is actually soteriological in that the martyr gets the opportunity to be ushered into the presence of God to join other martyrs already resting there.[169] Indeed, a couple lines later, Polycarp prays that he may be received in God's presence today.[170]

Two key phrases deserve a closer look because of their centrality not only in understanding the concept of death in the thought of Polycarp, but, also, in a larger scale, in the thought of many martyriological texts. These are: εἰς ἀνάστασιν ζωῆς αἰωνίου ψυχῆς τε καὶ σώματος ἐν ἀφθαρσίᾳ πνεύματος ἁγίου ("to the resurrection to eternal life, both of soul and of body, in the incorruptibility of the Holy Spirit").[171] This is extremely interesting given the fact that Polycarp sees all of these as taking place on exactly the same hour and day that he is executed. As I argue above, at this point, the concept of the difference in time between death and resurrection, that later came to be known as the "intermediate state," had not been fully developed. At this point in the history of the church, death was understood as the resurrection of the body and soul to eternal life and incorruptibility. In other words, just like Ignatius, Polycarp sees death as

---

167. Mellink, *Death as Eschaton*, 161.
168. Greenberg, *My Share of God's Reward*, 151.
169. Ibid., 152.
170. *Mart. Pol.* 14.2.
171. *Mart. Pol.* 14.2.

eschaton, bypassing the whole issue of the intermediate state, something that must wait until the work of the Apologists and Polemicists. As Mellink observes, "although allusions to the realm of the dead can be found in the New Testament and the Apostolic Fathers, systematic reflections on the issue of intermediate state developed later."[172] As I will show below, it is not a surprise that the friends of Polycarp who witnessed his death interpreted it as his "birthday."

In chapters 15 and 16, the author tells us about the actual execution of Polycarp. According to him, after Polycarp finished praying, the men charged with burning him alive lit the fire (15.1). As he continues, the reader is informed that although Polycarp was right there in the middle of the fire, he wasn't being burnt. As he explains, τὸ γὰρ πῦρ καμάρας εἶδος ποιῆσαν ὥσπερ ὀθόνη πλοίου ὑπὸ πνεύματος πληρουμένη, κύκλῳ περιετείχισεν τὸ σῶμα τοῦ μάρτυρος ("For the fire took the form of an arch like the sail of a ship filled by the wind and encircled the body of the martyr like a wall").[173] The failure of the fire to consume Polycarp, the author writes, is a miracle that was seen by the witnesses who then preserved it in order to tell the rest.[174] Whether this description of the incident is true or not, it clearly plays an important role in the understanding of the concept of death in the *Martyrdom of Polycarp*.

In the next statement, the author tells us that Polycarp's body was there "in the middle, not like flesh burning but like bread baking or like gold and silver being refined in a furnace."[175] The author then declares that γὰρ εὐωδίας τοσαύτης ἀντελαβόμεθα, ὡς λιβανωτοῦ πνέοντος ἢ ἄλλου τινὸς τῶν τιμίων ἀρωμάτων ("For we also perceived a very fragrant aroma, as if it were the scent of incense or some other precious spice").[176] According to the *Martyrdom of Polycarp*, Polycarp's death is presented as a sacrifice, a "precious gift prayerfully offered upon the altar of God."[177] Death, in other words, is a good and precious thing. Talking about this imagery as used in this text, Jefford makes the observation that:

172. Mellink, *Death as Eschaton*, 339.

173. *Mart. Pol.* 15.2. For more information of the invulnerability of the martyrs in Jewish culture, see Fischel, "Martyr and Prophet," 265–80.

174. *Mart. Pol.* 15.1.

175. *Mart. Pol.* 15.2. The wording here differs in that while Eusebius (*H.E.* 4.15.37) reads ὡς ἄρτος . . . πυρούμενος ("not like burning flesh but like gold and silver being refined in a furnace"), others have the word μέγα after furnace.

176. *Mart. Pol.* 15.2.

177. Jefford, *Reading the Apostolic Fathers*, 92.

This imagery is depicted in order to emphasize the pleasant nature of Polycarp's sacrifice. The incredible contrast created in the mind of the reader between the anticipated stench of a burning corpse and the unexpected aroma of freshly baking bread recalls the words of Ignatius, who previously had imagined that he himself soon would be ground by wild beasts to become the "pure bread of Christ" (*Romans* 4.1).[178]

Therefore, death here is understood as a purification process, with the fire being the instrument by which this process takes place.[179] Schoedel notes that this set the precedent such that later deaths of martyrs were referred to as "odor of sanctity."[180]

Last, we can also decipher more aspects of the concept of death according to the *Martyrdom of Polycarp* from the report concerning the treatment of Polycarp's remains. In chapter 17, the author informs us that when the jealous Evil One (ἀντίζηλος καὶ βάκανος καὶ πονηρός, a definite reference to the devil) observed the greatness of Polycarp's martyrdom, and especially the fact that Polycarp had now been "crowned with the crown of immortality and won the prize that no one could challenge," he was furious.[181] The phrase "crowned with the crown of immortality" (ἐστεφανωμένον τε τὸν τῆς ἀφθαρσίας στέφανον) is certainly a reference to the belief that Polycarp had, in death, achieved the state in which he will exist forever. Thus, it strengthens the conviction that by this time in Christian belief, the concept of an intermediate state pending the resurrection had not been developed. The emphasis, however, seems to be on the fact that Polycarp has already won the battle against the devil since the devil is depicted as having realized that Polycarp actually lived an "incomparable life."[182] As Bynum notes, "martyred flesh had to be capable of impassibility and transfiguration; suffering and rot could not be the final answer."[183] As she notes, "if flesh could put on, even in this life, a foretaste of incorruption, martyrdom might be bearable."[184] This was especially so given the cruelties that the martyrs had to endure at the time of their execution. As the writer indicates, it is this conviction of victory

---

178. Ibid.
179. For another example of this view of the role of fire, see 4 Macc 9:22.
180. Schoedel, *Polycarp*, 72.
181. *Mart. Pol.* 17.1.
182. Greenberg, *My Share of God's Reward*, 152.
183. Bynum, *The Resurrection of the Body*, 45.
184. Ibid.

over suffering and the resulting reward upon Polycarp that seems to have infuriated the devil. And, for this reason, the writer informs us that the devil incited Nicetes, the father of Herod to appeal to the magistrate not to release the body of Polycarp to the Smyrneans.[185] Thus, Polycarp's final achievements are "viewed through the lenses of athletic metaphor, much like that of Paul and other members of the Noble Death tradition...."[186] In this case, the rewarding is believed to take place immediately since it is believed to be the gift that God gives to the martyr. Therefore, "the impassibility of the risen body was stressed as a reward for such sacrifice or that terror of execution was allayed by the suggestion that a sort of anesthesia of glory might spill from the promised resurrection into the ravaged arena, making its experience bearable."[187] But, as I have argued, this reward and resurrection was believed to have taken place immediately after death during this stage in the development of the concept of death in Christianity. However, the treatment of Polycarp's remains suggests belief in the future resurrection of the body and the soul.

In chapter 18, the author gives us the final disposition of Polycarp's body. According to him, after seeing the opposition raised by the Jews, the centurion set Polycarp's body "in the middle and cremated it, as is their custom" (θεὶς αὐτὸν ἐν μέσῳ, ὡς ἔθος αὐτοῖς, ἔκαυσεν).[188] The author then notes that they took Polycarp's bones, which, according to him were "more valuable than precious stones and finer than gold," (τὰ τιμιώτερα λίθων πολυτελῶν καὶ δοκιμώτερα ὑπὲρ χρυσίον ὀστᾶ αὐτοῦ ἀπεθέμεθα), and they deposited them in a suitable place.[189] Although it is unclear where this "suitable place" was/is, the implication is clear: the Smyrneans

---

185. *Mart. Pol.* 17.2. According to Schoedel, Eusebius knew of many incidents whereby the remains of the martyr were not given up by the executors (Schoedel, *Polycarp*, 74 n. 17.1). See Eusebius, *H.E.* 5.1.36 for these examples.

186. Greenberg, *My Share of God's Reward*, 152. As the author informs us, the Smyrneans wanted to take Polycarp's body so that they can "touch his holy flesh" (καὶ κοινωνῆσαι τῷ ἁγίῳ αὐτοῦ σαρκίῳ). This phrase, literally "have a share/fellowship in his holy flesh," has been taken by some like Bowersock and Reeves to imply that their intention was to participate in a cannibalistic practice in which the eating of the flesh that had been dedicated to God would result in the participants becoming one with God. See Bowersock, *Fiction as History*, 193; Sanday, *Divine Hunger*.

187. Bynum, *The Resurrection of the Body*, 46.

188. *Mart. Pol.* 18.1.

189. *Mart. Pol.* 18.2.

took great care of Polycarp's bones since they believed that they were extremely precious.[190]

Even more significant is the author's comment that the Smyrneans were able to congregate at Polycarp's burial place with joy and gladness, as the Lord would allow them, in order to celebrate the "birthday of his martyrdom" (ἐπιτελεῖν τὴν τοῦ μαρτυρίου αὐτοῦ ἡμέραν γενέθλιον).[191] Clearly, therefore, death here is also understood as a "birthday." This comparison of death as being born, argues Lightfoot, refers to the fact that at death, the martyrs were understood as having been ushered into a higher life.[192] In a more elaborate study on the meaning of the word γυνέθλιον (literally, "birth day"), Jefford points out that the inauguration of the celebration of the deaths of martyrs as birthdays in early Christianity "illustrates a growing realization among early Christians that martyrdom on behalf of Christ was not an end to life itself, but was a rebirth into another existence—a second birthday as it were."[193] It is perhaps during these commemorations of the martyrs that early Christians heard the stories of the acts of the martyrs read to them as an attempt to prepare them for their own future martyrdom if need be.[194] According to Schoedel, the practice of referring to the death of a person as his birthday, a pretty popular practice in early Christianity, was actually borrowed from the Greek cult of the dead whereby "a man's (natural) birthday was the most important day of his commemoration."[195] In Polycarp, this practice has been transformed to refer to what elsewhere is referred to as the "resurrection" or the acquisition of immortality and/or incorruptibility of the soul. As I have noted, this transformation ("birthday") takes place instantaneously at death.

In summary, therefore, in both the surviving letter of Polycarp, bishop of Smyrna *To the Philippians* as well as the record of his martyrdom known as *The Martyrdom of Polycarp*, the concept of death is explained

---

190. According to Lightfoot, Polycarp's grave is mentioned to be "at Smyrna by one who lived in a neighboring city and had already grown up to manhood when the martyrdom took place, Polycrates of Ephesus writing soon after AD 190" (Lightfoot, *S. Ignatius, S. Polycarp*, 396).

191. *Mart. Pol.* 18.3.

192. Lightfoot, *S. Ignatius, S. Polycarp*, 396 n. 13.

193. Jefford, *Reading the Apostolic Fathers*, 93. With later theologians such as Origen, death by martyrdom was being compared to the ritual of baptism.

194. Kelley, "Philosophy as Training for Death," 725.

195. Schoedel, *Polycarp*, 76 n. 18.2.

using terms that are similar to those already used by his friend, Ignatius bishop of Antioch. These are *imitatio Christi*, going to one's place, and sacrifice.[196] In addition, however, the *Martyrdom of Polycarp* uses a term that we have so far not seen in the discussion of death in this stage in Christianity: birthday. As I have argued, this term most probably refers to the belief that all the eschatological promises to believers take place at the event of death: the resurrection of the body, the granting of the immortality to the soul and the body as well as the rewarding of the believer. To use Mellink's terms here, for believers at this point in the development of Christianity, "death is eschaton."[197]

Acts of the Christian Martyrs: Death As Witness

Although there is a great corpus of literature that has been identified as the hagiographical acts of martyrs, scholars have grouped them into two groups: the apocryphal acts of martyrs and the *acta sanctorum* or *acta martyrum*.[198] The first group of writings comprises of the Apocryphal New Testament, "telling of the deeds of and the deaths of famous apostles."[199] These include such texts as *The Acts of John*, *The Acts of Paul*, *The Acts of Andrew*, *The Acts of Peter*, and the *Acts of Thomas*. Several church fathers objected to the contents of these apocryphal texts, "partly because of their relatively recent composition, compared to the books that

---

196. Indeed, it can be argued that the concept of the *imitatio Christi* reaches its climax in the *Martyrdom of Polycarp*. As Jefford summarizes, "From the beginning to the end, the bishop's arrest, trial, and execution are painted against the canvas of similar events in the life of Jesus of Nazareth as they are recorded in the New Testament gospels. Thus it is that Polycarp serves as the host for a final meal, and agonizes in prayer immediately prior to his arrest by the authorities. He is escorted into the city on a donkey, is interrogated by an important Roman authority, and is then condemned to death with an eager agreement of the Jews. Although he is condemned to the flames, his body is pierced to ensure that he has died. All of these images are compared to the final days of Jesus' life in Jerusalem. Each image, in turn, is then recast according to the final hours of Polycarp's life in Smyrna. As the author states in 1.2, Polycarp waited to be betrayed as had the Lord. In 6.2, the bishop is brought to the arena for trial in order to participate in the fate of Jesus, just as his betrayers were to share in the punishment of Judas Iscariot, who previously betrayed his master" (Jefford, *Reading the Apostolic Fathers*, 94).

197. Mellink, *Death as Eschaton*, 339.

198. For an evaluation of hagiographical literature, see Barnes, *Early Christian Hagiography*.

199. Elliot, "Imitations in Literature and Life," 87.

eventually were promoted as canonical to form the New Testament, and partly because of their contents being magical, superstitious, uncritical or, (occasionally) tinged with Gnostic or other 'unorthodox' ideologies."[200] The second group comprises Christian hagiographical corpus which, unlike the apostolic apocryphal acts, "have a certain freshness and immediacy, suggesting a closeness to the facts, free from fanciful elements and relatively unadorned."[201]

Although because of the above-mentioned reasons it is hard to conclude much from the apocryphal acts, it seems fair to observe that in both of these kinds of writings, death is understood as a witness to the life and resurrection of Jesus Christ. Indeed, as Elliot suggests, there is a noted development towards this view of death that can be documented in the New Testament and early Christianity. The term μαρτυς first appears in Acts 1:8 and 22.[202] In these appearances, the witness to the death and resurrection of Jesus Christ is assumed to be verbal. However, by the time of the writing of the book of Revelation, those who were remembered as the μαρτυς were said to have made the ultimate sacrifice at the face of persecution. Specifically, in Revelation 16:6 and 17:6, reference is made to the blood of the saints and the martyrs. Again, in Revelation 20:4–6, reference is made to those who are "beheaded because of the testimony about Jesus Christ" (διὰ τὴν μαρτυρίαν Ἰησοῦ). This phrase becomes especially significant when we consider the fact that "Ἰησοῦ is an objective genitive here."[203] In other words, in the book of Revelation, a martyr is now defined as "a Christian believer who gives his or her life or allows his or her life to be taken specifically in times of persecution."[204] Thus, "the death itself thereby then becomes the *witness* and is testimonial."[205] This is a much nuanced understanding of Christian death through persecution. As Elliot further clarifies:

> The death of the Christian martyr is not suicide, which is negative. Martyrdom has to be presented and succeed as a positive act, a willing acceptance of fate for the purpose of maintaining and promoting one's faith. And it is obviously different from

200. Ibid., 89.

201. Ibid., 97. So far the standard text for these writings is Musurillo, *The Acts of the Christian Martyrs*. For pagan parallels, see Musurillo, *The Acts of the Pagan Martyrs*.

202. Elliot, "Imitations in Literature," 88.

203. Ibid.

204. Ibid.

205. Ibid.

modern military use, where a fallen combatant fighting a totalitarian regime, for example, may be described as having made the ultimate sacrifice—in effect as a martyr—and where heroes may be poignantly described on headstones and on war memorials as dying for a higher cause than self, such as for King and Country, *Vaterland*, or for *la république*.... Unlike such cases, Christian martyrdom requires a choice to have been available: death itself could have been avoided, albeit only at a price the Christian was unwilling to pay.[206]

Although I will come back to this, herein lies the difference between Christian martyrdom whereby death is clearly a witness of Christ's own death and resurrection and the Greco-Roman concept of the Noble Death.[207]

Although many examples can suffice from both the apocryphal acts and the *acta sanctorum* to illustrate the point that death was understood

---

206. Ibid., 88–89. As far as the reasons for the persecution of Christians are concerned, Frend notes that they were varied. For example, in some cases, Christians were persecuted when natural disasters occurred whose occurrence was attributed to Christians because they worshipped Christ and not Caesar. In other cases, there were specific policies laid down by some Roman emperors that almost always guaranteed a conflict with Christians. Speaking about Emperor Dominitian, for example, Frend notes that "other causes of tension were more directly due to the policy of the Emperor himself. First, financial stringency seems to have led him to take energetic steps to garner much proceeds of the 2 drachma contributions from the Jews for the benefit of the treasury. Secondly, his profound hostility towards any form of religious unorthodoxy resulted in the punishment of any prominent citizen who lapsed too blatantly into an external religion" (Frend, *Martyrdom and Persecution*, 212). As he continues, with Emperor Trajan, more serious accusations against Christians emerged as causes for persecution. These are cannibalism and incest. Trajan developed an edict known as the *collegia*, an edict which required stringent penalties for Christians. It was the standard trial document for Christians in the second century. "The *collegium* theory," he writes, "also would account for Pliny's reference to the common meals, which were the hallmarks of a *collegium*, and in the background lurked the fear of secret magic rites which could harm the community. Hence, the requirement of 'cursing Christ', implying the abjuration of a demonic name. His lurid description, too, of the vast numbers of both sexes from town and countryside alike who were tainted '*superstitionis istius contagio*,' points in the same directions.... Altogether, the active Christian *collegium* with its bishops and close-knit organization would appear to Pliny to be typical of the *inlicitos coetus* which it had been his duty to suppress" (Frend, *Martyrdom and Persecution*, 221–22). For further discussion on why Christians were persecuted, see Croix, "Why Were the Early Christians Persecuted?" 6–38.

207. Greenberg is certainly correct when he notes that although there are similarities between the noble deaths of Greek philosophers and Christian martyrs, there are certainly key dissimilarities also. (See Greenberg, *My Share of God's Reward*, 43–69).

as a witness in and of itself, two will serve us here. First, in a manner typical of the apocryphal acts of the apostles, we read in the apocryphal *Acts of Paul* concerning the death of Paul by beheading by the orders of Emperor Nero in the late 60s before Nero himself died, that:

> And among the many Paul was also in fetters. Those who were imprisoned with him looked at him, so that the emperor observed that he was the leader of the soldiers. And he said to him, "man of the great king, now my prisoner, what induced you to come secretly into the Roman Empire and to enlist soldiers in my territory?" But Paul, filled with the Holy Spirit, said in the presence of all, "Caesar, we enlist soldiers not only in your territory but in all lands of the earth. For thus we are commanded to exclude none who wishes to fight for my king. If it seems good to you to serve him, for neither riches nor the splendours of this life will serve you; but if you become his subject and beseech him you shall be saved. For in one day he will destroy the world." Having heard this Nero commanded all the prisoners to be burned with fire, but Paul to be beheaded according to the law of the Romans.[208]

It seems, therefore, that in this case, both the words of Paul as well as the whole event of his death through martyrdom serve as a witness to the work of Christ.

The same phenomenon is observable in the vast Christian hagiographical corpus known as the *acta sanctorum* (Acts of the Christian Martyrs). Although these are numerous, the ones that were written in the second century or whose recorded events are believed to have taken place in the second century include but are not limited to the *Martyrdom of Polycarp* (c. 167 or so), *The Acts of Justin and his Companions* (c. 165), *The Martyrs of Lugdunum* (Lyons, c. 177), *The Acts of the Scillitan Martyrs* (c. 180) as well as the *Martyrdom of Apollonius* (c. 180–185). Since the *Martyrdom of Perpetua and Felicitas* is reported to have taken place at the dawn of the third century (c. 203), it is slightly beyond the time period of our consideration here, pivotal as it is to later martyrdom stories in Christianity.

Although most passages from these writings can be cited as evidence that death is understood as a "witness," perhaps the record of the

---

208. *Acts of Paul*, Martyrdom 3, quoted in Elliot, "Imitations in Literature," 90. For a hermeneutical suggestion on how to study this corpus, see Bovon and Junod, "Reading the Apocryphal Acts," 161–71.

death of Justin in *The Acts of Justin and his Companions* is most illustrative. We read, concerning this martyrdom:

> The Prefect turned to Justin: "You are said to be learned. You think you know the true doctrine. Tell me: if you are scourged and beheaded, do you suppose that you will ascend to heaven?" "I have confidence," said Justin, "that if I endure all this I shall possess his mansions. Indeed, I know that for all those who live a just life, there awaits the divine gift even to the consummation of the whole world." The prefect Rusticus said: "You think, then, that you will ascend to heaven to receive certain worthy rewards?" "I do not think," said Justin, "but I have accurate knowledge and am fully assured of it." "Well then," said the prefect Rusticus, "let us come to the point at issue, a necessary and pressing business. Agree together to offer sacrifice to the gods." "No one of sound mind," said Justin, "turns from piety to impiety." The prefect Rusticus said: "If you do not obey, you will be punished without mercy." Justin said: "We are confident that if we suffer the penalty for the sake of our Lord Jesus Christ we shall be saved, for this is the confidence and salvation we shall have at the terrible tribunal of our Savior and Master sitting in judgment over the whole world." Similarly, the other martyrs said, "Do what you will. We are Christians and we do not offer sacrifice to idols." The prefect Rusticus passed judgment, saying: "Those who have refused to sacrifice to the gods and to yield to the emperor's edict are to be led away to be scourged and beheaded in accordance with the laws."[209]

Thus, not only is the death of these Christians presented in this report as witness, but it is also presented as salvation, with an emphasis on Christ's terrible tribunal as the judgment that is way above all earthly judgments. It is this judgment of Christ that the writer suggests the Roman prefect should be concerned with more than anything else.

In conclusion, therefore, in the apocryphal *Acts of the Apostles* as well as the *Acts of Christian Martyrs*, death is understood as a witness to the death and resurrection of Jesus Christ and its accompanying benefits. This understanding comes from both the statements that the martyrs make in their defense before their execution as well as the events surrounding the death itself together with their attitudes towards their deaths.

---

209. Elliot, "Imitations in Literature," 100.

CONCLUSION: MARTYRS' CONCEPT OF DEATH

The survey of the martyrs' concept of death leads to a number of key observations. First, although the martyrs use many terms contemporary in their cultural milieu to define and describe death, it is a mistake to assume that they use these terms the same way as their contemporaries use them. Rather, they adapted and modified the terms to help express and explain a distinctive Christian understanding of death that corresponded with the fact that Christ has already died, resurrected, and ascended to heaven. Thus, for the martyrs, a proper Christian view of death is neither a completely Hellenized view nor a view that is in complete contrast to those prevalent in these cultures. There is, in other words, a conversational "doing" theology going on, with an emphasis on terminological reinterpretation.

Second, the martyrs used terms that were more reflective of their various occasions than offering a complete theological system of death. As emphasized, many of the martyrs wrote under extenuating circumstances. Since they were not doing their theology at the comfort of their armchairs at home, what we have from them is an immediate reflection of death in view of the prospect of execution. Therefore, to demand that their writings on the subject of death be prescriptive and systematic is to ask them to do something impossible under the present circumstances. For a more nuanced and theologically systematic treatment of the concept of death in the second century, we must turn to the apologists. Although many of the apologists wrote under similar threats of persecution, in addition, they were now compelled to respond to philosophical questions about their faith in Christ. Whether the questions come from inside the church or outside, this compulsion offered the apologists an opportunity to reflect on many theological doctrines of the church. As a result, in them, we have an elaborate understanding of death that connects it to the entire program of God, showing both its necessity and the present state of the dead, whether believers or non-believers alike. This exploration is the subject of the next chapter.

CHAPTER 3

Death in Valentinian Gnosticism, Apologists, and Polemicists

INTRODUCTION

WITH THE EMERGENCE OF the apologetic literature, evidence of more reflection on the key theological subjects is seen as the apologists try to come to terms with the culture in which they lived. In their interaction with the culture, the apologists neither presented Christianity as a contrast to the culture nor saw both as identical. "Apologists," writes Grant, "do not completely identify themselves with the broader society, but they are not advocates of confrontation or revolution."[1] Rather, "they address their contemporaries with persuasion, looking for links between the outside world and their own group and thus modifying the development of both."[2]

The apologists offer the clearest demonstration of the thesis of this study. While making every effort to relate Christianity to the larger philosophical and cultural surroundings, the apologist also made sure that the content of his belief was uninterrupted. Though perhaps too razor-thinly

---

1. Grant, *Greek Apologists*, 9.
2. Ibid.

divided, Grant's explanation of the work of an apologist in the second century is helpful here. He writes:

> The apologist is not completely at home in either his own group or the larger society. He is too much of a generalizer for his own people, and too closely related to minority specifics for society at large. He stands on a borderline, overlapping parts of both areas but not fully identifiable with either part or the whole. His critics from within sometimes admit his "subjective" loyalty to the group's beliefs but they deny that it is "objective." When Loisy modernized Catholic history nearly a century ago, his opponents accused him of betraying Catholicism. There is something to such a charge, for an apologist's efforts are likely to produce significant changes in the ways the minority looks at itself. As he tries to present its ideas as persuasively as possible, the persuasion is likely to convert the converted and modify their ideas at least in form.[3]

While I contest Grant's classification of an apologist as being "not fully identifiable with either the part or the whole" on the grounds that most Christian apologists clearly identified themselves as Christians, I agree with him that there is modification taking place. In other words, the Christian apologist tries to make Christianity intelligible to the outside world while clearly retaining its inherent tenets.

One such key area where the apologists' modification took place is in their conception of death. Faced with the deeper questions of relating Christian beliefs to their changing philosophical culture, these Christians attempted to place Christian beliefs within the larger program of God. These questions are both internal and external. On the one hand, for example, gnostic groups presented challenges that needed an extremely careful and nuanced response. This is so because of the proximity of some of the gnostic language to orthodoxy since many of these groups claim to be interpreters of key biblical figures such as Paul.[4] On the other hand, as noted in chapter 1, with the presence of the Greek (Orphic) idea of the immortality of the soul, key apologists like Tatian, Justin Martyr, and Athenagoras were forced to sharpen the areas of agreement and disagreement between Christianity and the Greek philosophy's concept of death. Since I have offered an exploration into the Greek concepts of

---

3. Ibid.

4. For this observation concerning especially the Valentinians, see Thomassen, "Valentinian Ideas," 169. See also Lundhaug, "'These are Symbols and Likenesses," 187.

death in chapter one, it is in order to do the same here as far as Gnosticism is concerned in order to lay the ground for the discussion of the apologists' idea of death.

The Concept of Gnosticism

No discussion of second-century Christianity can be complete without taking into account the contributions of the groups that second-century Christian writers called the "gnostics."[5] Different scholars have offered different definitions of Gnosticism. Karen King defines it on the basis of some shared characteristics. For her, the "so-called Gnostic works provide evidence of wide of ethical orientations, theological and anthropological views, spiritual disciplines, and ritual practices, confounding any attempt to develop a single set of typological categories that will fit everything scholars have labeled Gnosticism."[6] In addition to these shared characteristics, it is also clear that there were discernible groups such as the Valentinians, the Marcionites, the Saturnilians and the Basilidians as early as the first part of the second century.[7] Daley's summary is more helpful. "Gnosticism," he writes, "was not simply a Christian heresy, nor was it [a] theologically coherent religious movement."[8] It was "rather a type of elitist religious thought, present in Jewish and philosophical pagan circles as well as in a fairly wide range of Christian ones, which claimed privileged access to a kind of knowledge that could revolutionize the believer's understanding of existence."[9] His definition, in other words, guards against treating the movement either monolithically or entirely outside Jewish and Christian circles. In a general manner, therefore, gnostics regarded the world of ordinary experience as of low grade of reality, "and promised escape from matter and union with the transcendent source of being to the favored few who accepted the esoteric knowledge that the group[s] possessed."[10]

---

5. Current scholars have cautioned us against classifying all these groups under the same umbrella of "gnostics" since there were many diverse groups that the Fathers addressed. For a current discussion of this issue, see King, *What is Gnosticism?*

6. Ibid., 213

7. Ibid. See also *Dial.* 35.2.

8. Daley, *The Hope of the Early Church*, 25.

9. Ibid.

10. Ibid. See also Rudolph, *Gnosis*, 115. This promise of escape provides a significant background towards understanding the gnostics' concept of death.

The question of the relationship of these groups with orthodoxy has been the subject of numerous debates over time. The essence of the discussion is the question of historiography. Although it is not possible to offer a full treatment of the well-worn historiographical discussions on this issue here, a brief sketch is necessary in order to locate the relationship between the second-century Christian apologists and Valentinianism.

Since perhaps the question of the relationship of orthodoxy and heresy is the most significant aspect of the self-definition of Christianity in the second century, a number of viewpoints have been advanced over the years in terms of response.[11] First, there is what has come to be known as the "traditional" (or classic) viewpoint. Summarized, this is the view that truth, unity and orthodoxy came first while heresy came later and was the minority view. That is, "the Church kept the Lord's teaching and the apostolic tradition untainted and pure."[12] Orthodoxy, according to this view, "was a line of tradition that represented the original apostolic teaching and thus represented 'authentic' Christianity, whilst alternative streams were considered to be aberrations that deviated from the 'true' Christianity of the orthodox."[13] In addition to some scriptural prophecies understood to predict the oncoming heresies (see, for example, Paul's words to the Ephesian church leaders in Acts 20), Eusebius made the famous remarks that after the demise of the apostles, "combinations of impious error arose by fraud and delusions of false teachers," setting the tone that would become the standard view for the better part of the history of Christianity.[14] Indeed, according to Eusebius, orthodoxy had no history *per se*. Only heresy had. As Pelikan summarizes, according to Eusebius, "orthodox Christian doctrine did not have a history, having been true eternally and taught primitively; only heresy had a history, having risen at particular times and through the innovation of particular teachers."[15]

Second, in the mid-1800s, F. C. Baur and the so-called Tübingen school argued that the relationship between orthodoxy and other groups

---

11. For the importance of this question as it relates to Valentinianism, see Hunt, *Christianity in the Second Century*, 10–17.

12. Bingham, "Development and Diversity," 48.

13. Hunt, *Christianity in the Second Century*, 10.

14. Eusebius *Ecclesiastical History*. 3.32.8. For Eusebius's *Ecclesiastical History*, unless otherwise stated, I am using Cruse, *Eusebius' Ecclesiastical History*.

15. Pelikan, *The Emergence of the Catholic Tradition*, 7–8. This comment is based on Eusebius *Ecclesiastical History*. 1.1.1 and 7.30.4; 31.1. See also Hultgren, *The Rise of Normative Christianity*, 7–8.

in early Christianity was characterized by a conflict, resolution, and synthesis. Focusing especially on the New Testament and owing his methodology to Hegel's dialectic, Baur "interpreted both the development of early Catholicism—as the synthesis of Jewish and Gentile Christianity in the primitive Christian community."[16] In other words, he viewed early Christianity as being a conflict between the particular form of Jewish Christianity (that of Peter) and the universalistic form of Christianity (that of Paul), forming a final synthesis of catholic Christianity.

Third, Adolf Harnack argued that although the gospel entered into the world not as a static doctrine "but as a joyful message and as a power of the Spirit of God," it stripped itself of these forms and "united and amalgamated itself with Greek science, the Roman Empire and ancient culture."[17] For Harnack, therefore, "doctrinal development in early Christianity . . . meant change in the gospel, its misdirection, its impairment."[18] According to him, this negative development of early Christianity crystallized during her fight with such groups as Gnosticism and Marcionism.[19] Harnack's sentiments continue to be evidenced in the writings of such scholars as Elaine Pagels who understand the development of Christian doctrines as originating from an attempt by Christian groups to "consolidate their group against the demands of a fellow Christian named Marcion, whom they regarded as a false teacher."[20]

Finally, Walter Bauer's book, *Rechtgläubigkeit und Ketzerei im ältesten Christendum*, which first appeared in 1934 and was translated into English under the title *Orthodoxy and Heresy in Earliest Christianity* in 1971, is still considered one of the most crucial works in the study of early Christianity.[21] In it, Bauer defended the thesis that, contrary to the assertions of Eusebius and most early church fathers, "in earliest Christianity, orthodoxy and heresy do not stand in relation to one another as primary to secondary, but, in many regions heresy is the original manifestation of Christianity."[22] Indeed, according to Bauer, not only did heresy precede orthodoxy, but, in some geographical regions, "heresies" were in the majority.

---

16. Livingston, *The Enlightenment and the Nineteenth Century*, 128.
17. Harnack, *The History of Dogma*, 7.272.
18. Bingham, "Development and Diversity," 49.
19. Svigel, "Second Century Incarnational Christology," 4.
20. Pagels, *Beyond Belief*, 6.
21. Bauer, *Rechtgläubigkeit und Ketzerei* and Bauer, *Orthodoxy and Heresy*.
22. Bauer, *Orthodoxy and Heresy*, xi.

While it is not possible to offer a thorough assessment of the reception of Bauer's thesis here, it would suffice to point out that it continues to receive mixed reaction among scholars today.[23] On the one hand, there are those scholars such as James Robinson and Helmut Koester who have accepted Bauer's thesis wholeheartedly.[24] On the other hand, there are those, like Henry Turner, who have offered negative reception of the Bauer thesis.[25] Finally, there are those whose views are seen as emanating from Bauer's conception of early Christianity as a struggle between orthodoxy and heterodox. Examples of these include James Dunn and Elaine Pagels.[26] By far, however, the most comprehensive response to Bauer's thesis was by Thomas Robinson.[27] After retracing Bauer's reenactment of the geographical development of heresy and diversity in the early church, Robinson concluded that Bauer's reconstruction of the history of the early church was faulty not only in minor details, "but at critical junctures."[28] Thus, according to him, "the failure of the [Bauer] thesis in the only area where it can be adequately tested [historical reconstruction] casts suspicion on other areas of Bauer's investigation."[29]

For our purposes here, while Bauer and others would consider groups like the Valentinians to be expressions of Christianity (and, to be fair to the Valentinians, they considered themselves as interpreters of Paul), their conceptions of some of the key aspects of Christianity indicate otherwise.[30] A key example is how they understood the concept of death. In their attempt to offer a concept of death that stands in between Neopythagorean ideas and Paul, they end up with a view of death that posits a departure of the soul from the body in order to head back to where it came from while never conceiving of the possibility of a future reunion with the body in the form of the resurrection.[31]

---

23. For an assessment of the earlier reception and critique of Bauer's thesis, see Bauer, *Orthodoxy and Heresy*, 266–316.

24. Hunt, *Christianity in the Second Century*, 11. See Koester and Robinson, *Trajectories*.

25. See Turner, *The Pattern of Christian Truth*.

26. Ibid. See Dunn, *Unity and Diversity* and Pagels, *The Gnostic Gospels*.

27. Robinson, *The Bauer Thesis Examined*. See also Jerry R. Flora, "A Critical Analysis of Walter Bauer's Theory."

28. Ibid., 203.

29. Ibid., 204.

30. Desjardins, *Sin in Valentinianism*, 16.

31. Thomassen, "The Valentinian School," 792.

In summary, therefore, Valentinianism was one of the most successful gnostic groups. It was founded by Valentinus around 140.[32] Much of its success came from its founder, Valentinus, who is believed to have lived between AD 100 ca. and ca. 175.[33] Valentinus' prudence was evidenced by his revision of classic gnostic tradition, "consciously adopting the language of the New Testament and stamping the result with his own rhetorical genius."[34] In so doing, he was able to bridge the gap between proto-orthodox Christianity and the gnostic religion. But, as I will argue, although Valentinianism used Pauline terminology, the meanings of these terms were changed.

From the works of Irenaeus, Hippolytus, and the Nag Hammadi tractate known as the *Tripartite Tractate* (NHC I,5), scholars have been able to decipher the main works of Valentinianism as follows: *The Gospel of Truth* (NHC I,3), the *Treatise on the Resurrection* (NHC I,4), the *Tripartite Tractate* (NHC I,5), *The Gospel of Philip* (NHC II,3), the *Interpretation of Knowledge* (NHC XI,1), and *Valentinian Exposition* (NHC XI,2) with the *Liturgical Readings* as well.[35] In order to be able to present the Valentinian concept of death, a brief analysis of its view of man and salvation is necessary. This is because, according to them, death is salvation (hence, the term *apolytrosis*, which means salvation or release, is used).

It is impossible to talk about the Valentinian thanatology without making a statement about both its anthropology and soteriology since these tenets serve as the background to its understanding of death. Particularly, since the concept of death is closely connected to their understanding of salvation, this forms a good beginning point towards understanding the Valentinian concept of death.

Generally speaking, two views have emerged concerning the origin and meaning of salvation in Gnosticism in general. On the one hand, there are those who have understood the gnostic salvation as being by nature. In this case, man is understood (at least in the case of the elect) to be in possession of some innate divine nature that needs to be saved. Thus, "though he [man] is a creature of psychic nature, bound to matter,

---

32. Ibid., 790.
33. Layton, *The Gnostic Scriptures*, xv.
34. Ibid.
35. Thomassen, "The Valentinian School," 790–91. With the exception of the *Treatise on the Resurrection* [*The Epistle to Rheginos*] whose Malcolm Peel's translation still remains the critical edition, for the Valentinian literature, I am using Meyer, *The Nag Hammadi Scriptures*.

he already bears the principle of salvation within himself: the pneumatic seed... this pneumatic particle has sunk into matter and must be liberated by the Saviour."[36] This "pneumatic man" is identified, in some gnostic circles with the "*nous*," with the Saviour, Christ, being its "prototype."[37] The "pneumatic man is latently present in the visible man and is enlivened by his prototype, the Christ."[38] In this case, salvation is understood as by nature, in which case, there is nothing "absolutely new introduced into the human race by means of redemption."[39]

On the other hand, there are those who argue that although mankind possesses this spark, it is half extinguished and, therefore, requires redemption from beyond itself. As Bousset summarized, "it is not the opinion of the Gnostics that the half-extinguished spark could, from its own nature and power, again be fanned and burst into flame. The elements of light ... are in hopeless captivity here below. [Thus] a redemption is required that comes down from above and comes in from without."[40] In this case, salvation is understood to come from outside of man and not from within himself.

Valentinianism, however, was able to deal with this discrepancy through its anthropology. For example, in the Nag Hammadi Valentinian treatise known as the *Tripartite Tractate*, man is often understood as divided into three groups. As Irenaeus elaborated, in this case, Valentinianism saw man as composed of three races with various designations (*Haer.* 1.6.1).[41] The material man, also known as the "left out one," would be considered unredeemable. The psychic one, who is also called the "one of the light," would be considered as redeemable if he, somehow, exercises his freewill. In this case, within the Valentinian gnostic system, "room is made for the exercise of free will and for the conversion in the intermediate sphere of the psychics."[42] Finally, there is the pneumatic man, the elect, whose destiny is favorable (although there is a group within

---

36. Zandee, "Gnostic Ideas," 41.
37. Ibid.
38. Ibid.
39. Bousset, *Kyros Christos*, 265.
40. Ibid., 266.
41. Roberts and Donaldson, *The Ante-Nicene Fathers*, 1.323–24. For an argument for post-Christian origins of Valentinianism, see McCue, "Orthodoxy and Heresy," 151–52. For an attempt to trace the life of Valentinus himself, see Stead, "In Search of Valentinus."
42. Zandee, "Gnostic Ideas," 51–52.

the pneumatics whose destiny seems unfavorable). Understood this way, therefore, the polarizing opinions of scholars like Karen King, which pits the Polemicists suggestion of gnostic salvation via human nature versus recent discoveries that suggest that gnostic redemption was from beyond human nature, is at least ameliorated, if not eradicated.[43]

A number of Valentinian texts describe both the origin of man as well as his present situation. Of all these texts, the *Tri. Trac.* (NHC I,5) is the most important source of Valentinian anthropology. Additionally, the same is true of the works of Irenaeus and Hippolytus. It describes the creation of the human in 104.18–106.25. Here, the author starts by noting that the creator created humanity after creating all the other things. He continues to note that the creation of man happened in the same way as that of everything else. That is, the creation of man was a presumptuous activity of the spiritual Word, meaning that "the human became like an earthly shadow, so that he would be of the same kind as those who are cut off on the right as well as the ones on the left, each of the orders forming."[44] In addition, he notes that the human being that was created was "deficient in such a way that he was [afflicted] by sickness."[45] However, most significantly, the author adds that, without the knowledge of it, the Word, through the creator Demiurge, gave man "something" that would enable him to "know that there exists something higher and realize that he needed [it]."[46] This "something" is what has been identified elsewhere as the "pneumatic seed."[47] He adds that, because of this implantation, we must "conclude that the soul of the first man derives from the spiritual Word, even if the creator thought that it was his."[48] The *Tri. Trac* also adds that, since the creator is able to procreate also, he "sent down souls out of his own substance."[49] These constitute the second kind of humanity in Valentinianism. Finally, "those on the left," a term probably used to some of the members of the All (the Pleroma), also "produced a sort of human

---

43. See King, *What is Gnosticism?* 282–83 n. 18.

44. Thomassen, "The Tripartite Tractate," 87.

45. Ibid.

46. Ibid.

47. Zandee, "Gnostic Ideas," 41. As Zandee further explains, this concept is comparable with Hellenistic conceptions whereby there are concepts of the function of the "nous" in respect to the "psyche."

48. Thomassen, "The Tripartite Tractate," 87.

49. Ibid.

being of their own, since they possess the imitation."[50] The end result, therefore, is a tripartite humanity, that is, a humanity that is "a depository of those on the left and those on the right, as well as of a spiritual Word."[51]

Evidently, it was this tripartite division of mankind that Irenaeus was referring to when he pointed out that the heretics divide man into a threefold of substances. According to him, the heretics held that those who are on the left hand are the material ones, and are, thus, "incapable of receiving any *afflatus* of incorruption" (*Haer.* 1.6.1).[52] Second, according to him, the "animal men," those who are on the right, are "instructed in animal things; such men, namely, are established by their works, and by a mere faith, while they have not perfect knowledge" (*Haer.* 1.6.2).[53] The heretics, he adds, saw those belonging to the catholic church as such persons. Finally, there are the "most perfect," as Irenaeus calls them. As he describes them, they see themselves as the elect seed, who "have grace as their own special possession, which has descended from above by means of unspeakable and indescribable conjunction."[54] Thus, without doubt, Irenaeus' understanding of Valentinian anthropology is quite in accordance to that of *Tri. Trac.* And, as aforementioned, this tripartite understanding of man plays an indispensable role in our understanding of Valentinian soteriology.

Concerning their soteriology, it is clear from the writings of the Valentinians that salvation involved at least some gaining of knowledge that would make it possible for there to be a "separation from the lower sensual elements of existence and surrender to the higher celestial world."[55] As the author of *Tri. Trac.* explained, because of the promise of Jesus, we have Christ as a deposit, "whose revelation and unification we have ministered to, this promise now enabled instruction and return to that which they had been from the beginning—that of which they possessed a drop inciting them to return to it—which is what is called redemption."[56] Thus, redemption involves both the acquisition of knowledge as well as the use

---

50. Ibid.
51. Ibid.
52. Roberts and Donaldson, *The Apostolic Fathers*, 1.323.
53. Ibid., 324.
54. Ibid.
55. Bousset, *Kyros Christos*, 267.
56. Thomassen, "The Tripartite Tractate," 92–93.

of it to return to where we came from. This return, otherwise known as *apolytrosis*, entails the Valentinian concept of death.

Death As Apolytrosis

Lewis has observed that the Valentinians (and perhaps, the Barbeliots), offer the most elaborate treatment of the concept of death in the second century.[57] These views can be primarily deduced from such rites as the Marcosian death rite and other key writings such as *The Treatise on the Resurrection [Epistle to Rheginos]*, *Tripartite Tractate* and the *Gospel of Philip*.[58] Irenaeus argued that, for the Marcosians, death means *apolytrosis* (literally, a "freeing" or "releasing" of the person from existential enslavement in which he lives as long as he is alive.)[59] With this understanding of death in Valentinianism, I will deal with the relevant sections of these writings here.

THE TREATISE ON THE RESURRECTION

Although a very short document, the importance of the Nag Hammadi Valentinian tractate known as *The Treatise on the Resurrection [Epistle to Rheginos]* (NHC I,4) cannot be overestimated.[60] This is because the writing "provides us with the first Gnostic document devoted exclusively to the subject of individual eschatology."[61] Although space does not allow me to explore the complete introductory details pertaining to this

---

57. Lewis, "*Apolytrosis*," 525. According to BDAG, the term ἀπολύτρωσις was originally used to refer to "buying back a slave." Thus, it meant setting free through payment. It means to "release from painful interrogation . . . release from captive condition, that is, release, redemption or deliverance" (Bauer, *A Greek-English Lexicon of the New Testament*, 115). Thus, it seems that Irenaeus is well within the semantic range of the meaning of this term in his refutation of the Marcosians here.

58. The Marcosians are believed to be the followers of the Valentinian teacher known as "Marcus the Magus," and whose death ritual is exposed at length by Irenaeus in *Haer*. 1.21.5.

59. Lewis, "*Apolytrosis*," 525.

60. The original document, written in Subakhmimic language, is less than eight pages in length.

61. Peel, *The Epistle to Rheginos*, viii. This conclusion of the place of *Treatise on the Resurrection [Epistle to Rheginos]* in the treatment of such subjects as death, survival of death and other related matters is also reached by Dale Goldsmith in Goldsmith, "*De Resurrectione*," 256.

key document, a few remarks are in order. As the title suggests, the literary form of this work is that of a letter, written to a certain Rheginos [Rheginus in newer translations]. Resembling a philosophical diatribe, the letter explores the subject of the doctrine of resurrection.[62] Although the work was probably used by the Sethian sect at the ancient city of Chenoboskion, the it is still Valentinian in nature.[63] The main reason for its presence in this ancient city is its close affinity with the teachings of Sethian Gnosticism.[64]

It has been suggested that the *Treatise on the Resurrection* was written by Valentinus himself in the 140s.[65] However, this view has not found much support amongst scholars. Instead, most scholars believe that the book was written by "a member of the Valentinian school in the late second century."[66] What is clear is that the treatise was written at a point in the history of the Church whereby her attempt to understand and explain the doctrine of the resurrection was a matter of great interest. According to Peel, this fits aptly with the late second century since it reveals the height of the church's struggle with those within herself who advocated the position that "the resurrection has already occurred [see, for example, the comment in II Tim 2:18 that λέγοντες ἀναστασιν ἤδη γεγονέναι)."[67] As Peel notes, the *Treatise on the Resurrection* evidences a developed view of what is called "pneumatic resurrection."[68] This is the belief that resurrection is obtainable in this life. Thus, this view fits squarely with Valentinian Gnosticism of late second century.[69]

Because of the nature of its content, the *Treatise on the Resurrection* is probably the most elaborate Valentinian document on the subject of

---

62. Thomassen, "The Treatise on Resurrection," 49. There is a debate as to whether the letter was an epistolary written for general circulation and that Rheginus was actually a fictitious figure or he was a real person to whom the letter was addressed. For the former view, see Malinine et al., *De resurrectione*, ix. Malcolm Peel, on the other hand, strongly defends the letter's addressee as a real individual, the writer's disciple, Rheginos (*The Epistle to Rheginos*, 10–12).

63. Peel, *The Epistle to Rheginos*, 12.

64. Ibid.

65. Ibid., 16–17. See also Malinine et al., *De resurrectione*, xxxi-xxxiii.

66. Svigel, "Second-century Incarnational Christology," 264.

67. Peel, *The Epistle to Rheginos*, 14.

68. Ibid.

69. See Lundhaug, "'These are Symbols and Likenesses of the Resurrection.'"

death and resurrection. The author's discussion of death comes in the midst of his discussion other aspects of his anthropology. His anthropology, which is clearly exposed in 45.39–46.2, is encapsulated through the use of such terms as "flesh" (σάρξ), "body" (σῶμα), "members" (μέλη), "thought" (ἄννοια?), and "mind" (νοῦς).[70] After a careful study of these words as they are used in the *Treatise on the Resurrection*, Peel concludes that the writer of the document exhibits a dualistic anthropology. That is, according to the writer of this letter, while the terms "body" and "flesh" denote the external corruptible nature of man, as well as the sphere of error and death, on the other hand, the terms "Members," "Mind," and "Thought" refer to an "inward, incorruptible nature" of man.[71] According to the writer, at death, therefore, the redeemed leaves behind the "body," with the resultant state being that of "absence" ('ἀπουσία), a state that is considered "gain" (47.17–20).[72]

But what is death, according to the writer of the *Treatise on the Resurrection*? Before looking at the specific passages where the writer either alludes to death or discusses it at length, it is important to make a comment concerning the author's semantics. That is, as some scholars have observed, although his theological terminology is remarkably similar to that of early Catholicism, this writer does not have the same exact meaning as that of the early church. Quoting Wright, for example, Svigel observes that although the writer of the *Letter to Rheginos* is clearly working with Paul's terminology in 1 Corinthians, the terminological likeness is only superficial.[73]

70. Peel, *The Epistle to Rheginos*, 112.

71. Ibid., 113.

72. *Treat. Res.* 47.17–20 reads: "The afterbirth (χόριον) of the body (σῶμα) is old age, and you exist in corruption. You have absence (ἀπουσία) as a gain."

73. Svigel, "Second-Century Incarnational Christology," 265. See also Peel, "The Treatise on the Resurrection," 166; Wright, *The Resurrection of the Son of God*, 540. A good example of this terminology is evidenced, for example, in the writer's seemingly orthodoxy explanation of the doctrine of the incarnation in 44.21–33 this way: "Now (δέ) the Son of God, Rheginos, was Son of Man. He embraced both of them, possessing the humanity and the divinity, so that on the one hand (μέν) he might conquer death through his being Son of God, and on the other (δέ) through the Son of Man the restoration (ἀποκατάστασις) to the Pleroma (πλήρωμα) might occur because (ἐπειδή) originally He was from above, a seed (σπέρμα) of Truth before this structure (σύστασις) had come into being," leading Svigel to comment that "one can find nothing in this quotation that could not be read in conformity with the catholic Incarnational narrative." (Svigel, "Second-century Incarnational Christology," 265). For a discussion of Gnostic eschatology and the New Testament, see Peel, "Gnostic Eschatology," 143–62. As well,

Terminology referring to the idea of death occurs in a number of places in this document. The writer of the *Treatise on the Resurrection* expresses the concept of death in the various forms of the Coptic term whose root form is *mot*. This term occurs in the intransitive verbal form (ἀποθνῄσκειν) in 48.22; 49.17, 19, 27, 28; in the qualitative form (probably νεκρός in 46.7, 17; 47.39; as well as a masculine substantive (θάνατος in 44.21, 28; 45.15, 35; 46.19.[74] In addition, the author uses some metaphors, which, in my opinion, reveal the real essence of his view of death even more clearly than the more direct terms already mentioned above. These include "departure" (47.22), "absence" (ἀπουσία—47.20), "to leave the body behind" (47.34–35), "suffering" (45.25), and "release" (49.33).[75]

According to the author of the *Treatise on the Resurrection*, perhaps echoing Pythagoreanism and/or the Stoics, death is understood as the cessation of life, the inevitable destiny of both the Elect and the non-elect.[76] In addition to the writer's contention that the Savior participated in death, his use of the first person plural "we" in 45.32–35 is also additional evidence that the Elect will participate in death since he, most certainly, sees himself as part of the Elect. The second and perhaps the most important aspect of death in the *Treatise on the Resurrection* is that it involves the "extinction of the life in the body and entails separation from it."[77] We read, for example, in 47.30–48.1, that

> But (ἀλλά) there are some (who) wish to understand in the inquiry about those things they are looking into, whether he who is saved, if he leaves behind his body (σῶμα), will be saved immediately? Let no one be given cause to doubt (διατάζειν) concerning this . . . indeed, the visible members (μέλος) which are dead shall not be saved.[78]

---

for a brief discussion of how gnostics read 1 Cor 15, see Pagels, "'The Mystery of the Resurrection,'" 278–87. According to her, Valentinians saw no "paradox" in Pauline eschatology as supposed in this text. Rather, "they insist that Paul's contradictory statements apply to different psychics and pneumatics respectively" (287).

74. Peel, *The Epistle to Rheginos*, 117.

75. Ibid.

76. This is especially so since the Savior himself also participated in death as shown in 46.16-19: "This is He of whom we say, 'He became the destruction,' as (ὡς) He is a great One." The phrase 'He became the destruction' here is understood to refer to the Savior's death.

77. Peel, *The Epistle to Rheginos*, 120.

78. *Treat. Res.* 47.30–48.1.

As I noted above, the author of the *Treatise on the Resurrection* seems to be using the term μέλος to refer to the "inward incorruptible nature" of man. Death, therefore, involves the separation of this invisible nature from the "visible members" of man. Thus, from this passage, it seems clear that death "involves disengagement from the corruptible body ... and that the body from which one is separated is recognizable by its dead, visible members."[79]

It is perhaps this advanced dualistic view of man that Irenaeus was talking about when he accused the Marcosians, a group within the larger Valentinianism, of a dualistic view by offering a detailed rendition of their ritual for death in *Adversus haereses* 1.21.5. Describing what has come to be known as the *apolytrosis* ritual within the Marcosians, Irenaeus wrote:

> Others still there are who continue to redeem persons even up to the moment of death, by placing on their heads oil and water, or the pre-mentioned ointment with water, using at the same time the above-named invocations, that the persons referred to may become incapable of being seized or seen by the principalities and powers, and that their inner man may ascend on high in an invisible manner, as if their body were left among created things in this world, while their soul is sent forward to the Demiurge. And they instruct them, on their reaching the principalities and powers, to make use of these words: "I am a son [υἱος] from the Father—the Father who had a pre-existence, and a son in Him who is pre-existent. I have come to behold [ἰδεῖν] all things, both those which belong to myself [τά ἀλλότρια καὶ τά ἴδια], and others, although, strictly speaking [παντελῶς], they do not belong to others but to Achamoth, who is female in nature, and made these things for herself. For I derive being from Him who is pre-existent, and I come [πορεύομαι] again to my own place [εἰς τά ἴδια] whence I went forth." And they affirm that, by saying these things, he escapes from the powers. He then advances to the companions of the Demiurge, and thus addresses them:—"I am a vessel [σκεῦος] more precious than the female who formed you. If your mother is ignorant [ἀγνόεις] of her own descent [ῥίζαν], I know myself, and am aware whence I am, and I call upon the incorruptible Sophia, who is in the Father, and is the mother of your mother, who has no father, nor any male consort [σύζυγος]; but a female springing from a female formed you, while ignorant of her own mother, and imagining that she alone existed; but I call upon her mother." And they declare, that when

---

79. Peel, *The Epistle to Rheginos*, 121.

the companions of the Demiurge hear these words, they are greatly agitated, and upbraid their origin and the race of their mother. But he goes into his own place, having thrown [off] his chain, that is, his animal nature. These, then, are the particulars which have reached us respecting "redemption." But since they differ so widely among themselves both as respects doctrine and tradition, and since those of them who are recognized as being most modern make it their effort daily to invent some new opinion, and to bring out what no one ever before thought of, it is a difficult matter to describe all their opinions.[80]

Thus, as Irenaeus reports, the purpose of this ritual (a combination of chrismation and invocation), is to help the individual's "inner human" to ascend successfully and invisibly through the cosmic realms back to the pleroma.[81] Because of the nature of the possible opposition along the way as the inner human returns to the pleroma at death, the defense is geared towards two possible opponents. As the reader can see, the first part of the defense is geared towards the principalities and powers (ἀρχῆς καὶ ἐξουσίας).[82] For this group, the dying person is advised to tell them that he is a son from the father, and he is heading back to where he came from. Thus, having spoken these words, the "inner human" is able to evade these principalities and authorities.[83] The second kind of defense is aimed at those who are around the Demiurge. As far as these are concerned, the person is instructed to inform them that he is a vessel which is more precious than the female who formed them (in other words, he is creationally superior to them). As Lewis notes, once the person speaks these words to them, the hostile powers become exceedingly disturbed, reviling (καταγνῶναι) their root and race of their mother. At this juncture, "the 'inner human' then casts off the 'chains' that bind it."[84] These "chains," according to Irenaeus, are the soul of the "inner human."[85] Thus, once these are cast off, the now

---

80. Irenaeus *Haer.* 1.21.5.

81. Lewis, "*Apolytrosis*," 529.

82. The phrase ἀρχῆς καὶ ἐξουσίας was quite common in the ancient world. Here, it is quite possible that the author is quoting Paul. See Rom 8:38; 1 Cor 2:6–8; Eph 1:21; 2:2. For an analysis of Paul's use of this phrase, see Forbes, "Paul's Principalities and Powers," 81–88.

83. Lewis, "*Apolytrosis*," 529.

84. Ibid., 530.

85. Ibid.

unfettered "inner human" continues its ascent back to its place (τὰ ἴδια), having now completed the process of *apolytrosis*.⁸⁶

On a more positive note, according to this author, death is not to be feared because it has lost its power, having been conquered by the Savior who is the Son of God. For example, in 44.25–29, the author writes that "possessing the humanity and the divinity, so that on the one hand (μέν) he might conquer death through his being Son of God."⁸⁷ Thus, as he continues to observe, the Son of God destroyed death by rising from among the dead (see 46.15–19). In other words, in his resurrection, the Savior "became the destruction of death"⁸⁸

In his understanding of death, therefore, the author of the *Treatise on the Resurrection* uses Pauline language quite frequently. In light of his emphasis that death is release from this worldly power, the writer implores Rheginus to know that death eventually comes no matter the longevity of one's life (49.17–24). But there is no need for Rheginus to be afraid of death since the Savior has conquered it. Indeed, death is "release," involving the departure/absence from the body (47.19–22). This language is reminiscent of Paul's words in 2 Corinthians 5:8. However, as Peel notes, there are two significant differences with Paul as far as his understanding of death is concerned. He writes:

> In his views on death . . . the author of our Letter [*Treat. Res*] reveals two decisive differences from the Apostle Paul whose language he echoes and cites. In the first place, whereas Paul can speak of death as "the last enemy to be destroyed" (I Cor. 15.25f), our author holds that it has already been destroyed and has lost all threat for the Elect. Consequently, for the author there can be no thought of an interim period or "sleep" (cf. I

---

86. Lewis, "*Apolytrosis*." It is important to note that key scholars today have cast some doubts on Irenaeus' representation of this Marcosian ritual. See, for example, Thomassen, *The Spiritual Seed*, 360–77. However, as Lewis argues, the fact that this ritual is also evident in other groups of Valentinianism in addition to the Marcosians serves as proof enough that Irenaeus was not mistaken in his understanding of the rite. In addition, as Lewis notes, in his *Refutation of All Heresies*, "Hippolytus of Rome (179–235) also briefly describes a rite of *apolytrosis*, in which the Marcosians 'speak in words that must not be divulged (ἀρήτω), placing hands on them for the receiving of redemption (ἀπολύτρωσις), which they claim cannot be spoken of casually (εὐκόλως) unless one were highly instructed (ὑπερδόκιμος), or when the bishop would come to say it into the ears ((πρὸ τὸ οὖς) of one ending this life (ὁ τελευτῶν)" (Lewis, *Apolytrosis*, 526). Hence, the ritual as well as its meaning seem to be well-attested.

87. *Treat. Res.* 44.25–29.

88. *Treat. Res.* 46.18–19.

Cor. 15.51) for the dead preceding the resurrection. But, second, and perhaps of greater importance, the author says nothing comparable to the Apostle's affirmation that the real "sting of death is sin" (I Cor. 15.56). Thus, Christ's defeat of death has nothing to do with the nullifying its power by taking upon himself the sin of the world. The author uses Pauline terms, but he knows nothing—or at least says nothing—of the Saviour's defeat of that death which is the "wages of sin" (Rom. 6.21, 23; 7.5; 8.6, 13; Gal. 6.7f.; James 1.15; etc). Consequently, the Cross is mentioned nowhere in our Letter, and salvation [death?] has to do with flight from a corruptible world rather than with the reconciliation of man to God.[89]

Peel's observation confirms my thesis that there is an implicit development of the understanding of the concept of death in the second century. In my opinion, although the writer of the *Treatise on the Resurrection* perhaps does not belong to the "intra-Christian" debates on the concept of the resurrection in the second century, he, nevertheless, belongs to the earlier understanding of death whereby there is no clear concept of the "inter-mediate" state. In other words, although it is highly likely that, as Peel contends, the author only sees the resurrection as having taken place since it will surely happen, nevertheless, the conclusion that by so strongly stressing the faith-view that the resurrection has already occurred, the author gives the impression of holding an over-realized eschatology, cannot be avoided.[90] In my opinion, according to the *Treatise on the Resurrection*, death is redemption (and, consequently, resurrection). He, in other words, attempts to interpret Paul, but falls short in some very key areas. For Paul and the Apostolic Fathers such as Ignatius of Antioch and Polycarp, the key difference with the *Treatise on the Resurrection* is the extreme dualism between the "internal members" and the "external members" of the person that this author exhibits as pointed out above.[91] And, therefore, according to this writer, there is no future resurrection since resurrection is entirely spiritual.

89. Peel, *The Epistle to Rheginos*, 122.
90. Ibid., 152.
91. Peel elucidates these differences when he writes, "Nevertheless, our author's negative evaluation of the 'world' and the corruptible body of 'flesh' does border upon a metaphysical and anthropological dualism which goes beyond Paul's views," (ibid., 149).

The Gospel of Philip

One of the most difficult documents to interpret is the late second-century Valentinian treatise known as *The Gospel of Philip* (NHC II,3).[92] Although scholars are in agreement that the *Gospel of Philip* is a "collection of teachings or statements on the sacraments," how to interpret these sacraments has been particularly puzzling.[93] As Lewis notes, the starting point for most analyses of this treatise is the statement that suggests that the author of the *Gospel of Philip* knew of five sacraments: "The Lord did everything in a mystery: a baptism and a chrism, a Eucharist, an apolytrosis and a bridal chamber."[94] Although such key questions as whether or not these five sacraments are separate events or stages of a single ritual (or even a combination) are worthy pursuing, they are beyond our concern here. Suffice it to say that this work "attests to a complex ritual system."[95]

The most significant discussion of the concept of death comes in the context of the author's discussion of the death and resurrection of Christ. Advancing what Svigel has appropriately termed as a polemic "directed against key aspects of the catholic Incarnational narrative (e.g., 55,23–28; 33–36)," the text advances a spiritual resurrection of Jesus since the author's view of physical death is that it is "an escape from the body."[96] For example, in 56,15–20, the author writes: "Those who say that the master died and then arose are wrong, for he first arose and then died. If someone is not first resurrected, wouldn't that person die? As God lives, that one would die."[97] Because of the extreme symbolism used in the *Gospel of Philip*, it is not easy to determine what the author has in mind here

---

92. For the dating of this document, see Isenberg, "The Gospel according to Philip." See also these helpful studies: Gaffron, "Studien zum koptischen Philippusevangelium," Sevrin, "Practique et doctrine des sacraments," Grant, "The Mystery of Marriage," Rewolinski, "The Use of Sacramental Language," Pagels, "Ritual in the Gospel of Philip," 280–91, Pagels, "The 'Mystery of Marriage' in the Gospel of Philip Revisited"; Segelberg, "The Coptic-Gnostic Gospel," Segelberg, "The Gospel of Philip and the New Testament"; Tripp, "The 'Sacramental System,'" 251–60; Stroud, "Ritual in the Chenoboskion," 30–35. For the argument that the Fathers also understood death as communal and the gateway to the eschatological ecclesial marriage, see Rush, "Death as a Spiritual Marriage," 94–101.

93. Lewis, "*Apolytrosis*," 548. For a more detailed analysis of the interpretive difficulties, see DeConick, "The Rite Mysteries," 229–31.

94. Lewis, "*Apolytrosis*," 548.

95. Ibid.

96. Svigel, "Second-century Incarnational Christology," 303.

97. *Gos. Phil.* 56,15–20.

when he talks of Christ's resurrection before death.[98] As Williams has suggested, the author of this treatise exposes a view of the resurrection that is full-blown realized eschatology. "It is obvious," he writes, "that for the author of Philip "resurrection" does not mean the resurrection of a person whose physical body has died. Resurrection means the birth of the soul and the birth of the soul and spirit within a spiritually dead ... individual at initiation."[99]

In addition to this passage on the resurrection and death of Jesus Christ, in a number of places the author of this treatise mentions either death or the soul's trial after death. For example, in 52,2–15, the author writes: "Heirs to the dead are dead, and what they inherit is dead. ... The dead inherit nothing, for how could a dead person inherit? If a dead person inherits the living, the living will not die and the dead will come to life."[100] It seems, however, the author is using death here metaphorically. "The language here suggests," writes Lewis, "that 'the dead' should be taken as a metaphorical expression for those who are spiritually asleep, thus the author offers a powerful critique of those who call themselves Christians and yet are so in name only."[101]

Additionally, in a text where the author is speaking of the nature of the resurrection he writes: "Some are afraid that they may rise from the dead naked, and so they want to arise in flesh. They do not know that it is those who wear the [flesh] who are naked. Those who are [able] to take it off are not naked."[102] Although Svigel sees this text as "quite clear" in its advancement of spiritual resurrection, there are still some pertinent questions as to what it teaches concerning the meaning of death.[103] For example, what does it mean to be "naked" and/or "clothed?" While Wilson

---

98. Clearly, this is a reversal of the catholic formula that "the Lord died first and then rose up." (See Williams, "Realized Eschatology," 10). As he points out, according to this author, indeed, the reverse was true! "In opposition to those who hold that 'the Lord died first and then rose up,' the writer forcefully affirms that the reverse was true ... and therefore the believer must also attain the resurrection in this life" (Williams, "Realized Eschatology," 10). Perhaps, what Svigel says about the *Gospel of Truth* may also apply here: "it appears to some scholars that the book was primarily written for Christians familiar with catholic Christianity, but not yet initiated into gnostic beliefs," (Svigel, "Second-century Incarnational Christology," 264).

99. Williams, "Realized Eschatology," 16.

100. *Gos. Phil.* 52,2–15.

101. Lewis, "*Apolytrosis*," 549.

102. *Gos. Phil.* 56,26–30.

103. Svigel, "Second Century Incarnational Christology," 303.

is certainly correct in holding that the idea of "naked" and "clothed" is a reference to the fact that the "Gnostic must rise [that is, resurrect through the initiation to the movement] in order to be stripped of the garment of the flesh [that is, die physically] and clothed in his heavenly robe," he does not tell the reader when this clothing with heavenly garments takes place or what it means.[104]

Finally, as Lewis observes, there are other key terms that the author of the *Gospel of Philip* uses frequently to refer to death. The treatise uses such key terms as "light, transformation, the passage out of this cosmos, and inheritance."[105] Interestingly, however, although this author, like that of the *Treatise on the Resurrection*, mentions the struggle of the soul as it journeys back to the Creator, emphasis is placed on ethical preparation instead of specific sacramental preparation to help the soul survive cosmic attacks on its ascent. Lewis summarizes:

> The author makes it clear that preparation for the soul's successful ascent after the death of the physical body comes not from magical passwords or even from the sacraments, but from sound ethical behavior, particularly from restraining the passions: "He who comes out of the cosmos ... and (thus) can no longer be seized ... on the grounds that he was in the cosmos reveals that he is above desire ... of the [. . .] and fear . . . . He is master over [. . .]. He is superior to envy . . . ." Controlling the passions has cosmological ramifications, since cosmic beings use the passions to entrap the ascending soul. These passions in fact originate in the Middle, and continue to dwell there with Achamoth. They exert direct control over the body, until the ascending spirit-soul aggregate can be stripped of their influence. The best protection from their power, advocates the *Gos. Phil.*, is to exercise *enkrateia*: "Fear not the flesh nor love it. If you (sg.) fear it, it will gain mastery over you. If you love it, it will swallow and paralyze you." The author then includes a final comment: "For it is good to come forth from the cosmos before one has sinned."[106]

Thus, according to the author of this treatise, death is the soul's ascent back to its creator. In spite of the soul's protection on its journey on the basis of the individual's ethical behavior, dangers along the way exist. In fact, there is the danger that the soul might end up in what the author

---

104. Wilson, *The Gospel of Philip*, 89.
105. Lewis, "Apolytrosis," 551.
106. Ibid. See *Gos. Phil.* 66.28–35.

calls the "Middle Place." This is the place in between the cosmos and the "resurrection," an evil place indeed. He writes, for example, in 66.9–21:

> A person is either in this world or in the resurrection—or in the middle place. May I not be found there! [in the middle place]. In this world there is good and evil, but the good of the world is not really good and the evil of the world is not really evil. After this world there is evil that is really evil: this is called the middle. The middle is death. As long as we are in this world, we should acquire resurrection, so that when we take off the flesh we may be found in rest and not wander in the middle. For many go astray on the way.[107]

This middle place refers to the "region between the Fullness [Pleroma] of the divine above and this world below."[108] Whether this is a precursor to the Roman Catholic doctrine of purgatory is unclear.

In conclusion, therefore, death according to the *Gospel of Philip* is the soul's flight back to the Pleroma. This journey starts at one's initiation to the group. This initiation is also known as the "resurrection." In order to assure this, one undergoes through the rite of the Chrism. As the author notes in 73.17–18, "It is an olive tree, and from it comes chrism, and from chrism comes resurrection."[109] And, as noted above, in addition

---

107. *Gos. Phil.* 66.7–21.

108. Scopello and Meyer, "The Gospel of Philip," 172 n. 68.

109. *Gos. Phil.* 73.17–18. The author elsewhere observes that death came into the world as a result of the "separation of the male and the female." He argues that this separation is healed by Christ: "Christ came to heal the separation that was from the beginning and reunite the two, in order to give life to those who died through the separation and unite them. A woman is united with her husband in the bridal chamber, and those united in the bridal chamber will not be separated again. That is why Eve became separated from Adam, because she had not united with him in the bridal chamber [ὁ νυμφῶν] (*Gos. Phil.* 70.9–22). Commenting on the role of the sacraments in this treatise, Deconick notes: "It seems then that the sacramental experiences allowed the believer to mystically penetrate the heavenly Temple as far as the veil of the Holy of Holies. Through the sacraments of initiation and the eucharist meals, the believer gazed upon the Spirit and was transformed into the Spirit, beheld the Christ and was transfigured into Christ. Moreover, by enacting the sacred marriage through properly directed sexual activity, the believer participated mystically in the hierogamy taking place behind the veil and thus influenced the harmony of the divine world. *Philip* reminds the believer that at this stage, the human is enacting the divine marriage, and in so doing: 'You saw the Father' (. . . (61:31). But complete transformation into the Father must wait until the Eschaton when 'you shall become Father' . . . (61:31). In that divine bridal chamber, the believer will see his angelic self, 'and what you shall [become]'. . . (61:32–35)," (Deconick, *The True Mysteries*, 258). My opinion is that, for

to the sacraments, the individual's ethical behavior assures the soul's clear path through the cosmos back to the Pleroma. Daley well-summarizes the treatise's view of death aptly: "The *Gospel of Philip* describes the goal of salvation [resurrection] as the consummation of a mystical marriage between the soul and truth or light, foreshadowed on earth in the community's liturgy of initiation (67.14–30; 84.20–86; 8; cf. *II Treatise of Great Seth* 57.7–27; 67.5–18)."[110]

The Gospel of Truth

In his *Haer.* 3.11.9, Irenaeus mentions that the Valentinians posses a work known as "The Gospel of Truth." As Thomassen and Meyer note, since the Nag Hammadi *Codex I* starts precisely with those words, "most scholars are therefore inclined to identify the tractate with the work mentioned by Irenaeus."[111] If this document is the same as what Irenaeus is talking about here, "we could date the text rather narrowly between 140 and 180 C.E."[112] It is even possible that this document was composed by Valentinus himself in the middle of the second century.[113]

As far as the message of the *Gospel of Truth* (NHC I,3 and XII,2) is concerned, the main focus is on how the Savior appeared on earth to bring the message of salvation to the world. Thomassen and Meyer's summary of how this message plays out in two different levels in this text is worth noting. They write:

> A peculiar feature of the text, however, is that the story of salvation seems to unfold simultaneously on two distinct levels. On one level we hear about the appearance of the Savior in the world of human beings: he taught them the truth, but he was persecuted by his enemies and was crucified and killed. However, his death brought life to mortal humans, and his instruction woke them up from forgetfulness and made them to return to the Father, the source of their being. Parallel with this account, however, another, more mythological story is told in the text as a kind of metanarrative. This story tells how the world came into

---

the Valentinians, there is no future eschaton. Rather, there is only a spiritual one. All the promises of the eschaton for the Elect become realized at death.

110. Daley, *The Hope of the Early Church*, 27.
111. Thomassen and Meyer, "The Gospel of Truth," 31.
112. Svigel, "Second-century Incarnational Christology," 261.
113. Ibid.

existence as a result of ignorance. Initially, the All, the Entirety of aeons or eternal realms, existed inside the Father, who was so vast and unfathomable that they were unable to perceive him. Because of this, ignorance, anguish, and terror took hold of the aeons; Error was produced instead of truth, and on this illusive basis the world was created as a solidification of ignorance and fear, a "fog."[114]

The *Gospel of Truth*, therefore, presents Jesus as the "revealer," being nailed on the cross and becoming the "fruit of the knowledge of the Father" (18,11–19,17). Thus, in this metanarrative, Jesus appears primarily as a revealer.

The concept of death is alluded to in two places and clearly discussed in one in the *Gospel of Truth*.[115] First, in 22,9–12, while talking about those whom the Father knows, the author notes that the person whom the Father knows find rest. In addition, that person knows where he has come from and where he is going. Second, in 24,14–21, the author alludes to the idea that whoever knows the truth through the revelation of the Son finds rest in the Father, rest that endures even after the individual dies. Third, and most significantly, the author of the *Gospel of Truth* explains in 41,8 that whoever has known the truth that is revealed by the Son will eventually "return and receive from that place [Pleroma], the place where they stood before, and they will taste of that place, be nourished, and grow."[116] He further clarifies:

> Their own place of rest is their fullness. All the emanations from the Father are fullness, and all his emanations find their root in the one who causes them all to grow from himself. He assigned their destinies. They all appear so that through their own thought [they might be perfected]. . . . Such is the place of the blessed, such is their place. There I shall dwell, to devote myself, constantly, to the Father of the All and true brothers and sisters, upon who the Father's love is lavished, and in whose midst nothing of him is lacking.[117]

Most probably, the author is here using the phrase "own place of rest" as a reference to the Pleroma. Thus, according to him, death is the soul's return to the Pleroma as well as the succeeding rest there. This flight

114. Thomassen and Meyer, "The Gospel of Truth," 31.
115. Daley, *The Hope of the Early Church*, 27.
116. *Gos. Truth.* 4.8.
117. *Gos. Truth.* 41.8—43.24.

constitutes the freeing of the soul since, according to the *Gospel of Truth*, "the physical world and presumably fleshly existence, is regarded as a temporary and undesirable imperfection (24,20–24; 25,3–6; 25,10–19)."[118] Consequently, the *Gospel of Truth* does not mention any time period between death and resurrection since death is the soul's regaining of the light. In other words, for its author, there is no future resurrection.

The Tripartite Tractate

A distinctly Valentinian treatise, the document known as the *Tripartite Tractate* (NHC I,5), is one of the largest documents discovered in Nag Hammadi. However, since this document has been reasonably dated in the first half of the third century, it is beyond the stated time period of this study.[119] I will only offer a brief summary of the document's view of death.

Many scholars see *Tripartite Tractate* as clearly divided into three parts—the first and the longest runs from 51–104 and deals with the Father, the Son and the emanation of the Pleroma (Fullness), the fall of the youngest aeon, and the creation of the cosmos.[120] The second narrative runs from 104,14—108,12 and discusses the creation of humanity. [121] Finally, in 108–38, the author deals with "the many confused opinions among people about the nature of the cosmos, the advent of the Savior, the establishment of the church, and the fates of the various categories of humans."[122] Obviously, the document's view of death occurs in this last part.

The discussion of death in the *Tripartite Tractate* occurs in the context of the author's discussion of redemption especially in 123,4—125,25. As Lewis points out, this section describes what looks like a "post-eschatological summary of salvation."[123] Set in the past tense, the author writes: "Once the redemption had been proclaimed, the perfect human immediately received knowledge so as to return swiftly to his unity, to the place from which he came."[124] Death, according to the author of the

---

118. Svigel, "Second-century Incarnational Christology," 263.

119. Thomassen, "The Tripartite Tractate," 60. See also Attridge and Pagels, "The Tripartite Tractate," 178.

120. Thomassen, "The Tripartite Tractate," 57.

121. Svigel, "Second-century Incarnational Christology," 284.

122. Thomassen, "The Tripartite Tractate," 57.

123. Lewis, "*Apolytrosis*," 546.

124. *Tri. Trac.* 123.8.

treatise, is the return of the soul to where it is supposed to have originated from. Whether there will be a final redemption at the Eschaton is not clear from this treatise, however. Strangely, *Tripartite Tractate* is virtually silent on the question of the resurrection. It neither condemns the fleshly concept of the resurrection as in the *Treatise on the Resurrection* (46,1–2) nor offers a reinterpretation of the "flesh" as a spiritual substance as in *Gospel of Truth*.[125]

The Interpretation of Knowledge

Dating from either towards the end of second century or early third century and perhaps written in Egypt, the *Interpretation of Knowledge* (NHC XI,1) stresses humility.[126] In order to understand the author's view of death, a brief comment about his soteriology and anthropology needs be made. Specifically, in 11,31–32, the author argues that the flesh that Jesus Christ was clothed is a "garment," which he elsewhere refers to as the "burden [that] you carry now . . . ."[127] Death, therefore, according to the author of the *Interpretation of Knowledge*, is the removal of this physical burden [the flesh], resulting in an escape from the material prison of the soul. This understanding is consistent with the conception of death in the other Valentinian documents that we have come across thus far. In other words, in these documents, the dualism between the soul and flesh is carried into death and beyond.

Summary of the Valentinian Concept of Death

A survey of these key Valentinian documents reveals a consistent concept of death. Death is the flight/escape/freedom of the soul back to where it came from. At least this understanding of death is consistently held to be true as far for the Elect in most of these Valentinian documents. Death for the Elect, therefore, is *apolytrosis*; the redemption of the soul, usually accompanied by some sacramental rituals aimed at ensuring the safe return of the soul to the Pleroma.[128] To some extent, as Lewis notes,

---

125. Svigel, "Second-century Incarnational Christology," 285.

126. Thomassen, "The Interpretation of Knowledge," 653.

127. *Interp. Know.* 10,37.

128. For similar rituals, see Segelberg, "The Coptic-Gnostic Gospel," 189–200, Buckley, "The Making of a Mandaean Priest," 195–210. For interpretive difficulties of

these Valentinian mortuary traditions may shed some light to the development of later, Catholic liturgics and sacramentalism.[129] But tracing this connection is beyond the scope of this book.

Death in Apologists and Polemicists

The Apologists and the polemicists operated in a slightly different theological and social environment from that of the Apostolic Fathers. While the concern of the Apostolic Fathers was with the internal issues affecting the church, that of the apologists and polemicists was much broader. Operating in the latter half of the second century, the apologists "attempted to establish communication with those outside the church—its Jewish and pagan despisers."[130] Because of this differing occasion, it is to be expected that their concept of death would be much broader than that of the Apostolic Fathers.

In them, we have the first comprehensive attempt to offer an understanding of death that explains it within the entire program of God on the earth. In their writings, a number of themes and emphases appear as they attempt to define death and show its purpose in God's program. In other words, in these works, death is mostly defined in terms of its functionality. While, on the one hand, they agreed with the gnostics that death involves the departure of the soul, on the other hand, they differed with them by insisting that there will be a future rejoining of the body and the soul. In other words, according to them, resurrection is not merely spiritual. That is, not only will there be some substantial continuity between the material individual and his resurrected state ["that which falls must rise"] but, also, most significantly, matter is not necessarily evil. As expected, they leave the questions of the exact nature of the resurrected body to the power and the wisdom of God, who, as they argue, is powerful and wise enough to create in the first place.

Also, on the one hand, in agreement with the Greek (Orphic) concept of death, the apologists taught that death is not the annihilation of the individual. Both agreed that the soul survives physical death. On the other hand, the apologists rejected the idea of the immortality of the

---

these rituals, see Buckley, "A Cult-Mystery," 570–81 and DeConick, "The Rite Mysteries," 225–31.

129. Lewis, "*Apolytrosis*," 559.

130. Dewart, *Death and Resurrection*, 57.

soul in the sense that it existed eternally even before the creation of the individual. For many apologists, as we shall see, the soul started to exist the moment a person began to exist. In what might be termed as a modified concept of the immortality of the soul, the apologists argue that although the soul permanently survives physical death, its state is conditioned upon its knowledge of God. I will come back to this as I discuss individual apologists.

Finally, as noted above, starting with the apologists and the polemicists, the purpose of death in God's program begins to emerge. Nicholas Vassiliades' fourfold summary is helpful here. He notes that according to the Fathers, death, first, halts our remaining in sinful nature. That is, "God has not inhibited the dissolution, the separation of the body and the soul" in order that evil shall not itself become immortal.[131] Since we have explored this point in chapter one, I shall not belabor it here again. Second, through death, the Lord benefited us by suppressing our arrogance, "the greatest of all evils."[132] He comments:

> We see death, yet many have dared to proclaim themselves gods! What would happen though, if we did not die? Consequently, with the decomposition of the body, God, at the very beginning, established the "foundation of humility," a virtue which rendered man beloved *per excellence* by God.[133]

Third, particularly for Irenaeus, the dissolution at death and the body's subsequent melting in the "crucible of the earth" is benevolent because, through that, it will be ready to be purified and brightened at the resurrection. That is, through death, mortality disappears, leaving the substance of the body for the resurrection.[134] Finally, death, "the greatest evil," is, changed by God to become the gateway for the reception of the heavenly and imperishable prizes. Although this concept seems to apply especially to martyrs, the apologists insist that death paves the way for resurrection. And, consequently, it is the resurrected bodies that will be able to either experience eternal blessedness or eternal punishment. Hence, death, the greatest of all evils that the devil introduced, "is changed by the most gracious and all-wise Lord into good; and in this

---

131. Vassiliades, "The Mystery of Death," 273.
132. Ibid.
133. Ibid.
134. Ibid.

way, the Lord guides man to eternal glory."[135] In addition, as far as the internal development of the doctrine of death is concerned, with Tertullian being our *terminus ante quem*, the possibility of an intermediate state of the souls between death and resurrection is now fully actualized.

I will assess the views of some of the most prominent apologists here. These are Aristides, Justin, Theophilus of Antioch, Tatian, and Athenagoras. My survey concludes with the works of the theologian and polemicist Irenaeus of Lyons, Clement of Alexandria and Tertullian of Carthage, who, by all estimations, close second-century Christian thought. Thus, for our purposes here, Tertullian acts as the bridge between second-century apologists and third-century theologians.

Aristides

Aristides is the earliest apologist whose writings we still possess. He addressed a "defense of Christianity to the Emperor Hadrian (117–138)."[136] Written perhaps as early as 145 C.E., the *Apology* makes the assertion that the world was made for the church since the church is the true Israel.[137] Aristides emphasized the ethical/moral uprightness of Christians as opposed to that of the Egyptians and Chaldeans. Aristides attributed this moral uprightness to the "expectation of a resurrection, followed by divine judgment and recompense for their deeds (*Apology* 15f)."[138] As expected, therefore, Aristides' concept of death is based on this eschatological expectation. As Daley summarizes, when a member of the Christian community dies, who was known to be virtuous, according to Aristides, "the Christians 'rejoice and thank God . . . as if he were only being transferred from one place to another'; but when a sinner dies, they weep bitterly over him because they know he is sure to be punished."[139] Aristides, however, does not say whether this judgment and recompense takes place immediately after death or during the eschaton. Aristides, therefore, does not offer any reflection on the possibility of the time period between death and resurrection. Death, for him, opens the way for either judgment or recompense.

135. Ibid.
136. Daley, *The Hope of the Early Church*, 20.
137. Frend, *Martyrdom and Persecution*, 249.
138. Daley, *The Hope of the Early Church*, 20.
139. Ibid.

Justin Martyr

In order to be able to properly assess Justin's understanding of death, a brief overview of his life, thought and intellectual milieu is necessary. As scholars have noted, our information concerning Justin's life comes almost entirely from his own writings. He was born at Flavia Neapolis.[140] A Greek-speaking non-Jewish, perhaps Samaritan by birth, "he did not hear of Moses and the Prophets until well into his life."[141] Although we do not know the exact date of his birth, details of his later life are much clearer. Grant observes that Justin's father's name was Priscus, which suggests that he was Greco-Latin.[142] He gives us details about his intellectual and religious pilgrimage in the first chapters of the *Dialogue*, canvassing through Stoicism, Peripatetic and Pythagorean philosophies before settling on Platonism. He tells us that he found fulfillment in Platonism, finally.[143]

Since Justin says that he became a Christian while in Platonism, the question of the relationship of that philosophy and his thought has been the subject of discussion ever since. As he reports in *Dialogue* 7, he met an old man who pointed him to the Hebrew prophets, who, according to him, are "certainly men more ancient than all those esteemed philosophers, both righteous and beloved by God, who spoke by the Divine Spirit, and foretold events which would take place, and which are now taking place."[144] Although this report of Justin's conversion has been assailed by scholars as idealized, in the final analysis, it seems hard to sustain such a proposition.[145] This is especially so if we consider the other motif that led to Justin's conversion in addition to his disappointment of philosophy: the steadfastness of the Christian faith in the midst of persecution. "I myself too," he writes, "I was delighting in the doctrines of Plato, and heard the Christians slandered, and saw them fearless of death," concluding that he "perceived that it was impossible that they could be living in

---

140. *1 Apol.* 1.

141. Barnard, *Justin Martyr*, 5. For a recent treatment of the life and thought of Justin, see Parvis and Foster, *Justin Martyr and His Worlds*.

142. Grant, *Greek Apologists*, 50.

143. *Dial.* 2. For a discussion on the question of whether or not Justin was schooled in Platonism, see Edwards, "On the Platonic Schooling," 17–34.

144. *Dial.* 7.

145. See, for example, Goodenough, *The Theology of Justin Martyr*, 58–59. For a defense of the possibility of the authenticity of Justin's conversion story, see especially Chadwick, "Justin Martyr's Defence," 275–97 and Barnard, *Justin Martyr*, 11.

wickedness and pleasure."[146] After becoming a Christian, Justin himself died as a martyr, earning the title "Justin Martyr," during the reign of Marcus Aurelius somewhere between AD 163 and 167.[147]

Although all agree that Justin's philosophical background plays an insurmountable role in his work as an apologist, how this takes place has been the subject of great contention among scholars in Justin's scholarship over the centuries. On the one hand, there are those who contend that Justin, finding no spiritual and intellectual help in philosophy, rejected it completely. In this case, his works are seen as being in complete contrast to Greek philosophy. Going back to the story of Justin's meeting with the old man as recorded in *Dialogue with Trypho* 4–6, it is pointed out that Justin came to the conclusion that there is a chasm between the philosophers and the Prophets in that while the former try to access the knowledge of God through the mind alone (and fail), the latter have this access through the Holy Spirit.[148] A more nuanced version of this view is that Justin underwent some methodological change between the *Apologies* and the *Dialogue*. According to Slusser, this change entails Justin moving away from philosophy to the degree that it would be even questionable to call him an "apologist."[149]

On the other hand, there are those who argue that, in Justin, we have the philosophizing of Christianity. According to Harnack, for example, Justin's description of Christianity was just a strategy to Hellenize Christianity.[150] This understanding fits with Harnack's historiography of Hellenization as the decline of the gospel. Thus; "Within Harnack's larger model, Justin's mimicry of philosophy was simply an example of creeping Hellenization through an evangelistic intention."[151] Indeed,

---

146. *1 Apol.* 8, 9.

147. Barnard, *Justin Martyr*, 13. For a response to the argument that Justin was the precursor to modern religious inclusivism, see Sparks, "Was Justin Martyr a Proto-Inclusivist?" 495–510. Sparks concludes that the view that Justin was a proto-inclusivist has been greatly exaggerated. Instead, "Justin should not be interpreted as a proto-inclusivist or as an early proponent of the fulfillment approach. Furthermore, if Justin was arguably one of the most sympathetic of early Christians to the pagan tradition, this gives some guidance on the limits of the patristic appraisal of the pagan culture" (509–10).

148. Adair, "Paul and Orthodoxy," 189.

149. Slusser, "Justin Scholarship," 20. For a discussion of the sources for Justin's *Dialogue*, see Skarsaune, *The Proof from Prophecy*.

150. Lyman, "Justin and Hellenism," 164.

151. Ibid.

since this picture presents Justin as neither a true Christian nor a worthy philosopher, it has been adopted especially in the post-colonial reading of Justin to portray him as using his "Greekness" as "a means of resistance to the Roman authority."[152] In this case, Justin is understood as bridging the gap between Greek philosophy and Christianity by creating an ideal, perhaps, a third hybrid. But this argument is questionable, given Justin's own admission that, "Christianity was the one, sure, worthy philosophy."[153] As Droge concluded, for Justin, "Christianity therefore is not one, or even the best, philosophy among many; it is the *only* philosophy insofar as it is the reconstitution of the original, primordial philosophy."[154] Thus, in Justin, it seems like there is more going on than mere Christianization of pagan philosophy.

So, how does Justin's work and thought relate to Greek philosophy? Or, is it even legitimate to ask the question, given the possibility that Justin is interacting with *philosophies* and not just one kind of philosophy? Indeed, a number of scholars have reached the conclusion that Justin is interacting with Middle Platonism, the kind of philosophy that was predominant in his day, and not Platonism *per se*. Basing his argument on the work of Copleston, Barnard concluded that "Justin's philosophical background is predominantly that of eclectic Middle Platonism, although it is well to remember that this was not a philosophical system, as such, but rather, a philosophical transition."[155] Likewise, Droge also noted that

152. Ibid., 166. An example is *1 Apol.* 2.1 where Justin asks: "Why do you persecute us when we say the same things as the Greeks?" For this postcolonial reading of early Christianity, see especially Lyman, "Natural Resources," 71–77; Lyman, "Hellenism and Heresy," 218–19; Lyman, "The Politics of Passing"; Rowe, "Adolf von Harnack," 69–98; Rajak, "Talking at Trypho"; Bhabha, *The Location of Culture*; Young, *Biblical Exegesis*.

153. Barnard, *Justin Martyr*, 7.

154. Droge, *Homer or Moses?* 72.

155. Barnard, *Justin Martyr*, 37. See Copleston, *A History of Philosophy*. According to Copleston, Greek philosophy underwent these three stages of development: 1) the period between the end of fourth century BC and mid-first century BC in which Stoic and Epicurean philosophies were founded. In addition, some kind of eclecticism is evidenced during this time in the schools of Middle Stoa, the Peripatetic and the Academy. 2) the period between the first century BC and mid-third century AD characterized by eclecticism and skepticism. Evidentially, there is also an attempt during this time to return to philosophic "orthodoxy," resulting in the conflict evidenced in Middle Platonism, resulting in some kind of amalgam and transition philosophically. This period coincides with the time span of the life and works of Justin Martyr. 3) Finally, the third period runs from mid-third century AD to mid-sixth century AD. This period sought to combine all the valuable aspects of philosophy and religious

"Justin's argument for the superiority of Christianity is based on a theory of the history of philosophy which derives from middle Platonism."[156] In this case, Justin tried to find areas of agreement especially between the philosophy of the Platonists and the Stoics. Again, Droge's summary here is noteworthy. He writes:

> Indeed, according to Justin, Socrates himself was a precursor of Christ inasmuch as he too tried to deliver humanity from the power of the demons by means of "true reason" (*logos alēthēs*). Likewise, Plato was correct in teaching that God is transcendent, as well as immutable, impassible, and nameless. He was also correct when he declared in *Timaeus* (41ab) that the cosmos is created and perishable. Furthermore, Plato was right in his teaching about the soul, that it is related to God, that it possesses free will, and that it suffers punishment after death. Admittedly, in some things Plato was mistaken, as the "old man" pointed out to Justin, chiefly in believing that the soul is immortal and suffers punishment [immediately] after death in the form of metempsychosis.[157]

The same agreement and disagreement is also evident in Stoicism. Again, Droge notes:

> He [Justin] praises the Stoics above all for their admirable moral teaching (*Apol.* 2.8.1). They also approximate the truth in their doctrine that the cosmos is subject to cataclysms and conflagrations. The last cataclysm was the flood of Deucalion, whom Justin identifies with the biblical hero Noah (*Apol.* 2.7.2–3); the coming conflagration is a shadow of the eschatological fire of God's judgment (*Apol.* 1.60.8–9).[158]

Revealed herein is a methodology that realizes, borrows and modifies existing "parallels" to cleverly create a distinctive Christian worldview that is commensurate with Justin's understanding of revealed truth. That is, "while it is true that he grants a certain legitimacy to some of

---

doctrines from the east and the west into one comprehensive whole, with the philosophy of Plotinus being dominant (Barnard, *Justin Martyr*, 28–29).

156. Droge, "Justin Martyr," 305.

157. Ibid., 306. For a complete comparison of points of agreement between Christianity and Platonism, see Chadwick, *Early Christian Thought*, 12 and 128 nn. 19–23. See also *1 Apol.* 25.2, 61.11, 63.1, *2 Apol.* 6.1, 12.4, *Dial.* 5.4. For a fine discussion of the concept of *logos spermatikos* in Justin, see Holte, "Logos Spermatikos," 109–68.

158. Ibid.

the opinions of the philosophers, it would be wrong to assume that Justin's main intention is to reconcile Christianity to Greek philosophy."[159] This observation is clearly contrary to what Harnack called "the universal-historical alliance between ecclesiastical Christianity and Greek philosophy."[160] As Wolfson observed, Justin like Philo and Paul, argued that philosophy could be critiqued on two grounds. First, as far as its substance is concerned, there is "falsity in many of its doctrines."[161] As Justin pointed out, the philosophers have not always accurately understood the modicum of truth that was contained in their philosophy, perverting it often.[162] Second, together with the other church fathers, Justin argued that the philosophers had also disagreed amongst themselves. As he put it, they had often contradicted themselves.[163] Thus, it seems like Justin is willing to use the Greek philosophers' *methodology* while clearly critically evaluating their *content* in order to offer a distinctive Christian view. He intends to prove the superiority of Christianity. This approach, I argue, is clearly observable in his concept of death.

Justin fought two fronts in his defense of Christianity. On the one side, he was faced with Jewish opponents who rejected Christ as the Messiah while on the other hand he was faced with pagan philosophy. His works are geared towards responding to these threats. As far as the Jews are concerned, Justin wrote what we know as *Dialogue with Trypho*. To the Romans, he wrote two *Apologies*. Both help explain aspects of Christianity in the mid-second century.[164]

As noted, Justin's focus in the *Dialogue with Trypho* is to show that Jesus Christ is the Messiah. As the title suggests, it is a dialogue with Trypho, a Jew, concerning how Justin got converted through his interaction with another converted Jew, whom he calls an "excellent man ... a Hebrew of the circumcision."[165] As the discussion progresses, it quickly

---

159. Ibid., 306–7.

160. Harnack, *Lehrbuch der Dogmengeschichte*, 1.498.

161. Wolfson, *The Philosophy of the Church Fathers*, 1.16.

162. *1 Apol.* 44.

163. *2 Apol.* 10, *Dial.* 2.

164. For a discussion of the works of Justin, see Barnard, *Justin Martyr*, 14–26. For a discussion of how Justin's works relate to other key writings of his time, see Foster, "The Relationship between the Writings of Justin Martyr," 104–12; Skarsaune, "Justin and His Bible," 53–76.

165. *Dial.* 1. Unless otherwise states, I am using Roberts and Donaldson, *Ante-Nicene Fathers*, vol 1.

turns to a discussion on the concept of the soul. Indeed, Justin's entire concept of death is subsumed in his understanding of the soul. After helping Justin understand that the philosopher's ideas about the soul being immortal are mistaken since such a view suggests that if this is the case, then the soul is "plainly unbegotten," the Old Man had proceeded to help Justin understand what happens to the souls after death. In what has been understood as the first major conversation on the soul in the apologists, the *Dialogue with Trypho* goes into great lengths to explain that, for the soul, there is a time difference between death and resurrection. For example, in chapter 80, while defending his belief in the resurrection, Justin writes:

> For if you have fallen in with some who are called Christians, but who do not admit this [truth], and venture to blaspheme the God of Abraham, and the God of Isaac, and the God of Jacob; who say there is no resurrection of the dead, and that their souls, when they die, are taken to heaven; do not imagine that they are Christians, even as one, if he would rightly consider it, would not admit that the Sadducees, or similar sects of Genistæ, Meristæ, Galilæans, Hellenists Pharisees, Baptists, are Jews (do not hear me impatiently when I tell you what I think), but are [only] called Jews and children of Abraham, worshipping God with the lips, as God Himself declared, but the heart was far from Him. But I and others, who are right-minded Christians on all points, are assured that there will be a resurrection of the dead, and a thousand years in Jerusalem, which will then be built, adorned, and enlarged, [as] the prophets Ezekiel and Isaiah and other declare.[166]

Thus, as we have argued, the apologists' conception of world history in light of God's program now includes the time difference between death and resurrection. After death, the souls of the departed are said to be in a "waiting" place, which, as we will see, Justin and others call "Hades." He is careful, however, to separate two waiting places. He notes that while the souls of the pious remain in a better place, those of the wicked remain in a worse place, waiting for the judgment.[167] And, as he notes in chapter 80, any denial of the existence of such a place as well as believe in the resurrection, is exposed as not Christian in the *Dialogue with Trypho*. But what is death according to him?

166. *Dial.* 80.
167. *Dial.* 5.

Because of the occasion within which Justin was writing his *Apologies*, most of his comments about death are subsumed within the themes of God's judgment of the wicked, and the vindication of the righteous. Although there are many places where we can appeal to in order to get his concept of death, these three suffice: *1 Apol.* chapter 11, 18, and 57. As we know them, the Apologies were written primarily to demand justice for the persecuted Christians. In chapter 11, Justin seeks to clarify what kind of kingdom Christians are looking forward to. He explains that had Christians been waiting for a human kingdom, then they would have denied Christ at the face of persecution. However, since they are waiting for the kingdom of God, death is part of that expectation. He writes:

> And when you hear that we look for a kingdom, you suppose, without making any inquiry, that we speak of a human kingdom; whereas we speak of that which is with God, as appears also from the confession of their faith made by those who are charged with being Christians, though they know that death is the punishment awarded to him who so confesses. For if we looked for a human kingdom, we should also deny our Christ, that we might not be slain; and we should strive to escape detection, that we might obtain what we expect. But since our thoughts are not fixed on the present, we are not concerned when men cut us off; since also death is a debt which must at all events be paid.[168]

Thus, according to Justin, death is the punishment associated with believing in Jesus Christ. However, because of his view of the future, he can comfortably say that Christians are not worried when men cut off their heads. Justin's understanding of the future as it relates to death saturates the *Apologies*.[169]

In chapter 18, Justin further clarifies that the souls of the departed exist in a sensation as they wait to be reunited with their bodies after the resurrection. He writes:

> For reflect upon the end of each of the preceding kings, how they died the death common to all, which, if it issued in insensibility, would be a godsend to all the wicked. But since sensation remains to all who have ever lived, and eternal punishment is laid up (i.e., for the wicked), see that ye neglect not to be convinced,

---

168. *1 Apol.* 11.

169. For a complete evaluation of Justin's eschatology, see Barnard, "Justin Martyr's Eschatology," 86–98.

> and to hold as your belief, that these things are true.... Let these persuade you that even after death souls are in a state of sensation; and those who are seized and cast about by the spirits of the dead, whom all call dæmoniacs or madmen; and what you repute as oracles, both of Amphilochus, Dodana, Pytho, and as many other such as exist; and the opinions of your authors, Empedocles and Pythagoras, Plato and Socrates, and the pit of Homer, and the descent of Ulysses to inspect these things, and all that has been uttered of a like kind. Such favour as you grant to these, grant also to us, who not less but more firmly than they believe in God; since we expect to receive again our own bodies, though they be dead and cast into the earth, for we maintain that with God nothing is impossible.[170]

Justin, therefore, sees souls continuing in a conscious existence after death. As Gousmett notes, although in Justin we do not have a fully developed doctrine of the intermediate state (this has to wait until Irenaeus of Lyons), "given his comments that the souls of the righteous do not enter heaven before the resurrection, and that eternal punishment is kept in store for the wicked, it would seem that the dead are in some kind of conscious state, but have not yet received their reward either good or bad."[171]

Finally, in *1 Apol.* 57, Justin argues that the reason why Christians do not fear death is that, in essence, death is freedom from all suffering. He writes:

> For we do not fear death, since it is acknowledged we must surely die; and there is nothing new, but all things continue the same in this administration of things; and if satiety overtakes those who enjoy even one year of these things, they ought to give heed to our doctrines, that they may live eternally free both from suffering and from want. But if they believe that there is nothing after death, but declare that those who die pass into insensibility, then they become our benefactors when they set us free from sufferings and necessities of this life, and prove themselves to be wicked, and inhuman, and bigoted. For they kill us with no intention of delivering us, but cut us off that we may be deprived of life and pleasure.[172]

In other words, according to Justin, although the persecutors of Christians thought they were doing great harm and disservice to

---

170. *1 Apol.* 18.
171. Gousmett, "Shall the Body Strive and Not be Crowned?" 66.
172. *1 Apol.* 57.

Christians for they thought they were sending them to non-existence because they did not believe in life after death, in contrast, they were actually relieving Christians of the sufferings and necessities of this life. In other words, according to him, death, for a believer, is salvation or freedom from the sufferings of this world.

In conclusion, therefore, death according to Justin Martyr is both punishment that we must all necessarily endure if we are believers in Christ as well as freedom from the sufferings and necessities of this world. In addition, as I have pointed out, with Justin, we begin to see a clear separation between death and resurrection, something that we haven't seen with the earlier fathers.

Theophilus of Antioch

Theophilus of Antioch's views are very similar to those of Justin since they fought the same philosophical battles. However, in anticipation of the thought of Irenaeus of Lyons on the subject of death, Theophilus starts to tie his understanding of death with the grand scheme of God's salvific plan for humanity. Particularly, in *To Autolycus* 2.26, Theophilus writes:

> And God showed great kindness to man in this, that He did not suffer him to remain in sin for ever; but, as it were, by a kind of banishment, cast him out of Paradise, in order that, having by punishment expiated, within an appointed time, the sin, and having been disciplined, he should afterwards be restored. Wherefore also, when man had been formed in this world, it is mystically written in Genesis, as if he had been twice placed in Paradise; so that the one was fulfilled when he was placed there, and the second will be fulfilled after the resurrection and judgment. For just as a vessel, when on being fashioned it has some flaw, is remoulded or remade, that it may become new and entire; so also it happens to man by death. For somehow or other he is broken up, that he may rise in the resurrection whole; I mean spotless, and righteous, and immortal. And as to God's calling, and saying, Where art thou, Adam? God did this, not as if ignorant of this; but, being long-suffering, He gave him an opportunity of repentance and confession.[173]

---

173. Theophilus *To Autolycus* 2.26. Unless otherwise stated, I am using Roberts and Donaldson. *Ante-Nicene Fathers*, vol. 2. For Theophilus' exegetical methods, see Schoedel, "Theophilus of Antioch," 279–97, esp. 280–91.

Therefore, in Theophilus of Antioch, we begin to see an attempt to define death in such a way that connects it with God's plan of redemption. According to him, death is the process through which God molds the broken vessel, the human being who has been corrupted by disobedience in order to make him like new again. This theme will be finally elucidated by Irenaeus of Lyons.

In addition to seeing death as the remolding of the human vessel, Theophilus also argued that death is the gateway to the necessary time of final recompense. "Central in Theophilus' hope, too," writes Daley, "is in a sense of the appropriateness of a final divine recompense after death: justice demands that the believer be made immortal in body and soul and see God worthily in a new and incorrupt life (1.7; 1.14; cf. 2.26)."[174] Without death, according to Theophilus, it is impossible for justice, that is, the joining of the body and soul in an incorruptible union, to be served. Indeed, Theophilus is the first noted theologian to speak in terms of *theosis* while referring to the Christian fulfillment, which is the individual's ultimate nature after the reception of the incorruptible body and soul, a possibility only achievable through death. Daley, again, summarizes, for Theophilus:

> The place of this transformation from a human to a divine mode of life will be Paradise, a place "intermediate between earth and heaven" (2.24); there those who have sought for God and kept his commandments will rediscover the original harmony of created order (2.17), and receive new, unparalled gifts that will allow them to share in the nature of God (2.26).[175]

In Theophilus, therefore, we have the assertion that death is the necessary way through which the human vessel, the rejoined body and soul, can be brought to a state to enjoy the benefits of Paradise. It is, in other words, the way to proper *theosis*.

Tatian

Tatian was one of the most influential thinkers in the second century. However, as many have observed, a clear understanding of his thought has been challenged by Irenaeus' accusation that Tatian was actually a gnostic. As Dewart observes, however, "the justice of the accusation [by

---

174. Daley, *The Hope of the Early Church*, 24.
175. Ibid.

Irenaeus] is still debated."[176] Starting the accusation, Irenaeus, in his *Haer.* 1.28.1, claimed that after the martyrdom of Justin, "Tatian apostatized from the church and set down his own teaching."[177] Irenaeus accused Tatian of inventing a system of "invisible Æons," combining the teachings of Valentinus, Marcion, and Saturnus, and declaring marriage as nothing but corruption and fornication.[178] Thus, Irenaeus saw Tatian as showing adherence to both Encratism and Valentinianism.[179] This accusation was successfully repeated by such Fathers as Clement of Alexandria (*ca.* 150–215 CE), Hippolytus (*ca.* 160–235 CE), Eusebius (*ca.* 260–339 CE), and Epiphanius (*ca.* 315–402 CE).[180]

A key current defender of the view that Tatian was a heretic is Robert Grant.[181] Arguing for a late composition of Tatian's *Oration to the Greeks* around 177 or 178, Grant "claims that Tatian uses terminology from the Valentinian pleromic myth," asserting that Tatian "spoke of 'better aeons' above."[182] However, not everyone agrees with this conclusion concerning Tatian. For example, in a recent study of the accusation of Tatian of heresy, Emily Hunt concludes:

> I believe that in Irenaeus' charge of Valentinianism and Encratism, we are faced with political propaganda rather than a true representation of Tatian's views. At the end of the second century some fairly major changes were happening within western Christianity; the stream that was to become known as "orthodoxy" was beginning to achieve dominance, and the consolidation of that power involved an increasing intolerance towards more extreme Christian groups and a formalization of the content of mainstream Christian teaching. . . . At any rate, Irenaeus' claim of apostasy seems convenient way to discredit Tatian whilst retaining the teaching of Justin for orthodoxy.[183]

---

176. Dewart, *Death and Resurrection*, 83.
177. Hunt, *Christianity in the Second Century: The Case of Tatian*, 20.
178. *Haer.* 1.28.1. See also *Haer.* 1.26.1.
179. Hunt, *Christianity in the Second Century*, 20.
180. Ibid., 20–21. See Clem. *Strom.* 3.82.2, Hipp. *Refutation of all Heresies.* 8.16; 10.8, Eus. *E.H.* 4.29, and Epiph. *Panarion.* 46.1.6-7. See also Koltun-Fromm, "Reimagining Tatian," 1–30. On Tatian's anthropology, see Elze, *Tatian und seine Theologie*, 88–100; Whittaker, *Tatian: Oratio ad Graecos.* On his use of *psyche*, see Toews, "Biblical Sources," 100–108.
181. Grant, *Greek Apologists*, 113. See also Grant, "The Heresy of Tatian," 62–68.
182. Hunt, *Christianity in the Second Century*, 22.
183. Ibid., 177.

L. W. Barnard has argued successfully that the best way to resolve this issue is to take a closer look at the chronology of events in Tatian's life, an aspect on which Robert Grant relies a lot in his conclusions that Tatian was a gnostic heretic. While Grant had dated the composition of *Oratio* about 176, "or, probably late 177 or early 178, on the grounds of clear chronological notices on the work itself," Barnard thinks otherwise.[184] On the basis of a critical comment made by Eusebius in *E.H* 4.16, she argues that most likely, the composition of *Oratio* can be dated at around *ca*. 160 or a few years before. Based on this dating of *Oratio*, Barnard deduces that "we would suggest that Irenaeus, who knew that on leaving Rome Tatian had embraced extreme views, had no real knowledge when the *Oratio* had been written and assumed that it belonged to the time when Tatian had defected, after Justin's death."[185] In this case, therefore, Irenaeus' accusation of heresy on the part of Tatian is based on ignorance and not politics. Furthermore, Barnard sees this clear-cut ascribing of heresy on the part of Tatian as odd, given what we have also learned from Eusebius concerning the personage of Tatian. She writes:

> This clear-cut theory of Tatian's heresy, however, runs somewhat counter to Eusebius's statement that Tatian had been the teacher of Rhodon, after the death of Justin—and that Rhodon combated Marcion heresy—and that Tatian had also written a book of questions of biblical writings, in which he promised he would explain what was hidden and obscure in the biblical writings, which no doubt included the Old Testament. . . . This is very odd if Tatian was the arch-heretic and follower of Marcion's brand of Gnosticism for there is no suggestion that Rhodon and Tatian held divergent views.[186]

It is hard to make a decision either way on this brilliant student of Justin Martyr. While most of the accusation is based on his joining the group known as Encratism later in his life, it seems like his concern for Christian sexual abstinence was based on his understanding of Paul and his conviction that this abstinence was "in order to gain salvation and immortality."[187] That is, in order to attain salvation, according to Tatian, one had to practice sexual abstinence. This understanding of Christianity,

---

184 Barnard, "The Heresy of Tatian—Once Again," 1. See also Hunt, *Christianity in the Second Century*, 3–4.

185. Barnard, "The Heresy of Tatian," 3–4.

186. Ibid., 3. See also Eus. *H.E.* 5.13.

187. Gaca, "Driving Aphrodite From the World," 28.

argues Barnard, was originally part of the Roman church's interpretation of the Bible. And, certainly, in the Syriac-speaking church of the East, Tatian's beliefs were not considered strange as such.

I think what we have in Tatian is an attempt to exercise spiritual discipline as much as possible for the purpose of the attainment of salvation. This is perhaps something akin to the step that Tertullian took later of joining the Montanists. While we are not given any reasons for Tatian's encratism, it seems like Tatian was only attempting to understand and follow Paul, and, perhaps, some aspects of the Valentinians.[188] Like Justin, he was an eclectic Christian philosopher.

But what about Irenaeus' accusations that Tatian was a heretic? Were they all based on "politics" as scholars like Emily Hunt claim, or was there something else going on? I think if we understand Irenaeus correctly, it is incorrect to argue that only ecclesial politics were behind his accusation of heresy on the side of Tatian. I agree with Barnard that whatever it is that caused this accusation, it is not ecclesial politics. Irenaeus, as many have observed, was a bishop whose concern for his flock and their spiritual well being surpassed everything else in his life. Since, as Daley put it, "Irenaeus' theology is essentially a plea for the validity of ordinary Christian life and tradition," anything that seems to threaten this proposition is treated with suspicion by him.[189] Thus, rather than seeing Irenaeus' accusation as purely political, it is better to see his point in light of his protection of his flock from any hint of heresy. It is perhaps akin to what Wilbur Smith once remarked that he could smell heresy one mile away![190] That is, Irenaeus is offering a cautionary note upon his flock in light of the existence of such threatening groups as the gnostics and the Marcionites. As for Tatian, "certainly, as with the other apologists, his beliefs are not circumscribed by the purpose of his writings and it should be unwise to assume that his ascetic-encratism was the whole of his Christianity."[191] Nevertheless, he opened the door for such kinds of extreme interpretations of the Bible later.

Tatian's two surviving works are the *Oration to the Greeks* and the *Fragments*. His only clear discussion of the concept of death comes

---

188. For attempts to explain the reasoning behind Tatian's Encratism, see Gasparro, *Enkrateia e antropologia*, 32–56, Vööbus, *A History of Asceticism*, 11–12, and Brown, *The Body and Society*, 92–96.

189. Daley, *The Hope of the Early Church*, 28.

190. Marsden, *Reforming Fundamentalism*, 149.

191. Barnard, "The Heresy of Tatian," 10.

in the *Oration* as he responds to the claims of some philosophers that the soul is by nature, immortal. According to him, this is not the case, however. Instead,

> The soul is not in itself immortal, O Greeks, but mortal. Yet it is possible for it not to die. If, indeed, it knows not the truth, it dies, and is dissolved with the body, but rises again at last at the end of the world with the body, receiving death by punishment in immortality. But, again, if it acquires the knowledge of God, it dies not, although for a time it be dissolved.[192]

To Tatian, therefore, death is a temporary dissolution of the body and the soul to await resurrection. This happens only to those who know God. For Tatian, in order for the soul and the body to be able to attain immortality, it must know God. On the other hand, "the soul ignorant of the truth does, however, die, to rise again later at the end of the world along with the body, to suffer death [again] by immortal punishment."[193] Thus, "Tatian is saying that God grants a certain life apart from the body to the souls of the just, but it is clear that his understanding of normal and full life is that of the soul and body together."[194] That is why he sees death as the dissolution of the soul and the body.

While Tatian's view of death is much more detailed than this brief outline here, it is clear that all of his views on death are based on his understanding of God. While rejecting the Platonic idea of a natural concept of the immortality of the soul, Tatian locates the beginning of one's soul in God Himself. In addition, he bases the future recreation of the soul and the body squarely on the power and wisdom of God. Pelikan's summary is worth noting here. He writes:

> Like his argument against the preexistence of the soul, Tatian's rejection of natural immortality is fundamentally theocentric. "Not existing before I came to be, I did not know who I was, and existed only in the potentiality of fleshly matter; but having come to be after being nothing, I have through my birth become certain of my existence." This is his case against preexistence, and in the next sentence he continues: "In the same way, having come to be and through death existing no longer, shall exist again just as previously I did not exist but came to be." As the basis for this expectation he cites his conviction that "God the

192. Tatian *Oration to the Greeks*, 13.
193. Dewart, *Death and Resurrection*, 83–84.
194. Ibid., 84.

Sovereign, when He pleases, will restore to its original state the substance that is visible to Him alone." Neither for his original birth out of nothingness of nonbeing nor for his ultimate rebirth out of the nothingness of death can man take credit, but it belongs to God's sovereignty and discretion to create a human being in the first place and to re-create him after he has been annihilated by death.[195]

Thus, instead of the Platonic idea of death as either a destruction of the flesh in order to allow the soul to continue in its natural immortality or the recycling of souls in bodies (metempsychosis), Tatian insisted that death is a temporary dissolution of the body and the soul in order to pave way for their ultimate once-for-all rejoining by God for their eternal existence as one entity forever. But the quality of this future union depends on the soul's "participation in the immortality and incorruptibility of God."[196] In short, Tatian, while agreeing with the Greeks and the Romans on the concept of the existence of the soul beyond physical death, clearly disagrees with them in arguing for a future reunification of the body and the soul through the miracle of the resurrection, based on the resurrection of Christ, the basis of the Christian hope, and the power and wisdom of God.[197] Since He was powerful and strong enough to do it once (for there was a time we were not), God has no problem doing it again (recreation).

Athenagoras

Although very little is known about the so-called Athenian philosopher, some call Athenagoras the "most eloquent of the early Christian apologists."[198] According to Daley, Athenagoras composed his *Plea for Christians* about the year 177.[199] A praiseworthy document, the *Plea* was "an apology for Christians to the emperors Marcus Aurelius and Commodus during their tour of the eastern empire."[200] His message in the *Plea* can be summarized as follows:

195. Pelikan, *The Shape of Death*, 17–18.
196. Ibid., 18.
197. Ibid., 22.
198. Hill, *Regnum Caelorum*, 107.
199. Daley, *The Hope of the Early Church*, 23.
200. Hill, *Regnum Caelorum*, 107.

Like Justin, Athenagoras stresses the moral importance for Christians of their hope the resurrection and a future life, both because it entails the prospect of judgment (12) and because it affirms so concretely the value of human existence (31). Only divine being is eternal of its own nature (4); but the Christian expects to share in God's imperishability, since we shall abide near God and with God, free from all change or suffering of the soul—not as flesh, even though we shall all have flesh, but as heavenly spirit (31). Humans who "fall" in the coming judgment will also endure "in fire"; no one will simply be annihilated.[201]

Before discussing even the more important document known as the *Treatise on the Resurrection*, it is helpful to note that the *Plea* clearly offers Athenagoras' concept of death. For example, in chapter 31, Athenagoras offers a thorough description of what he believes happens at death and thereafter. He writes:

> For if we believed that we should live only the present life, then we might be suspected of sinning, through being enslaved to flesh and blood, or overmastered by gain or carnal desire; but since we know that God is witness to what we think and what we say both by night and by day, and that He, being Himself light, sees all things in our heart, we are persuaded that when we are removed from the present life we shall live another life, better than the present one, and heavenly, not earthly [ἐπουράνιον, οὐx ἐπίγειον] (since we shall abide near God, and with God [μετὰ θεοῦ καὶ σὺν θεῷ], free from all change or suffering in the soul, not as flesh, even though we shall have flesh, but as heavenly spirit), or, falling with the rest, a worse one and in fire; for God has not made us as sheep or beasts of burden, a mere by-work, and that we should perish and be annihilated. On these grounds it is not likely that we should wish to do evil, or deliver ourselves over to the great Judge to be punished.[202]

It seems, therefore, according to Athenagoras, immediately after a believer exits from this present life, he moves to the heavenly existence, "abiding near God and with God."[203] Although Athenagoras, just like Justin, conceives the heavenly life that believers go to live as a life that is "free from all change and suffering," he does not have a clear elucidation

---

201. Daley, *The Hope of the Early Church*, 23.

202. Athenagoras, *Plea*, 31. Unless otherwise stated, I am using Roberts and Donaldson, *Ante-Nicene Fathers*, vol 2.

203. Hill, *Regnum Caelorum*, 107.

of the waiting time period between death and resurrection. This leads Hill to comment that "Clearly, Athenagoras is a great distance from the chiliastic notion of subterranean waiting in the interim between death and resurrection."[204] Perhaps exposing what we have seen with most other writers of the second century, as Hill notes, to Athenagoras, the "soul created by God is immortal (*Plea* 27; Tertullian, *Res.* 13, 14) and is saved to dwell with him in heavenly life."[205]

The second document attributed to Athenagoras is the treatise entitled *On the Resurrection of the Dead*. Questions on its association with Athenagoras' name have been raised in modern scholarship.[206] The basis for the opposition is mostly the argument that the treatise is a third-century anti-Origenist polemic.[207] However, the weight of the evidence favors the attribution of the work to Athenagoras. In this treatise, we have "perhaps the earliest full-fledged apology, on philosophical grounds, for Christian hope in the resurrection of the body; [and, in fact] the work could also be called the earliest essay in Christian anthropology."[208] In this work, Athenagoras goes into great depths to argue for his belief that resurrection basically means the reconstitution of the bodies that we currently have with their souls, from which they are temporarily separated at death (chapter 25). By implication, therefore, Athenagoras sees death as the temporary separation of the flesh and the soul. Recognizing the difficulties that are involved in such a view (chapter 4), Athenagoras argues that God's knowledge and wisdom and creative power are able to effect such a reconstitution. In addition, "the author argues that the matter which truly belongs to the essence of an individual human body can never be assimilated by another being to become part of its central identity."[209]

In summary, therefore, death, according to Athenagoras, is the temporary separation of the soul and the flesh to be reconstituted later.

---

204. Ibid., 107–8.

205. Ibid., 108.

206. Those who argue against Athenagoras' authorship include Grant, "Athenagoras or Ps.-Athenagoras?" and Schoedel, *Athenagoras*. As Daley points out, both of these authors locate the work within the anti-Origenist movement of the third century. For a defense of Athenagoras' authorship, see Barnard, *Athenagoras*.

207. Daley, *The Hope of the Church*, 230 n. 4.

208. Ibid., 23.

209. Ibid. For example, in chapter 7, he goes into a very lengthy defense of the reconstitution of all the fleshly elements in spite of where they might have finally ended up in the chain of consumption.

However, as I noted above, Athenagoras does not have a clear view of the "waiting place" before this reconstitution takes place. But his concept of death is clearly an expansion of the earlier views which lumped all the events of the eschaton together with death.

Irenaeus

Irenaeus of Lyons (ca. 125–200) was the famed bishop of Lyons (in modern-day France). Although it is not easy to come up with a clear-cut reconstruction of his life, scholars are fairly in agreement over some of the key events in his life. According to Osborn, the church of Lyons, which Irenaeus served as the bishop, probably started in the middle of the second century.[210] Irenaeus explains that when he was young, he saw Polycarp, bishop of Smyrna, at the royal court in Smyrna. This probably took place in 155/6. That is why Irenaeus names Polycarp as the most influential person in his life.[211] Concerning how events culminated into Irenaeus' writing of his most important work *Adversus haereses* [Against Heresies], Osborn summarizes:

> Irenaeus travelled (by way of Rome) to the great city of Lyons, situated at the confluence of the Rhône and the Saône in the center of Celtic Gaul, which at that time stretched from the Seine to the Garonne. During the persecution of the church at Lyons in 177, he carried a letter from the confessors in Lyons to Eleutherus, bishop of Rome. It is possible that Irenaeus was already bishop of Vienne and that he took over the care of both churches when Pothinus died. This would explain why Irenaeus was not himself in prison at that time. Irenaeus' journey, "for the peace of the churches," was on behalf of the confessors at Lyons. . . . In the same year Pothinus, bishop of Lyons, died in prison, and Irenaeus succeeded to his office. Irenaeus' participation in current controversies extended into Victor's tenure as bishop of Rome. His *Against heresies* was written at Lyons.[212]

Before looking at Irenaeus' specific ideas about the concept of death, a statement or so about his general thought pattern is in order. This is because his entire discussion of death is within his larger theological

---

210. Osborn, *Irenaeus of Lyons*, 2. For a summary of his thought, see Smith, "Chiliasm and Recapitulation," 313–31.

211. Osborn, *Irenaeus of Lyons*, 3.

212. Ibid., 4.

framework. Better known for his fight against "gnostic theosophy," Irenaeus understood everything within the concept of the doctrine of recapitulation.[213] In other words, everything makes sense if it is viewed within the ultimate purpose of God as revealed in the life and work of His Son, the Lord Jesus Christ. Thus, "by his life, death and resurrection, Christ corrected what had gone wrong in Adam and perfected what was begun in Adam."[214]

Within this prism, Irenaeus understood death as the limit that God has set to man's sin. While discussing why God drove man away from Paradise after his transgression, Irenaeus says that God "set a bound to his [state of] sin by interposing death, and thus causing sin to cease, putting an end to it by the dissolution of the flesh, which should take place in the earth, so that man, ceasing at length to live in sin, and dying to it, might begin to live for God."[215] This statement comes within Irenaeus' larger discussion of why God drove Adam out of Paradise in the first place. He writes, for example, in the first part of this verse, that "Wherefore also He drove him out of Paradise, and removed him far from the tree of life, not because He envied him the tree of life, as some venture to assert, but because He pitied him, [and did not desire] that he should continue a sinner forever, nor that the sin which surrounded him should be immortal, and evil interminable and irremediable."[216] Thus, as Irenaeus sees it, death is the process through which God chose in order to make sure that man does not remain in his state of sin forever. Osborn summarizes Irenaeus' view of death as the limiting of human sin as well as the gateway to living with God this way: "Like a grain of wheat the body must die in order to live (5.7.2). That flesh which is now under the dominion of death shall put on incorruption and immortality (5.13.3). Death shall be defeated and the flesh shall emerge from its dominion."[217]

---

213. The phrase "gnostic theosophy," as a description of the conglomeration of the heresies that Irenaeus addressed, occurs at the back cover summary of Osborn's, *Irenaeus of Lyons*.

214. Osborn, *Irenaeus of Lyons*, 14

215. *Haer.* 3.23.26.

216. Ibid. Indeed, this thought is followed up later by John of Damascus, when he writes: "It was necessary that what was made of earth should return to earth, and thus be assumed to heaven. It was fitting that the earthly tenement should be cast off, as gold is purified, so that the flesh in death might become pure and immortal, and rise in shining immortality from the tomb." (Allies, *Treatise on Images*, 3.)

217. Osborn, *Irenaeus of Lyons*, 137.

Irenaeus also understands death as the process that God uses to cleanse and renew the body of the effects of the original sin. While arguing for the Christian belief in the resurrection of the dead, Irenaeus notes that although in death our bodies go into corruption, "they do not perish, for the earth, receiving the remains, preserves them, even like fertile seed mixed with more fertile ground."[218] He concludes, therefore, that "although the body [at death] is dissolved at the appointed time, because of the primeval disobedience, it is placed, as it were, in the crucible of the earth, to be recast again, not then as this corruptible [body], but pure, and no longer subject to decay."[219] According to Irenaeus, therefore, death is the purifying process that purges the body of its inherent corruption in order to make it ready to live with God forever. According to him, "the flesh would thus be saved through death and resurrection."[220] Pelikan summarizes Irenaeus's view of death within the matrix of the death and resurrection of Christ this way: "In the midst of life we are in death, for death is the end of life. Yet in the midst of death we are in life, for life is the end of death."[221]

Finally, as I indicated above, in the thought of Irenaeus, the reflection on the concept of the intermediate state between death and resurrection is completed. Specifically, in *Haer.* 5.31, Irenaeus "criticizes the Gnostic heretics who affirm that after death they will ascend above the heavens unto the Father."[222] He points to Christ's descent to Hades, arguing from several texts in the Old and New Testament, "and draws the conclusion that the disciples of Christ await the same lot."[223] He writes:

> Since, again, some who are reckoned among the orthodox go beyond the pre-arranged plan for the exaltation of the just, and are ignorant of the methods by which they are disciplined beforehand for incorruption, they thus entertain heretical opinions. For the heretics, despising the handiwork of God, and not admitting the salvation of their flesh, while they also treat the promise of God contemptuously, and pass beyond God altogether in the sentiments they form, affirm that immediately upon their death they shall pass above the heavens and the Demiurge, and go to the Mother (Achamoth) or to that

218. Irenaeus *Fragments From the Lost Writings of Irenaeus*, 12.
219. Ibid.
220. Gousmett, "Shall the Body Strive and Not be Crowned?" 44.
221. Pelikan, *The Shape of Death*, 101.
222. Mellink, *Death as Eschaton*, 335.
223. Ibid.

Father whom they have feigned. Those persons, therefore, who disallow a resurrection affecting the whole man (*universam reprobant resurrectionem*), and as far as in them lies remove it from the midst [of the Christian scheme], how can they be wondered at, if again they know nothing as to the plan of the resurrection? For they do not choose to understand, that if these things are as they say, the Lord Himself, in whom they profess to believe, did not rise again upon the third day; but immediately upon His expiring on the cross, undoubtedly departed on high, leaving His body to the earth.[224]

Thus, according to Irenaeus, following the pattern of Jesus Christ during the time between his death and resurrection, all believers will go away to the invisible place that has been allotted to them by God to await the resurrection. The identity of the exact location of this waiting place will have to wait for Tertullian, who will finally declare that Hades is a "subterranean region," in his *De anima*, 55.

Clement of Alexandria

One of the hardest Fathers to classify is Clement of Alexandria (d. 215). Described by Pelikan as the saint who, like Tatian, is unwelcome in the hall of the saints, Clement was known to perhaps love creation too much.[225] The first representative of the Alexandrian Christian tradition of appropriating from the broader Greek tradition, Clement "draws on both the intellectualist, anthropocentric speculations of Platonic and Stoic cosmology, and on the esoteric, mythically couched revelations of the New Testament apocrypha and Gnostic documents" to construct his thought.[226] While his treatise on the resurrection is lost, his teaching on the subject can be pieced together from his other writings.[227]

Pelikan sees Clement's view of death as a "circle" of immortality. Borrowing from the Platonic idea of the pre-existence of the soul,

---

224. *Haer.* 5.31
225. Pelikan, *The Shape of Death*, 34.
226. Daley, *The Hope of the Early Church*, 44.
227. Dewart, *Death and Resurrection*, 114. His existing works include *Exhortation to the Heathen*, the *Instructor (Paedagogus), Stromata* and *(Miscellanies)*. Those that are believed lost include *On the Salvation of the Rich Man, Excerpts of the Prophets* and *Extracts from Theodotus*. For a thorough discussion on the works of Clement of Alexandria, see Ferguson, *Clement of Alexandria* and Lilla, *Clement of Alexandria*.

Clement argues that it is inconceivable to think of the vast complexity of the human soul as suddenly bursting upon the sky of reality "like a nova, without even a glimmer of anticipation."[228] According to him, just like the soul continues to exist after death, it must have, somehow, been existing before birth. However, Clement's Christianity would not allow him to accept this Platonic concept without some qualification. Thus, he argues that our pre-existence before birth, was in God, and not independent of Him. He writes, for example, in *Protr*:

> But before the foundation of the world were we, who, because destined to be in Him, pre-existed in the eye of God before,—we the rational creatures of the Word of God, on whose account we date from the beginning; for "in the beginning was the Word." Well, inasmuch as the Word was from the first, He was and is the divine source of all things; but inasmuch as He has now assumed the name Christ, consecrated of old, and worthy of power, he has been called by me the New Song. This Word, then, the Christ, the cause of both our being at first (for He was in God) and of our well-being, this very Word has now appeared as man, He alone being both, both God and man—the Author of all blessings to us; by whom we, being taught to live well, are sent on our way to life eternal.[229]

By the "we" here, Clement is referring to the elect, those who were destined to be "in him."[230]

However, since, as Pelikan puts it, Clement is "too much a Christian to take over the Platonic notion [of the immortality of the soul] uncritically," his concept of the immortality of the soul is a qualified one.[231] After asserting the beliefs of Platonic philosophers on the immortality of the soul in *Strom*. 5.14, Clement "lists ideas from among the Greek philosophers which both agree and disagree with the Old Testament."[232] He attributes the differences to a misunderstanding on the part of the Greek philosophers.[233] For Clement, therefore, the soul is not preexistent

---

228. Pelikan, *The Shape of Death*, 35.

229. *Protr*. 1.

230. Pelikan, *The Shape of Death*, 37–38.

231. Ibid., 35.

232. Toews, "Biblical Sources," 212.

233. Ibid.

as a free entity. Rather, it "owes its origin to creation through the eternal Logos, the same Logos in whom the saints are predestined."[234]

One of the enduring difficulties in assessing Clements's concept of death is this conception of the lofty origin of the soul as, perhaps, opposed to the body. Asked in other words, the question is simply this: how is Clement's concept of the soul different from that of Platonists? What makes it "Christian," so to speak? Or, even more telling, how about his claim that Christianity is the "true gnosis?" How is his claim "to possess a secret tradition, neither published in the New Testament nor known to the common people," different from the claims of the gnostics?[235] Although space does not allow us to explore this question deeper here, taken in their entirety, the works of Clement suggest that he clearly differentiated his understanding of Christianity from that of the gnostics. For example, he would not allow the unity of the supreme God to be threatened by gnostic aeons or spirits. And neither would he accept any threat to the historical reality of the birth, death, and resurrection of Christ, realities that form the foundation of the church.[236]

With this conception of the soul, then, how does Clement define death? Although Clement does not answer this question directly, we are able to decipher its answer from a number of his comments here and there. First, Clement declares that the body is the "soul's tomb" in *Strom.* 3.11 and 77.3.[237] Although this understanding is reminiscent of the Platonic concept of *soma sema*, Clement does not go to the extent of denigrating the body, as Platonists did. Rejecting Platonic and some Christian' denigration of the body, Clement argued for the harmonious functioning of the body and the soul.[238] Second, death, according to him, is the "separation of the body and the soul."[239] Indeed, Clement argues that death is good since it is the "dissolution of the chains that bind the soul to the body."[240] To him, death is good since it is a "liberation from the bonds of the present life."[241] Finally, death is a separation from sin, a

---

234. Pelikan, *The Shape of Death*, 38.
235. Pelikan, *The Emergence of the Catholic Tradition*, 96.
236. Ibid.
237. Toews, "Biblical Sources," 213.
238. Pelikan, *The Shape of Death*, 41.
239. Ibid., 45.
240. Ibid.
241. Ibid., 45–46.

fellowship of the soul. In what he perceives as a "hazarded" view of death, Clement writes in *Strom.* 4.3:

> The assertion, then, may be hazarded, that it has been shown that death is the fellowship of the soul in a state of sin with the body; and life the separation from sin. ...The severance, therefore, of the soul from the body, made a life-long study, produces in the philosopher gnostic alacrity, so that he is easily able to bear natural death, which is the dissolution of the chains which bind the soul to the body.[242]

Here, Clement is offering his literal interpretation of the words of Paul in Romans 6:20–23 in order to define death as a fellowship of the soul that frees it from sin.

In conclusion, just like in many other areas of his thought, Clements's view of death is conceived within the larger and complex Platonic background. Scholars have struggled to state clearly how different Clement's view of death as the freeing of the soul from the chains of the body is from Platonism. However, as already indicated above, there are key differences. I agree with Pelikan's assessment that there are at least two key differences between Clements's view of death and that of Platonists. First, the conception of death as freeing the person from sin and temptation is consistent with Christian and not Platonic eschatology. Second, "Christian eschatology further softens the terror of death by holding forth the prospect of a better life beyond the grave."[243] This is the hope of the resurrection, which Platonism does not have.

Finally, concerning where the souls of the dead are, Clement makes it clear that the souls of the righteous and those of the wicked are in different places. He writes, for example, in *Strom.* 6.6: "For who in his senses can suppose the souls of the righteous and those of sinners in the same condemnation, charging Providence with injustice?"[244] Toews notes that this general argument is based on the concept of God's justice as well as the believe that, according to 1 Peter 3:19–20, the souls of the unrighteous were preached to by Christ between his death and resurrection. Thus, since, according to this argument, the souls of the Gentiles who died before Christ were preached to in Hades, each soul has had the

---

242. *Strom.* 4.3.
243. Pelikan, *The Shape of Death*, 47.
244. *Strom.* 6.6

opportunity to move from Hades to Paradise.[245] Clement refers to the place of the souls of the righteous through the use of several terms such as being "raised to God," resemblance of God and becoming the divine likeness and likeness of the holy image of the souls of the righteous upon death.[246] In other words, he sees the souls of the righteous as in Paradise and not in Hades.

Tertullian

The other key respondent to Gnosticism was the North African theologian, Tertullian of Carthage (ca. 160–220). Although his death falls slightly beyond our time frame here, he, nevertheless, provides significant help towards the understanding of the concept of death in late second-century Christian thought. An impassioned and brilliant Carthaginian lawyer, Tertullian's thought "drew freely on biblical eschatology and on the writings of earlier Christian writers, particularly Justin and Irenaeus."[247]

Although Tertullian deals with the question of death in a number of places, it is in his *A Treatise on the Soul* where his understanding of what death is comes out clearly. He writes, for example, in chapter 51, that "the operation of death is plain and obvious: it is the separation of body and soul."[248] In so defining death this way, Tertullian is waging a double-edged war on both the Platonic idea of the immortality of the soul as well as those who insisted the soul, at death, leaves the body progressively. He continues:

> Some, however, in reference to the soul's immortality, on which they have so feeble a hold through not being taught of God, maintain it with such beggarly arguments, that they would fain have it supposed that certain souls cleave to the body even after death. It is indeed in this sense that Plato, although he despatches at once to heaven such souls as he pleases, yet in his *Republic* exhibits to us the corpse of an unburied person, which was preserved a long time without corruption, by reason of the soul remaining, as he says, unseparated from the body. To the

---

245. Toews, "Biblical Sources," 216. For the concept of Christ's descend to Hades, see Daniélou, *The Theology of Jewish Christianity*, 1.233–48 and Bass, "The Battle for the Keys."

246. Toews, "Biblical Sources," 217–18.

247. Daley, *The Hope of the Early Church*, 34.

248. Tert. *On the Soul*, 51. Unless otherwise stated, I am using Roberts and Donaldson, *Ante-Nicene Fathers*, vol. 3.

same purport also Democritus remarks on the growth for a considerable while of the human nails and hair in the grave. Now, it is quite possible that the nature of the atmosphere tended to the preservation of the above-mentioned corpse.[249]

To Tertullian, this separation of the body and soul is immediate and final at death. As he notes, had we to view the departure of the soul from the body as occurring in "particles," then we would have to also divide death into various levels of operation.

As expected, Tertullian then embarks on an elaborate attempt to explain what happens to the soul after death. Tertullian rejects the views of the Pythagoreans, Empedocles, and Plato, that the soul is immortal. He, as well, rejects the Stoics' concept of the existence of the soul in "mansions above."[250] He also disagrees with Plato that this "waiting place" of the souls is not for everyone, but "only of those who have cultivated their philosophy out of love to boys."[251] Since Tertullian bases his understanding of what happens to the soul after death to what happened to Christ, he argues that all the souls of the dead descend to Hades. He defined Hades as "a vast deep space in the interior of the earth, and a concealed recess in its very bowels," a place "that is in the secret inner recess which is hidden in the earth, and enclosed by the earth, and superimposed on the abysmal depths which lie still lower down."[252] He sees this place as serving as the "reception room" (*hospitium*) for all the dead, villains and heroes alike. He bases his argument on the both the story of Lazarus and Dives and Christ's *descensus ad infernos* after his death. As Daley summarizes, according to Tertullian,

> There [in Hades] souls live "in exile" (56) until the time of their resurrection, unchanged in age and from the time of their death ... and unable to escape, even in response to the summons of sorcerers (57). Tertullian conjectures that "the soul undergoes punishment and consolation in Hades in the interval, while it awaits its alternative of judgment in a certain anticipation of gloom and glory" (58).[253]

In contrast to other thinkers of the time that see neither the soul nor the body as able to feel by itself without the other, Tertullian sees the

249. Ibid.
250. Ibid., 54.
251. Ibid.
252. Ibid., 55.
253. Daley, *The Hope of the Early Church*, 36.

soul as possessing, albeit subtle and very limited, a genuine corporeality. But his conception of Hades involves two regions, a good and a bad one.[254] In *Adv. Marc.* 4.34, Tertullian, for example, notes that the souls of believers are received in Abraham's bosom, "a temporary receptacle place of faithful souls, where we find drawn, even now, an image of the future."[255] Sinners, on the other hand, "begin already in Hades to suffer for their sins—especially sins committed through the soul alone."[256]

Therefore, according to Tertullian, death is the separation of the soul and the body. The soul is not immortal. And, neither does it leave the body progressively, as some philosophers of the day argued. As soon as it leaves the body, it goes to the waiting place known as Hades. Hades is a two-leveled enormous subterranean place. Here, souls of believers find reception and joy in Abraham's bosom while sinners suffer some initial punishments especially for sins committed in the soul. In the end times, all will be resurrected in the flesh for "only that can rise that has fallen," that is, the flesh.[257] Tertullian's discussion on death is tailored as a response to the Marcionites and Valentinians.

CONCLUSION

In this first part of the work, I have argued that although there are myriad of opinions concerning the concept of death in second-century Christian thought, there is a traceable development as well. In the earliest writings, the focus is on the concept of death as it functions to encourage such Christian disciplines as church unity and personal holiness. This is especially so with such writings as *1 Clement* and *The Shepherd of Hermas*. However, with the onset of persecution, the Christian' conception of death shifts its focus to such understandings of death as discipleship, sacrifice, and imitation. This is true with such writers as Ignatius of Antioch and Polycarp of Smyrna. The same was true with other writings such as the apocryphal *Acts of the Apostles* and the *Acts of the Christian Martyrs*. The second-century Christian concept of death reached its climax with the works of the apologists and the polemicists, where it was now clearly placed within God's grand salvific program.

254. Ibid. Cf. *An.* 7; *Res.* 17.
255. *Marc.* 4.34.
256. Daley, The Hope of the Early Church, 37. See also *Res.* 17; *An.* 58; 35.58.
257. *An.* 46.18.

CHAPTER 4

Treatment of the Dead in the Second Century

THIS CHAPTER EXAMINES THE attitudes towards the dead as well as the treatment of the dead in second-century Christianity. This is necessitated by the realization that no evaluation of the concept of death in any time period can be complete without discussing the attitudes towards and the treatment of the material remains. Once again, capturing what I consider to be the exact need for this study, Peter Brown made this remarkable observation, that "Apart from the beautifully written study of Jeroslav Pelikan, *The Shape of Death: Life, Death and Immortality in the Early Fathers* (New York: Abingdon, 1962), we lack a study of the meaning of death in early Christian world," adding that this gap is also clearly seen in the Christian "expression in burial practices and attitudes to mourning" during that period.[1] Since we have addressed the first concern in the previous chapters, this chapter deals with the latter part of Brown's concerns, which is by no means less in importance than the former.

At the heart of the matter is whether or not there was a change of attitude towards the dead and, if so, what accounts for such a change. The ultimate question, in keeping up with our thesis, is how the Christian approach to the dead related to the existing Old Testament and Greco-Roman attitudes and practices on this subject. I argue that the historically documented change of the disposal of the dead bodies from the three key

---

1. Brown, *The Cult of the Saints*, 158 n. 6.

methods practiced in the Greco-Roman culture, that is, cremation, burial and mummification to only inhumation, was the result of the changing view of death resulting from the teachings of Christianity.

In order to fully investigate and understand the attitudes and treatment of the dead in second-century Christian thought, it is imperative that we look at the same attitudes and practices in both the Old Testament and the immediate Greco-Roman culture. This is the subject of the first part of this chapter. In the second part, the attitudes and the treatment of the dead by second-century Christians are evaluated.

TREATMENT OF THE DEAD IN THE OLD TESTAMENT

The question of the attitudes to and treatment of the dead in the Old Testament has, in the scholarly levels, been dominated by the issue of whether or not the Israelites had an elaborate cult of the dead. As defined by one of its greatest proponents, Elizabeth M. Bloch-Smith, the cult of the dead is the "belief in the empowered dead, with the attendant practices stemming from that belief."[2] More significantly, the cult of the dead is a phrase that is used to refer to a veneration of the dead, veneration that is comparable to that accorded to the deities as well.[3]

While some of the proponents of this view, like Rachel Hallote, do not take the efforts to either define or defend the cult of the dead in Israel, others are more nuanced in their approach.[4] Mention should be made here of Elizabeth Bloch-Smith.

A key proponent of the existence of the cult of the dead in Israel, Bloch-Smith adduces both archeological and biblical evidence to back up her conclusions. With her groundbreaking *Judahite Practices and Beliefs about the Dead* as well as the key succeeding article already mentioned, she points to both biblical and archeological arguments for the cult of the dead in Israel.[5] A number of these deserve mention here.

---

2. Bloch-Smith, "The Cult of Death in Judah," 213. For an even more elaborate exposition of this view, see Bloch-Smith, *Judahite Burial Practices and Beliefs*. See also Schwally, *Das Leben nach dem Tode*, 35.

3. Spronk, *Beatific Afterlife*, 247.

4. Hallote, *Death, Burial, and Afterlife*, 54.

5. For a discussion of biblical arguments for the cult of the dead in Israel, see Heidel, *The Gilgamesh Epic*; Healey, "Death, Underworld and Afterlife"; Lewis, *Cults of the Dead*; and Tromp, *Primitive Conceptions of Death*. For an archeological approach, see Meyers, "Secondary Burials," 15–17; Abercrombie, "Palestinian Burial Practices";

First, she observes that the choice and nature of burial places in both Judah and Israel spoke more of the cultural attitudes towards death than other possible factors like geology and topography. That is, since both pit graves and bench tombs are documented in both the highlands and the lowlands of Israel and Judah, we can conclude that "culture and not geology was the determining factor in choice of burial type."[6] So, what is this culture of death that determined the burial types in Israel and Judah, according to her? She notes that as far as the treatment of the bodies that were either buried in cave and bench tombs, there was no difference. In both cases, bodies were "dressed and adorned with jewelry."[7] Other key provisions for the dead included such items as pottery, tools, household items, and personal possessions. Of particular concern are the food items and "female pillar figurines."[8]

According to proponents of the cult of death, these provisions accorded to the dead at burial were either considered as for protection, for the dead were considered more vulnerable than the living, or, paradoxically, for the invocation of the powers of the dead on the living based on fear of the dead. For many proponents of the cult of death in Judah and Israel, the latter is most probable. "In sum," writes Bloch-Smith, "the ancestral dead with supernatural powers, residing in the tomb which constituted a physical claim to the patrimony, made the cult of the dead an integral part aspect of Judahite and probably also Israelite society."[9] Indeed, for many, this concept of the dead as powerful and able to somehow affect the affairs of the living, accounts for the continued veneration of the dead. As Spronk notes, there are "indications of an Israelite belief in the dead being able to help or harm the living."[10] Thus, to avoid the latter, the dead were venerated.

The other set of evidence that Bloch-Smith adduces is a set of some key Old Testament texts. These include, but are not limited to, the multiple prohibitions against the contact between the living and the dead in the Old Testament.[11] Of special concern to her are those texts that

---

Gonen, "Burial in Canaan"; and Rahmani, "Ancient Jerusalem's Funerary Customs," 234. Rahman concludes by rejecting the existence of such a cult in Israel.

6. Bloch-Smith, "The Cult of Death in Judah," 216.

7. Ibid., 218.

8. Ibid.

9. Ibid., 222.

10. Spronk, *Beatific Afterlife*, 251.

11. See, for example, Deut 18:10–11; Lev 20:6, 27; 1 Sam 28:8–9; Isa 65:2–6.

either refer to the dead as *'elōhîm* or suggest the feeding and rendering of sacrifices to the dead. She writes:

> Biblical stories and injunctions support the reconstruction of mortuary practices proposed on the basis of physical remains. Feeding the dead, even tithed food, is well attested in the Bible as it is in the ground. The dead were regarded as divine beings, and so were entitled to the tithe. *'Elōhîm* is unequivocally used for the dead in Samuel in the story of Saul and the woman of En-Dor (1 Samuel 28). Isaiah 8:19 provides a second example of *'elōhîm* referring to the dead.[12]

Thus, according to her, all these practices indicate that the Israelites practiced an elaborate cult of the dead. This cult was based on the fear of the powers of the dead. In other words, it was an elaborate attempt to please the dead in order to both invoke their bestowal of goodness to the living as well as avert misfortune for the living since they were believed to have the power to do so.

What about those numerous biblical prohibitions against any contact between the living and the dead? How do the proponents of the cult of the dead in ancient Israel interpret these biblical texts? A cursory overview of many of the proponents of this view shows an understanding of these prohibitions as actually a political attempt either by the "official" religion to suppress other views concerning the dead, or, in the case of Saul, to consolidate his political power over the entire nation of Israel. For example, after observing that the cult of the dead in Israel was clan-based, Hallote then concludes, concerning Saul's prohibition against consulting the dead during the monarchy:

> This natural cohesion of tribal units was in direct opposition to the goals of Israel as a single political state. Citizens of the state needed to exchange their tribal loyalties for the greater good of the kingdom, or else the entire kingdom would be threatened. Without loyalty to the central authority, the king would not be able to effectively lead an army, or organize public works projects, or show a united front to an army. Tribal and clan ties undermined the centrality of the monarchy, always threatening to break it into its original tribal units.[13]

---

12. Bloch-Smith, "The Cult of Death in Judah," 220. For a recent treatment of the so-called witch of En-Dor, see Smelik, "The Witch of Endor," 160–79.

13. Hallote, *Death, Burial, and Afterlife in the Biblical World*, 62. It should be noted that not all equate the cult of the dead in Israel with ancestor worship. For a helpful

Not surprising, therefore, she sees the intensification of the objections to the cult of the dead by the government of Judah after the fall of the Northern kingdom to the Assyrians in the eighth century B.C.[14] She sees this intensification in such prophets as Isaiah (see Isa 65:2–6, for example).

Bloch-Smith argues for religious-politico-economic reasons for these prohibitions, on her part. Arguing for the intensification of these prohibitions starting from mid-eighth century B.C.E., she proceeds to conjecture what she believes are the reasons for these prohibitions. She writes:

> If the cult of the dead was an integral aspect of Judahite society ... why was there an "official" attempt to suppress certain aspects of it? The late eighth-seventh-century B.C.E. Hezekian-Josianic reforms were initiated to resanctify the people of Israel and centralize the Yahwistic cult in Jerusalem. As part of the effort to centralize both worship and cultic personnel, the dead were deemed an inappropriate source of knowledge. Formally, the dead could be consulted at various locales, either directly or with the aid of shrine or *bāmôt* personnel, prophets or necromancers.[15]

However, with the need to centralize the cult of Yahweh, the cult of the dead had to be eliminated, she argues. Additionally, the cult of the dead posed an economic threat to the profession of the priesthood in Israel, Bloch-Smith contends. She concludes:

> The death cult legislation, while set within the framework of a religious reform, was also economically advantageous for the Jerusalem Temple cult. The prescriptions guaranteed the self-styled "legitimate" priests their livelihood, first, in their role as the only acceptable intermediaries to the true source of knowledge, and, second, in the form of the tithe. Tithed food was no longer to be diverted to the dead.[16]

Of course, this last remark assumes that the amount of food that was used for the purpose of keeping up with the cult of the dead, through sacrificing to the dead, was large enough to affect tithing in the Temple!

In summary, therefore, according to the proponents of the cult of the dead in Old Testament Israel, the Jewish attitudes and treatment of

---

discussion of the key differences between both, see Kim, "Cult of the Dead," 14 n. 2.

14. Hallote, *Death, Burial, and Afterlife in the Biblical World*, 63.

15. Bloch-Smith, "The Cult of Death in Judah," 223.

16. Ibid.

the dead were based on an elaborate cult of the dead, similar to those of her neighbors. This cult involved both the funerary treatment of dead bodies (clothing, send-off food, tools, and other particulars) as well as the continued sacrifices to the dead with the goal of invoking the blessings of the dead to the living based on the conviction that the dead possessed an inordinate power to affect the state of the living. Biblical prohibitions against necromancy, according to this view, are actually politically, professionally, and economically-driven.

The question before us, however, is whether or not everyone agrees with this assessment of the attitudes to and treatment of the dead in the Old Testament. A significant number of scholars do not see enough evidence to arrive at the conclusion that Old-Testament Israel practiced an elaborate cult of the dead. For example, Klass Spronk, after assessing most of the archeological and biblical evidence adduced in support of the cult of the dead in Israel, is skeptical of such an elaborate phenomenon. Concerning food offerings, for example, he helpfully observes:

> Such food-offerings are often regarded as indications of a cult of the dead. However, without further information about the state of the dead there is no reason to assume that offering of food and drink points to something else than the normal care for the dead, because they were believed to live on in more or less the same way as before death. For this reason, also the archeological data which are interpreted as indicators of repeated offerings brought to the grave ... cannot be regarded as definitive proof of an Israelite cult of the dead.[17]

In other words, according to him, there is no clear evidence for an elaborate cult of the dead in the Old Testament. He further clarifies that "clear evidence of a cult of the dead practiced by Israelites is scarce."[18] Thus, although he sees traces of a possible "royal cult for the dead," that is, the burial of kings with elaborate ceremonies, there is no evidence for an elaborate cult of the dead.[19]

Others have reached similar conclusions.[20] Roland de Vaux, on his part, argues that the ceremonies of the dead in ancient Israel were merely a duty that the Israelites had to pay for the dead as "an act of filial piety,"

17. Spronk, *Beatific Afterlife*, 248.
18. Ibid., 249.
19. Ibid., 250.
20. For a succinct summary of these scholars, see Kim, "Cult of the Dead," 13–14 n. 1.

in which the dead were honored and not worshipped.[21] G. E. Wright, as well, insists that there was no sacrificial offerings were ever made to the dead in the Old Testament. According to him, these festivals were actually events in which focus was on God's revelatory events in the history of Israel. "The focus of attention," he writes "is on the will and acts of God, especially as revealed in historical events."[22] Likewise, Peter Ellis argues that the God of the patriarchs, as revealed in Genesis, leaves no room for the worship of anything else. However, whether the Israelites knew this truth and practiced it well always enough is another question. Thus, according to him, the question of whether or not the Israelites worshipped their dead is indeterminate.[23] Schmidt argues that the existence of mortuary data by itself does not presuppose or necessitate the belief in the power of the dead as believed to be expressed in the cult of the dead.[24] Finally, although Kautzsch admits that ancestor worship prevailed in the pre-Mosaic period, and that it is possible that the generations that came after them would be inspired to do the same, he also notes that this is the viewpoint of archeology and not biblical theology. "If ancestor Worship ever prevailed in the pre-Mosaic period," he writes, "—and it is psychologically quite possible that respect for the dead bodies and the tombs of parents inspired at least tendencies to a kind of Ancestor Worship,—no consciousness of this survived to historical times."[25] However, "the whole question . . . has at best been an interest from the point of Archeology but not of Biblical Theology."[26]

So, where does this discussion leave us? Did Jewish attitude and treatment of the dead suggest or include the cult of the dead? With the scarcity of clear evidence for a full-blown cult of the dead in the Old Testament, it seems in order to conclude that the existence of such a cult is improbable. As suggested by Vaux, what we have in the Old Testament is perhaps what we have had in all cultures in history: an attempt to treat the dead with honor and respect, realizing the shock and trepidation that death is associated with. I believe that Martin-Achard is correct, agreeing with both Dhorme and Bertholet in noting that we need to be a bit

21. Vaux, *Ancient Israel*, 61.
22. Wright, *The Old Testament against Its Environment*, 101.
23. Ellis, *The Yahwehist*, 101.
24. Schmidt, *Israel's Beneficent Dead*, 45–46.
25. Kautzsch, *Dictionary of the Bible*, 5.615.
26. Ibid.

cautious in interpreting Old Testament funerary rites. As he notes, "these [funerary rites] must have had various meanings in the course of the history of the Chosen People; moreover confronted by death, man experiences a multitude of contradictory emotions; at one and the same time, the departed inspires him with pity and terror."[27] In other words, since the Israelites were not immune to the universal fear of death that is evidenced by everyone when faced with death, their response would exhibit this attitude. Historically and even today, Christians evidence the same attitudes, even though they are in possession of the complete revelation of God in the form of the written word.[28] Martin-Achard rightly concludes:

> Old Testament mourning ritual is thus to be explained in terms of the paradoxical attitude that man in general, and the Israelite in particular, adopts in the face of death; the dead are endowed with higher knowledge, they possess a quasi-divine power; they must be honored, and at the same time all contact with them must be shunned and all possibility of return to the land of the living must be forbidden them. Therefore a stringently prescriptive code of taboos regulates funerary ceremonials, in order to prevent the power of the dead, his *mana*, from spreading and contaminating the clan or the whole people; thus whatever has been in contact with the dead must be put away or destroyed. But, from another angle, the perished are poor beings, insubstantial shades, strengthless, and at the mercy of the living; they are especially dependent on their kinsmen; it is these who will provide them with the lodging, food, and clothing they need, which will revive their failing power.[29]

---

27. Martin-Achard, *From Death to Life*, 26. See also Dhorme, "L'idée de l'au-delà dans la religion hébraique," 113 and Bertholet, *Die israelitischen Vorstellungen*. I can personally testify to this observation. A few years ago, my father suddenly passed away and was buried in my absence. When I visited his grave, my younger brother asked me to stand on it for a picture. Although I did not tell him, I instinctively felt the impulse not to, feeling that I was actually standing on him personally!

28 By this comment, I do not mean that second-century Christians did not have complete revelation from God. Rather, I am more interested in the dissemination and the circulation of the NT documents, which, by all standards, were still being circulated as individual documents amongst churches and individuals by this time. In other words, the document we know as the New Testament did not exist as a single collection by this time.

29. Martin-Achard, *From Death to Life*, 26–27.

I see this paradox as a better explanation of the attitudes and treatment of the dead in the Old Testament. This paradox, I will argue, continues in early Christianity.

As far as the funeral and burial practices of the Jews (whether in Palestine or in Diaspora) are concerned, not much seemed to have changed from ancient Israel to the time immediately preceding the birth of Christianity. They continued to bury their dead ones in family tombs. According to Klaas Spronk, the normal procedure would be to bury the departed in a tomb possessed by the family. However, the very poor would be occasionally buried in anonymous graves reserved for ordinary people. Because of matters of hygiene (bearing in mind the hot nature of the climate in that region of the world whereby decomposition of a dead body would start to take place rapidly after death), burial took place the same day. The only exception to this general practice would be in cases of either soldiers killed in battle and/or cases of punishment.[30] Cremation was not practised in Israel. As Johnston notes, cremation may have been practised in other regions, like in the land of the Moabites (see Amos 2:1). Finally, burial was followed by a period of mourning. It is not clear how long mourning lasted. Generally speaking, mourners would "weep, tear their clothes, wear sackcloth, uncover and/or dishevel their hair, cover themselves with dust, sit and sleep on the ground, walk barefoot and fast (Gen 37:34f.; 2 Sam 1:11f.; 13:31, etc)."[31] As noted above, these practices continued from the Old Testament times through the Intertestamental period to the New Testament times without any major noticeable changes.

In summary, therefore, when it comes to the attitude towards and treatment of the dead in the Old Testament, scholarship has revolved around the question of whether or not this constituted a cult of the dead. Proponents of the cult of the dead in the Old Testament interpret all the funerary and subsequent rites towards the dead as constituting perhaps a worship of the dead. They see evidence for this in both archeology and the Bible. Opponents of this view explain the archeological evidence that suggests a veneration of the dead as the paradoxical response towards death that all of us tend to have as we face the deaths of our loved ones. This involves both respect of the dead as well as an attempt to, as much as possible, be detached from them. It is the attitude of respect and/or fear

---

30. Spronk, *Beatific Afterlife*, 238.
31. Johnson, *Shades of Sheol*, 48.

and pity. I see the latter as presenting a better accounting of the evidence concerning the attitudes and treatment of the dead in the Old Testament than the former.

TREATMENT OF THE DEAD IN THE GRECO-ROMAN CULTURE

There is clear evidence that second-century Christian practice of disposing the dead was greatly influenced by the attitudes towards the dead of the Greeks and the Romans. However, for the Christians, all the Greco-Roman practices in honoring and disposing the dead were completely modified to reflect a distinctive Christian view of death in light of the death, burial and resurrection of Jesus Christ. But first, what were these attitudes and practices by the Greeks and Romans towards their dead?

The Greeks and Their Dead

Although our period of consideration is AD 200s when the cultures of the Greeks and Romans had merged in to what is now known as the Greco-Roman culture, preparations for this final merger started way earlier among the Greeks. From the earliest times, the Greeks had an elaborate "business of passing from here to there."[32] This involved a number of stages that would help carry a person through dying, being dead and uninterred to being dead and interred. This process was based largely on the Greeks' conception of what it means to be dead.

As Garland notes, the attitude towards the dead among the Greeks started with the dying person. Assuming that the death was not sudden, there are six observable features that were common in Greek deaths. These are, (1) the ritual bath (Alkestis, Socrates and Oedipus), (2) the committal of one's children to the safe care of others (Alkestis and Oedipus), (3) the settling of one's affairs (Socrates), (4) the prayer to Hestia (Alkestis and Ajax), (5) the prayer for safe passage to Hades (Socrates and Ajax), and (6) the farewell to one's family and friends.[33]

After the *psychê* left the body either through the mouth or through an open wound, at which point the Greeks believed death to have taken place, preparations for the body's disposal started. Although originally

32. Garland, *The Greek Way of Death*, 13.
33. Ibid., 16.

the Greeks conceived the departure of the *psychê* from the body as painless (actually, a release since the body was considered as the prison of the soul), this would later change. Starting from Plato in the fourth century, the struggle of the *psychê* to be released from the body starts to be noted. A phenomenon known as *psychorrhagêma*, this struggle is observable later in Christian eschatology.[34] But, as we have seen with many other beliefs and practices, a Christian modification of the phenomenon took place as well.

As far as the funeral is concerned, the Greeks held to the conviction that the importance of death demanded that the passage be marked with ceremony, a ceremony that proved quite uniform in spite of the changing views of the soul.[35] In agreement with most cultures of antiquity, the Greeks believed that if the dead are not send away through the proper ritual, their spirits may come back to haunt the living. Thus, elaborate funeral rituals were practiced. Indeed, in some cases, as Felton notes, perhaps to make sure that nothing was missed, some cities would hold annual ceremonies to honor the dead.[36]

Scholars have noted a number of steps that would be involved in the Greek funerals. Although an elaborate treatment of this ritual is impossible here, a summary is in order. First, as Garland notes, the funeral ceremony involved there key steps. These are, first, there was the laying out of the body (*prothesis*). Second, there was the conveyance of the body to its place of interment (*ekphora*). Finally, there was the actual interment itself, which involved either cremation of inhumation.[37] As far as the first step is concerned, we note that immediately after death, the eyes of the dead were closed. Although the practice may have started purely as cultural, later on, it seems to have achieved a theological significance. "An inscription found at Smyrna possibly dated to the third century B.C.," writes Garland, "suggests that the closing of the eyes was believed to secure the release of the *psychê* from the body."[38] Other practices here would include the washing

---

34. Ibid., 19.

35. Felton, "The Dead," 86–87.

36. Ibid., 87.

37. Garland, *The Greek Way of Death*, 21.

38. Ibid., 23. Garland notes an interesting innovation of this practice later whereby there was the placing of an obol (coin) between the deceased as a payment to Charon for being carried across the river Styx. This sounds very similar to the later Valentinian ritual of apolytrosis whereby the dying is taught incantations to help him go through the various archons on his way back to Demiurge. The purpose seems to make sure

of the dead, which was done normally by the women of the household, the clothing of the body and the placing on to the bed (*klinê*). In addition, other objects like branches were also placed on the bier. Concerning the purpose of this practice, it seems like it "was to enable the mourners to sing a funeral dirge in honor of the dead in order to satisfy the claims of duty and to appease the soul of the departed."[39]

Concerning the *ekphora*, there seems to have been an elaborate wheeled hearse. Whether this cart that carried the vase with the body was always pulled by horses or not remains a matter of scholarly debate. What is clear is that the cortège was led by a woman, had other women walking beside it, and was followed by a man "carrying no weapons who appears to be holding a conversation with the corpse," perhaps "reproaching him [the dead] for having abandoned his relatives."[40] Either with the use of family members as the pallbearers or using hired ones, the bier was escorted with music to the place of disposition.

Finally, as far as the disposition of the body is concerned, the Greeks used both cremation and inhumation, with "the popularity of one method or the other [being] varied over place and time."[41] That is, "archeological evidence indicates that throughout Greece, and Mycenae, in particular, inhumation prevailed from ca. 1650 to ca. 1200 B.C."[42] Such variations can be seen elsewhere at different times. However, no explanation is presented for either of these methods of body disposal among the Greeks. As I will show here below, a clear preference of inhumation over cremation during the advent of the Christian era takes place.

As far as the actual rites of the disposition of the body whether cremation or inhumation, sacrifices were involved. These included gifts that the deceased received commensurate to his/her status in life. "Earthen vessels," writes Burkert, "some containing food and drink, represent the minimal requirement, though the symbolic function of the gift means that the miniature vessels of no practical use may be substituted."[43] Secondly, there would be what was known as "destructive sacrifices," which were

---

that the departed do not necessarily come back!

39. Ibid., 30.
40. Ibid., 32–33.
41. Felton, "The Dead," 87.
42. Ibid.
43. Burkert, *Greek Religion*, 192. See also Hom. *Il.* 23.166–76.

"motivated by the helpless rage which accompanies grief."[44] Weapons and tools are broken. In some cases, "dogs and horses, and even the servants and the wife of the dead man may be killed."[45] As Garland summarizes:

> Increasing evidence is coming to light which demonstrates that in exceptional circumstances ritual slaughter took place at the graveside from the Protogeometric though the Classical period. Homer's description of the funeral of Patroklos as performed by Achilles refers to the slaughter of twelve Trojan youths, two dogs and four horses, sacrificed upon the dead man's pyre.[46]

Homer's descriptions have been independently confirmed by a recent excavation done jointly by the Greek Archeological Service and the British School of Athens at Lefkandi.[47] But, as noted above, it seems that this practice only applied to some and not all cases.

Finally, the disposition of the body would be accompanied by a banquet. Probably involving animal sacrifices, this was the climax of the funeral. Known as the *perideipnon*, this banquet was not held at the graveside. Instead, it was held at the home of the family of the deceased.[48] As Homer reports, during the presumed burial of the son of Aeacus,

> he made a funeral feast to satisfy their hearts. Many sleek bulls [πολλοὶ μὲν βόες ἀργοί] bellowed about the knife, as they were slaughtered, many sheep and bleating goats, and many white-tusked swine, rich with fat, were stretched to singe over the flame of Hephaestus; and everywhere about the copse the blood ran so that one might dip cups therein.[49]

The reasoning behind this kind of banquet was the belief that the deceased was now at a banquet of his own. The funeral would conclude with an assignment of new roles to the living as well as the marking of the grave with a stone sign, a *sema*.[50] The sign served as the proclamation of the dead to all eternity. According to Burkert, the continued honoring of the dead

---

44. Ibid., 193.
45. Ibid.
46. Garland, *The Greek Way of Death*, 35.
47. Ibid.
48. Felton, "The Dead," 87–88.
49. Hom. *Il.* 23.26–34.
50. Burkert, *Greek Religion*, 193.

involved "general celebrations with which the city honors [sic] its dead every year: days of the dead, *nekysia*, or days of the forefathers, *genesia*."[51]

As expected, the funerary and subsequent rites performed upon the dead among the Greeks, just like the Jews, have generated a debate on whether or not they constitute a cult of the dead. However, just as we noted with the Old Testament funerary and subsequent honor customs to the dead, it seems that there is not enough evidence to support the existence of a full-blown cult of the dead among the Greeks as well. Burkert is most probably correct when he observes that the "understandable awe which inhibits speaking or even thinking about death means that certain manners of speech are observed without the import of the words ever being made explicit."[52] In other words, what we have is an attempt to honor the dead, to sever any possible interaction between the living and the dead, as well as strengthen family ties for the living. All records indicate a continued attempt by the living Greeks to be as separate as possible from the dead.[53] Hence, there is no evidence for the existence of a cult of the dead among the Greeks.

The Romans and Their Dead

Turning to the Romans, we note great similarities with the Greeks as far as the attitudes towards and the treatment of the dead is concerned. As with the Greeks, family members played a significant role in the event of the death of a loved one. As Toynbee notes, when it became apparent that death was imminent, the close family members would gather around the dying one.[54] "The nearest relative present gave the last kiss to catch the soul, which, so it was believed, left the body with the final breath."[55] The same relative would then lament the dead intermittently until the disposal of the body.[56]

A key funeral rite involved the dressing of the corpse. In the case of a male, the corpse was dressed in a Roman toga, followed by the laying of a wreath on the head "particularly in the case of a person who had earned

51. Ibid., 194.
52. Burkert, *Greek Religion*, 191.
53. Felton, "The Dead," 99.
54. Toynbee, *Death and Burial*, 43.
55. Ibid., 43–44.
56. Ibid., 44.

one in life."⁵⁷ These would be powerful Roman citizens. Again, as was the case with the Greeks, the corpse also had a coin placed in its mouth "to pay the deceased's fare in Charon's barque."⁵⁸ With the clothing, the placing of the wreath as well as the placing of the coin in the corpse's mouth, the body was now ready for either laying-in-state for the great or the disposal of the body for everyone else.

As historians have observed, the Romans had elaborate laws for the disposal of their dead. According to Hopkins, these laws included the existence of burial clubs. These functioned the same way as modern-day death insurances, guaranteeing both a burial place for the dead as well as the continued support for the widowed.⁵⁹ In addition, the existence of these clubs suggests the urbanization of the Roman societies since they "helped men to cope with an anxiety that they would perhaps die without kin or cash with which to provide a proper burial."⁶⁰ Generally, many of these laws were aimed at protecting the welfare of the living.⁶¹

In terms of the funeral itself, like the Greeks, the Romans practiced both cremation and inhumation. However, there seems to have been a difference in terms the funeral between the rich and the poor. While the bodies of the rich would lay-in-state sometimes for a whole week, the poor were carried to their cremation or inhumation in a cheap bier (*sandapila*) as soon as possible after death.⁶² The funeral procession, which, for the Romans, took place at night under the lighting of torches, would involve the relatives, friends and other invited persons. All Roman bodies were to be buried outside the city, a practice that was laid out in the Twelve Tablets, and was followed up to the late Empire with a only a few exceptions.⁶³ Accompanied by such essential rites like the throwing of a little earth on the corpse (or the cutting off a fraction of the corpse in the case of cremation), the body would then be either cremated or inhumated in the place of disposal. While the poor were laid directly in the earth, notes Toynbee, the rich would be placed in richly carved sarcophagi, with "the moderately well-to-do in less elaborate sarcophagi

57. Ibid.
58. Ibid.
59. Hopkins, *Death and Renewal*, 211–13.
60. Ibid., 213.
61. For a complete function of these laws, see Davies, *Death, Burial and Rebirth*, 146–50.
62. Toynbee, *Death and Burial*, 45.
63. Ibid., 48–49.

of marble, stone, terracotta, lead, or wood."[64] Early Christians, regardless of their social status, were buried on shelves "cut in the rock walls of hypogea and catacombs."[65]

Post-funeral rites among the Romans included the sacrifice of a pig on the graveside, making it thus officially a grave as well as the holding of a funeral ceremonial feast at the grave of the deceased on the day of the funeral.[66] However, the continued practice of yearly commemoration of the dead accompanied by the eating of funerary meals by family and friends at the deceased's birthdays has caused scholarly difficulties. Do we, for example, read from these commemorations a Roman cult of the dead? Again, as we have seen with both the Jews and the Greeks, there does not seem to be enough evidence to lead to the conclusion that the Romans practiced an elaborate cult of the dead (which would include the veneration and worship of the dead). Wrestling with this issue, Hopkins concludes that what we have with these commemorations is recognition by the mourners that the dead survive death as individuals, and, consequently, show that the mourners had a "strong yearning for the dead loved one, [and that] they have a vivid image of his or her face, and imagine that, one day soon, they will meet again."[67] Thus, these commemorations seem to serve a psychological need rather than as evidence for an elaborate cult of the dead.

Christians and Their Dead

Historians of early Christianity have, for quite some time now, wrestled with two pertinent questions concerning the Christian attitude and treatment of the dead. These are, first, were Christian approaches to the dead different from those of the surrounding cultures, and, second, if so, whether or not these differences can be accounted for theologically or otherwise. I will argue here that while some practices towards the dead among early Christians are in conformity with the existing Greco-Roman practices, there is also a marked contrast commensurate with their Christian views of death. In contrast to a number of social historians of this period of time, I argue that some key writings of the Fathers suggest

---

64. Ibid., 49.
65. Ibid.
66. Ibid., 50–51.
67. Hopkins, *Death and Renewal*, 227–29.

a theological attribution to these changes. I conclude the section with wrestling with the question of whether or not we have a trace of a possible cult of the dead among Christians this early as it is much evidenced clearly in the medieval times.

Disposal of the Christian Dead

In agreement with the Greeks and the Romans, Christians' treatment and attitude towards the dead started when it was clear that a loved one would not live anymore. Coleman's summary of the "final practices" towards the dying is helpful. He writes:

> The greatest attention was bestowed by the early Christians upon the dying, and the highest respect entertained for their final counsels, instructions and prayers. Their [the dying] exhortations to surviving friends, and their prayers in their behalf, were treasured up with pious care. Their will in regard to the disposal of their effects, and the appropriation of them for objects of charity and benevolence, were religiously observed. The sign of the cross was administered to them. The bishop and the several orders of the clergy, as well as relatives and friends, sought to offer them consolation. Prayers were offered in the church for them. Friends pressed around them to give, and receive parting kiss, and the last embrace. To such as were restored to Christian fellowship in their dying moments, the sacrament was administered. This was afterwards united with the ceremony of extreme unction.[68]

---

68. Coleman, *The Antiquities*, 411. Praxton notes that Christians followed the Roman ritual of separation between the dead and the living known as the *ordo defunctorum*. It included these key steps: "1. As soon as they see him approaching death he is to be given communion even if he has eaten that day, because the communion will be his defender and advocate at the resurrection of the just. It will resuscitate him. After the reception of the communion, the Gospel accounts of the passion of the Lord are to be read to the sick person by priests or deacons until his soul departs from the body. 2. Immediately after the soul has left the body, the response *Subvenite sancti dei* is said, followed by the verse *Suscipiat te Christus* and a psalm (*In exitu Israel* [113] or *Dilexi quonium* [114]) with the antiphon *Chorus angelorum*. 3. Afterword the body is washed and they place it on a bier. After it has been placed on the bier and before it is taken from the house, the priest says the antiphon *De terra formasti me* and a psalm (*Dominus regit me* [22], *Gaudete iusti* [32], or *Dominus regnavit* [92]). 4. The body is carried to the church and placed therein to the accompaniment of psalms and antiphons (e.g., the antiphon *Tu iussisti nasci me domine* and Psalm 41, *Quemadmodum*). 5. And when it has been placed in the church everyone should pray for its soul without intermission until the body has been buried. They should chant psalms, responses, and lessons from the book of Job. The vigil should be celebrated for him at the proper hour, but without

Hence, the picture presented by Christians is both of concern for the dying, like the Greeks and the Romans, but also, in contrast to them, the concern is governed more by hope than hopeless despair.[69] More evidence for these differences will come up as we look at the deposal of the bodies of the dead among Christians.

In addition to these practices, Christians also practiced the closing of the eyes of the deceased, which was done by his close relatives and friends. Although, as we have seen, this was common among the surrounding cultures, as far as Christians are concerned, it was done for different reasons consistent with their believe in the resurrection of the dead at the end times. As Coleman notes, "to the early Christians this [closing of the eyes] was an emblem of the peaceful slumber of the deceased, from which he was expected to awake at the resurrection of the just."[70] Hence, as we saw with the use of κοιμᾶσθαι, the practice points to a belief in a peaceful rest as the dead await their resurrection at the end of time. This is consistent with the later Christian phrase, "*Requiescit in Pace*"—R.I.P ["she rests in peace"], a phrase that later became predominant on Christian tombstones.[71]

It is on the subject of the disposal of the dead where much scholarly discussion has taken place. After a loved one died, early Christians would normally wash the body and clothe it in linen, preferably white linen. The corpse would then be laid in repose, being frequently anointed and embalmed as it awaited proper burial. In contrast to the Jews, Christians normally deposited their dead in a coffin. After this, the coffin would be available for viewing by the public while awaiting burial.[72] During this time, the last rites were administered upon the dead. However, "the wailings of mourning women were, on no account, allowed as was customary among the Jews and many pagan nations."[73] Instead, "such lamentations

---

Alleluia. 6. When the body is placed in the tomb they sing the antiphon *Aperite mihi portas iustitiae* and the psalm *Confitemini* [117]" (Praxton, *Christianizing Death*, 39.)

69. Even before it was clear that a person was dying, all efforts were done to restore his failing health. According to Praxton, there was extensive use of oil medicinally (Praxton, *Christianizing Death*, 27–32).

70. Coleman, *The Antiquities*, 411.

71. Hopkins, *Death and Renewal*, 232.

72. The use of coffins was in contrast to the Jewish practice of burying the dead only in wrapped linen.

73. Ibid.

were exceedingly incongruous to Christians who regarded death as no loss, but unspeakable gain."[74]

As far as the actual method of the disposal of the body is concerned, with the onset of Christianity, historians have noted, there was a change in the treatment of dead bodies. There was, in other words, a change from cremation, inhumation, and mummification as the methods of the disposal of the dead to inhumation as the preferred method. This change was noticeable in the entire Roman Empire. Although it is not clear when this preference was finally fully made among Christians, by the fourth century AD, inhumation had clearly become the preferred method of the disposal of the dead. Coleman sees this practice as old as Christianity itself.[75] On the other hand, Rebillard sees this change as having taken place in the second century since cremation was still the norm in the first century.[76] While Nock is unclear on the timing of this change, he sees it as having taken place during the time of the Roman Empire.[77] In any case, by the fourth century, it is clear that inhumation had become the standard practice of disposing the dead among Christians.[78]

Before looking at the possible reasons for the change from cremation to inhumation, a word is in order as to why the Romans and Greeks practiced cremation. Not much is available in terms of the reasons for this practice. However, according to Pliny the Elder, the Romans avoided inhumations because these were prone to grave robbery. According to him, cremation was instituted in Rome after it was known that the bodies of soldiers were being dug up.[79] With the lack of more information on

---

74. Ibid.

75. Ibid., 408.

76. Rebillard, *The Care of the Dead*, 79.

77. Nock, "Cremation and Burial," 321. For the care and treatment of the dead in early Byzantium, see Kyriakakis, "Byzantine Burial Customs," 32–72.

78. Daniel-Rops, *The Church of the Apostles*, 206.

79. Rebillard, *The Care of the Dead*, 79. "According to Pliny the Elder (23–79)," writes Rebillard, "inhumations are more vulnerable to tomb violations than cremations: "Cremation was not actually an old practice at Rome: the dead used to be buried. But cremation was instituted after it became known that the bodies of those fallen in wars abroad were dug up again. All the same, many families kept on the old ritual; for instance, it is recorded that nobody in the family of the Cornelii was cremated before Sulla the dictator, and that he had desired it [cremation] because he was afraid of reprisals for having dug up the corpse of Gaius Marius" (*Natural History* 7.187). The greater vulnerability is the only reason Pliny offers to explain abandoning inhumation for soldiers who die in foreign lands as well as for Sylla fearing to see his own body dug up out of revenge" (ibid).

why cremation was practiced, it is impossible to speculate beyond the possibility that this was done to prevent grave theft.

There are a number of reasons given for the change from cremation to inhumation as the method of the disposal of the dead which coincided with the spread of Christianity in the Roman Empire. This change was especially noticeable among Christians. As Nock and Toynbee point out, there was increased concern among Christians to treat cadavers gently and to minimize images of violence in the afterlife.[80] Again, while discussing Christian art, as well, Latourette mentions the fact that the burial catacombs of Christians underwent some changes. "Christians disapproved cremation," he writes, "the form of disposing of the dead normally followed by pagans, and held that the body should be buried intact."[81] Although Latourette does not discuss this, the question certainly needs to be asked: why did Christians prefer inhumation?

Bynum observes that the reason as to why burial changes took place in the Roman world in the second and third centuries is a matter that continues to be debated.[82] This change, dating probably at the reign of Emperor Trajan (d. 117), has been hard to account for. On the one hand, many have argued that this change was actually based on the Christian understanding of death. Daniel-Rops, for example, wrote in the 1960s:

> Why did the Christians adopt this custom rather than that which was far more common—and more economical—at Rome, namely, that of cremating corpses, of placing the ashes in urns, and of setting the urns out in *columbaria*, "pigeonries"? Possibly because inhumation seemed more respectful treatment for a body destined to be resurrected. Perhaps to conform to the custom which had been followed in the burial of Jesus. Or

80. Toynbee, *Death and Burial*, 48; Nock, "Cremation and Burial," 321. See also Praxton, *Christianizing Death*; Rush, *Death and Burial*, 24.

81. Latourette, *A History of Christianity*, 251. Indeed, it has been noted that the earliest Christian prayer over a corpse reflects their thought on God. "It is worth noting here," writes Bynum, "that the oldest extant Christian prayer over a corpse stresses the contrast between an incorruptible God and creatures who must be lifted from change into changelessness. 'God, you who have the power of life and death, God of the spirits and lord of all flesh . . . you who change and transform and transfigure your creatures, as is right and proper, being yourself alone incorruptible, unalterable, and eternal, we beseech you for the repose and rest of this your servant. . . . [R]efresh her soul and spirit in green pastures . . . and raise up the body in the day which you have ordained.'" Quoted in Bynum, *The Resurrection of the Body*, 46 n. 101.

82. Bynum, *The Resurrection of the Body*, 51. For these debates, please, see Leclerq, "Incineration," 7.502–8, and Cumont, *After Life*.

the explanation may be simpler: because according to biblical tradition which the Christians observed, there was never any question of cremating the dead.[83]

In other words, according to him, this change was based purely on Christian belief; either the conviction that there will be a resurrection or because the Bible does not prescribe cremation as a method for the disposal of the dead. Similarly, while discussing the rise of the Christian catacombs, Alice Mulhern comments, "The Christians, it should be noted, had chosen inhumation, rather than cremation, a choice which perhaps related to the Christian belief that the soul and body would be reunited at the time of the final judgment."[84]

Davies is even more candid. According to him, the change was influenced by the events of the life of Jesus—his death, burial, and resurrection. "The death, burial and resurrection of Jesus," he writes, was symbolically consonant with death and burial of later generations of Christians."[85] Furthermore, Christians saw inhumation as consistent with the underlying motif of the Garden of Eden whereby God forms the first man from the "pre-moistened 'dust of the ground' into which the 'breath of life' is given and to which he is fated to return after disobeying the divine command not to eat of the tree of the knowledge of good and evil."[86] In other words, for Davies, inhumation is not just another method of the disposal of the dead preferred by Christians. Rather, it also fits in the larger program of God, which started in the Garden of Eden, and will be completed at the resurrection, which is the Christian hope.

On the other hand, the theory that the change took place because Christians were opposed to cremation on the basis of their eschatology has been vigorously challenged. One such key challenge was by Nock, who, in 1932, argued that this change had nothing to do with religious beliefs. According to him, the rise of Christianity cannot be offered as the cause for this change because "chronology and the distribution of the phenomena are fatal to that supposition."[87] In addition, Nock also refuted the possibility that this change could be accounted for in terms of the growth of mystery religions. According to him, this change can be

83. Daniel-Rops, *The Church of the Apostles*, 206.
84. Muhlhern, "The Roman Catacombs," 31.
85. Davies, *The Theology of Death*, 113.
86. Ibid., 112.
87. Nock, "Cremation and Burial," 321.

accounted for purely on the grounds of changing fashion. After offering a number of reasons as to why the change had nothing to do with religious convictions, he concludes that it "remains that it was a change of fashion," further clarifying:

> In respect to this change from cremation to burial, the word "fashion" needs a little explanation, for the change is a considerable one. By fashion we mean the habits of the rich, which gradually permeated the classes below them. Burial seems to have made its appeal to them because it presented itself in the form of the use of sarcophagus. This was expensive and gratified the instinct for ostentation. The richest could build mausolea. Many whose resources would not suffice for that could be afford sarcophagi, which might well appear a more solid and adequate way of paying the last honors to the dead.[88]

However, although Nock's article has been the basis for much of the subsequent argument that the change from cremation to inhumation was not based on any religious conviction, it is important to note that his article was purely focused on this change as it relates to mystery religions and not Christianity. Furthermore, Nock seems to contradict himself when, for example, he says that this change had nothing to do with economy while concluding that the change had something to do with economy.[89]

While it is true that is hard to pinpoint one aspect as the single cause of this change, be it religious or economic, it helps, as far as Christianity is concerned, to take a look at how early Christians themselves explained this change. Indeed, even before the emergence of Christianity, the Persians are noted as having opposed what they termed as the "cult of fire" in the third century B.C. This is a term used in reference to the cremation of dead bodies. As well, first century Greek military physician Discorides is reported to have complained, "Burn not Euphrates, Philonymus, nor defile Fire for me. I am a Persian as my fathers were, a Persian of pure stock, yea, master," instructing that "to defile [me by] Fire is for us bitterer

---

88. Ibid., 328.

89. For example, while discussing the changes in the Eastern part of the Empire, Nock notes that "in this whole area inhumation is at most times much the commoner custom, perhaps because simple burial in the ground without costly receptacles was cheaper than burning" (ibid, 327). However, when it comes to drawing his conclusion on the reasons for the change in the entire Roman empire, he notes that it seems that both the rich and poor adopted burial perhaps to cut the cost of disposing their dead (ibid., 358).

than cruel death. But wrap me up and lay me in the ground."[90] Thus, in this case, cremation was prohibited on the basis of the pollution believed to be caused by fire on the corpses.

Christians offer an explanation for this change on the basis of their conception of the soul. Although some scholars like Bynum and Louis-Vincent Thomas see the reason for both cremation and inhumation in early Christianity in purely biological terms, that is, "efforts to mask, and therefore in some ways to deny, putrefaction," Christian writers of this period seem to offer a different explanation for the change.[91] According to most, the body needs to be buried whole in order to be raised whole. This is the message of a number of key second-century apologists and other writings. For example, in the *Acts of Paul* (ca. 160), the metaphor used for dead bodies is that of seeds that have been planted whole. The writings of these key apologists offer a glimpse into the attitude of Christians towards the bodies of their dead in the second century. First, while discussing the bodies of the Christian dead, Justin Martyr draws on the metaphors of seeds and semen to stress the power of God in preserving the Christian bodies in order to recreate them with all organs complete.[92] Secondly, Athenagoras, in *On the Resurrection of the Dead* (*De ressurectionae*), argued that it is important that the body be well-kept since, in the end, both man's soul and body must be reconstituted.[93] God needs the same body in order to recreate the person anew. He clearly argues that it will not be the same person unless the same body is restored to the same soul. He observes that "Since the law of nature ordains the end not absolutely, nor as the end of any men whatsoever, but of the same men who passed through the previous life; but it is impossible for the same men to be reconstituted unless the same bodies are restored to the same souls."[94]

Even in situations whereby the bodies have been disparaged, Christians held that "God can reunite the fragments that have been entirely resolved ... into their constituents."[95] But Christians argued that they should not be the ones who initiate the disparaging of the bodies, as was the case with cremation. Even more pointed is his argument in *Legatio*, a

---

90. Rebillard, *The Care of the Dead*, 80.
91. Bynum, *The Resurrection of the Body*, 52. See also Thomas, *Le cadavre*.
92. *1 Apol.* 18–21, 51–52.
93. Athenagoras, *The Resurrection of the Dead*, 25.
94. Ibid.
95. Bynum, *The Resurrection of the Body*, 32.

Christian response to accusations of cannibalism. Athenagoras asks, how can someone who believes in the resurrecting accept to become a tomb for those who will rise again (chs. 35–37)?

> What man who believes in a resurrection would offer himself as a tomb for bodies destined to arise? For it is impossible at one and the same time to believe that our bodies will arise and then eat them as though they will not arise, or to think that the earth will yield up its dead and then suppose that those whom a man had buried within himself not reclaim their bodies.[96]

The same attitude towards the dead is evidenced in the writings of Theophilus of Antioch in his *Ad Autolycus*. In his response to the pagan Celsus who found the idea of the resurrection repulsing and ludicrous (who wants to recover his body back, he wondered), Theophilus argued that even pagan philosophers join the Hebrew prophets in declaring that God cares for not only the living but the dead as well.[97] Going even further, the apologist Aristides praises Christians for burying their dead, arguing for a proper burial of the righteous' body.[98]

The most elaborate argument against cremation on the basis of the Christian view of the body and the soul, however, came from Tertullian, a key link between second-century apologists and third-century theologians. As earlier-noted, in his pivotal treatise *On the Soul*, Tertullian objected to the views that seemed to indicate that the soul was somehow attached to the body after death. He wrote:

> And yet even this partial survival of the soul finds a place in the opinions of some men; and on this account they will not have the body consumed at its funeral by fire, because they would spare the small residue of the soul. There is, however, another way of accounting for this pious treatment, not as if it meant to favour the relics of the soul, but as if it would avert a cruel custom in the interest even of the body; since, being human, it is itself undeserving of an end which is also inflicted upon murderers.[99]

In other words, Tertullian, although rejecting the teaching that a residual particle of the soul remains in the body after death, nevertheless,

---

96. Athenagoras, *Legatio and De resurrectione*, 85. For Athenagoras, unless otherwise stated, I am using Schoedel's translation.

97. *Autol.* 2.38.

98. Quasten, *The Beginnings of Patristic Literature*, 1.171.

99. Tert. *De anima* 51.4.

argued that there is another possible accounting for a proper treatment of the body that prohibits cremation. That is, since the soul survives death (and, consequently, the human entity), Christians should encourage a respect for the tomb instead of cremating the body "since to preserve the buried body is to preserve the soul as well."[100]

One interesting observation is how non-Christians interpreted Christians' treatment of their dead in the second century. A number of these are recorded to have ridiculed the belief in the resurrection as the reasoning behind Christians' shunning of cremation as the proper method of the disposal of their dead. For example, as Rebillard observes, the pagan Caecilius Natalis "rejects belief in the resurrection as absurd, then pretends to wonder if that is why Christians shun cremation."[101] Writing in the second half of the second century, Minucius Felix notes in *Octavius*:

> And, not content with this wild opinion, they add to it and associate with it old women's fables: they say that they will rise again after death, and ashes, and dust; and with I know not what confidence, they believe by turns in one another's lies: you would think that they had already lived again. It is a double evil and a twofold madness to denounce destruction to the heaven and the stars, which we leave just as we find them, and to promise eternity to ourselves, who are dead and extinct—who, as we are born, so also perish! It is for this cause, doubtless, also that they execrate our funeral piles, and condemn our burials by fire, as if every body, even although it be withdrawn from the flames, were not, nevertheless, resolved into the earth by lapse of years and ages, and as if it mattered not whether wild beasts tore the body to pieces, or seas consumed it, or the ground covered it, or the flames carried it away; since for the carcasses every mode of sepulture is a penalty if they feel it; if they feel it not, in the very quickness of their destruction there is relief. Deceived by this error, they promise to themselves, as being good, a blessed and perpetual life after their death; to others, as being unrighteous, eternal punishment. Many things occur to me to say in addition, if the limits of my discourse did not hasten me. I have already shown, and take no more pains to prove, that they themselves are unrighteous; although, even if I should allow them to be righteous, yet your agreement also concurs with the opinions of many, that guilt and innocence are attributed by fate. For whatever we do, as some ascribe it to fate, so you refer it to God: thus

---

100. Rebillard, *The Care of the Dead*, 82.
101. Ibid.

it is according to your sect to believe that men will, not of their own accord, but as elected to will.[102]

Thus, the ridiculing here seems to be based on the fact that although Christians believe that the body feels no pain after death, they still think it does, somehow. However, Christians did not ascribe to a simplistic connection between inhumation and a belief in the resurrection. Rather, it seems like their emphasis was on adhering to the custom of the Jews, that is, honoring the body through keeping it in a tomb as it awaits the resurrection. As with the use of such key metaphors like that of a seed buried, to the Christians, "a body may dry into dust or dissolve into liquid or reduce into ashes of fade into smoke; however it is, every corpse is withdrawn from us but its elements are preserved in the safekeeping of God."[103] In other words, the Christian attitude was that, as much as possible, they should preserve the body of the departed intact. The most reliable way to do that was through inhumation. But if this is not possible, then the power and the wisdom of God are able to preserve the essential elements of the dead for the purpose of the future resurrection.

In conclusion, while it is hard to ascribe a single reason to the noted change from cremation to inhumation as the proper method of the disposal of the dead between the second and third centuries in the Roman Empire, Christians generally utilize their views of the body and the soul to explain the change. Whether this change is tied to their belief in the resurrection is yet to be firmly established. But as far as second-century Christians are concerned, any opportunity to preserve the body intact is a better option than other methods of disposal since it encourages respect for the dead and emphasizes their belief that the soul is alive as

102. Felix, Oct. 11.1–5.

103. Rebillard, The Care of the Dead, 83. An interesting incident is reported by Eusebius concerning the attempt by the Roman governor of Lyons in 177 to prevent Christians from burying their dead martyrs in the hope to prevent the resurrection. "To these," he writes, "they afterwards add other accounts, saying 'the bodies of the martyrs after being abused in every possible manner, and thus exposed to the open air for six days, were at length burned and reduced to ashes by the wretches, and finally cast into the Rhone that flows near at hand, that there might not be a vestige of them remaining on the land. These things they did as if they were able to overcome God, and destroy their resurrection (παλιγγενεςίαν) as they themselves gave out that they might not have any hope of rising again, in the belief of which, they have introduced a new and strange religion, and contemn the most dreadful punishments, and are prepared to meet death even with joy. Now we shall see, whether they will rise again and whether their god is able to help them, and rescue them out of our hands'" (Eusebius, E.H. 5.1.62–63).

well. Hopkins is certainly correct in noting that in contrast to their pagan neighbors, "Christian attitudes [towards death] were much more positive. Christians believed in Christ's death and resurrection; they hoped for life everlasting for themselves, and many of them believed in the resurrection of the body."[104] This attitude, I have argued, is evidenced in the disposal of the dead bodies.

Finally, when it comes to the places of Christian interment in the second century, discussion has focused on whether or not Christians had their own separate places for burial as well as whether or not we can detect a "Christian cult of the dead" as early as the second century. Although Christians did not have their own separate burial places this early, their funeral services were distinctively different from those of the Greeks and the Romans. Instead of holding the funerals at night, we are told, Christians held them in broad daylight. After holding a public procession carrying the body on a bier, they buried it, as noted above, during a service punctuated by the recital of psalms and celebration of the Eucharist. Although we do not have enough information concerning exactly what happened at the graveside, there is evidence that a Eucharist celebration was part of the funeral rites for Christians. For example, according to the apocryphal *Acts of John*, we have a report of the burial ceremony of the wife of Andronicus of Ephesus, Drusiana, presumably conducted by the apostle John. The text reports that John and Andronicus, together with the other brethren "went back at the break of the day to the tomb in which Drusiana had been for three days" so that they may break bread there.[105] Many commentators take this to refer to the practice of funerary Eucharist. Noting that the Lord's Supper was administered at the graveside, Coleman adds the comment that "By this rite, it was intimated that the communion of saints was still perpetuated between the living and the dead."[106] In other words, "It was a favorite idea that both [the living and the dead] still continued [to be] members of the same mystical body one and the same on earth and in heaven."[107] Thus, with Christians, in contrast to the Greeks and the Romans, we do not see

---

104. Hopkins, *Death and Renewal*, 230–31.

105. Rebillard, *The Care of the Dead*, 124.

106. Coleman, *The Antiquities*, 413. Since early Christians did not see death as afflictive but a joyful event, they severely reproved the Jewish and Roman custom of hiring women to make lamentations, discarding the Jewish badges of morning in the form of sackcloth and ashes (ibid., 414–15).

107. Ibid.

the immense attempt to break the relationship between the dead and the living. I will come back to this continued relationship as I talk about the commemoration of the dead in early Christianity.

When it comes to the places of the actual burial, there is also a noticeable continuity and change reflective of the Christian understanding of death. Although Christians did not originally have separate burial places for their own, this would eventually change, with the most change being noticed in the fourth and fifth centuries AD. At first, in conformity with the existing stipulations concerning the disposal of the dead, Christians buried their dead outside the cities. They buried them in the public places where everybody else was buried. These public places were designated in accordance to the Jewish and Roman laws.[108] Whether this practice was based on the belief that dead bodies polluted the cities, or on something else, continues to be matter of scholarly debate.

On the one hand, there are those who have insisted that since bodies were considered as pollutants in the Old Testament and the Greco-Roman culture, it was ordered that they be buried outside the residential places of the living. Supporting this view, McCane sees this as one of the areas whereby early Christians parted ways with the Jews. He writes:

> The first significant aspect of death ritual on which Jews and Christians eventually came to disagree was the social location of the human corpse. Initially, Christians and Jews in Palestine shared a common presumption about corpse impurity: they agreed that the dead were impure, and they regarded this impurity as a contamination that was to be avoided. On this basis both Christians and Jews customarily located the dead outside the margin of the social network. In the fourth century however, the situation began to change. Explicitly denying the impurity of the human corpse, Christians begun to treat the dead bodies, or parts thereof, in ways that had previously been regarded as inappropriate. In particular, Christians consciously violated the social spaces and locations that had formerly off-limits. Christian dead were brought into the center of public space and given a prominent role in public worship.[109]

Thus, a changing view of death also caused the change of the location of the dead from outside cities into the cities themselves. Indeed, although this time period is beyond the limits of our concern in this

108. Ibid., 409.
109. McCane, *Roll Back the Stone*, 112.

work, by the fourth century, historians have noted, the Christian dead had already been brought into the center of the cities. However, not all Christians were buried inside the city, thanks to the first three centuries of persecution when many Christians could only bury their dead in their hiding places.[110] However, my point here is that the long-standing separation between the dead and the living was no longer a factor for second-century Christians.

On the other hand, there are those who see these burial places outside the city as having nothing to do with the perceived pollution of living by the dead bodies. For example, Brown vehemently insists that there was no automatic resentment of the dead bodies in the Greco-Roman culture. He writes:

> I would stress this. I do not wish to imply that classical Greece and Rome were marked by an automatic sense of pollution by the dead, or that Christianity suddenly removed that sense. Other peoples' dead were the problem: one's own dead or those of one's city if sufficiently validated by custom, were not an object of repugnance or a source of supernatural danger.[111]

However, it seems like Brown does not take into account the fact that, with the few exceptions of some of the most important people in society like emperors, everyone else was buried outside the city. It did not matter, in other words, whose dead it was. The rules stipulated that the dead be deposed outside the cities.

In conclusion, it seems like what we see here is the carrying out to the fullest implications the changed view of death on the part of early Christians whereby death is no longer viewed as "afflictive but a joyful event" in light of the Christian hope of the resurrection.[112] This gradual reflection and change would now extend to not only the attitudes towards death and the funeral rites, but also, most significantly, to the burial places. The catacombs, that is, the "gigantic, fantastically large cemeteries in which generations of Christians interred their dead," could now be located inside cities instead of outside them.[113] Fontaine captures this

---

110. Coleman, *The Antiquities*, 421.
111. Brown, *The Cult of the Saints*, 133 n. 18.
112. Coleman, *The Antiquities*, 414.
113. Daniel-Rops, *The Church of the Apostles*, 205. Daniel-Rops notes that these catacombs (Greek *kata kumben*, meaning "hollow land" or "near the dell"), are located in many cities of late antiquity, with those in Rome being the largest. They are found in Rome, Sicily at Syracuse, in Tuscany, in Africa (Hadrumetes), in Egypt and Asia Minor.

gradual but significant development in the Christian change of burial places and what most probably led to it this way:

> We see, on the one hand, the continuation of the ancient practice of pagan necropoli located on the exit roads of the cities and the concomitant separation of the cities of the living and the cultic sites of the dead: and on the other hand we see the gradual introduction of what Saint Augustine called the *communio sanctorum*, in which the dead project themselves into the lives of the living. The Christian dead, since their *dies natalis* alive in God, have a presence as real as the living, and they come to play a larger and larger part in the liturgies of the community. In this sense, what we see is the "procession of the dead into the cities of the living," an interpenetration of the two cities, that of the dead and that of the living, a process which a new face to the cities of late antiquity and above all to the history of the Middle Ages.[114]

The result of this "Christianization of death," was the emergence of Christian burial places inside the city, which, by the fourth century, were "styled κοιμητήρια, places of repose, cemeteries, denoting hereby, not only that the dead rest from their earthly labors and sorrows, but pointing out the hope of future resurrection."[115] Indeed, as evidence shows, Christians were not only interred inside the city, but were also buried in such places as church compounds and even under church altars. As Webb notes, the remains of such key early church fathers as Clement of Rome and Ignatius of Antioch are interred under the high altar of the upper church of San Clemente in Rome.[116] But such privileged burial would only apply to the clergy and nobility.[117] In other words, Christian theology allowed the bringing together of the dead and the living in one place, perhaps even sharing in fellowship with one another.

The most famous seem to be those at Rome, especially the catacomb at Commodilla on the Ostian Way, and the "regions" of St. Priscilla, St. Domitilla and Ostrianus. The body of St. Paul is believed to be resting in the cemetery at Commodilla (ibid., 205–6)

114. Fontaine, "Discussion," in *Actes*, 152.
115. Coleman, *The Antiquities*, 409.
116. Webb, *The Churches and Catacombs*, 88.
117. Ibid., xxiii.

AN EARLY CHRISTIAN CULT OF THE DEAD?

Scholars are in agreement that during the medieval times, there was an elaborate Christian cult of the dead.[118] The question of the possibility of an early commemoration of the dead, which is a commonplace in medieval Christianity, has been prompted by the report of the treatment of the body of Polycarp of Smyrna according to the *Martyrdom of Polycarp*. As we noted in chapter two, according to this document, a contest concerning the disposal of the burnt body of Polycarp emerged after the "ἀντίζηλος καὶ βάκανος καὶ πονηρός" ("the jealous and envious Evil One") became envious after seeing that Polycarp had "now [been] crowned with the crown of immortality and had won the prize that no one could challenge," inciting Nicetes, the father of Herod and brother of Alce, to appeal to the magistrate not to give the Christians the body of Polycarp for burial.[119] The interesting reason that the Evil One gives is that the Christians may "abandon the crucified one and begin to worship this man [Polycarp]."[120] Even more interesting is the fact that the phrase translated "touch his holy flesh" (that is, ποιῆσαι καὶ κοινωνῆσαι), may also mean "*to commune with*, or possibly, *to receive as part of*."[121] This is because, taken at its face value, the phrase may connote cannibalistic intentions on the part of these Christians. However, as Holmes observes, it is very likely that what we have here is the start of the Christians' obsession with relics.[122] In other words, these Christians are interested in keeping some parts of Polycarp's bones as relics.

Second, assuming, as many have done, that the "Evil One" here is a reference to Satan, one would wonder why Satan would be interested in protecting the worship of his nemesis, the "crucified one," Jesus Christ. In any case, the Christians are reported to have taken the bones of Polycarp, τὰ τιμιώτερα λίθων πολυτελῶν καὶ δοκιμώτερα ὑπὲρ χρυσίον ὀστᾶ αὐτοῦ ἀπεθέμεθα ("which are more valuable than precious stones and finer

---

118. See, for example, Praxton, *Christianizing Death*; Schmidt, *Ghosts in the Middle Ages*; Lauwers, *La mémoire des ancêtres*. For a recent evaluation of the biblical basis for the veneration of the saints, see Frazier, *Holy Relics*.

119. *Mart. Pol.* 17.1–2.

120. Ibid., 17.2. But the Christians make it quite clear that, although they love the martyrs who are disciples and imitators of the Lord, they worship only the Son of God (see *Mart. Pol.* 17.3).

121. Holmes, *The Apostolic Fathers*, 325 n 17.1.

122. Ibid

than refined gold") and deposited them in a suitable place.[123] Again, the Christians report that there they continued to gather (i.e., in the "suitable place"), to celebrate Polycarp's "birthday" (the day he was born in heaven through death) in "commemoration of those who have already fought in the contest and also for the training of those who will do so."[124] Thus, the question that scholars have wrestled with is whether or not this annual commemoration points to an early Christian "cult of the dead."[125]

This issue has led some scholars to suggest that this part of the *Martyrdom of Polycarp* is a later interpolation. Von Campenhausen, for example, regards this section as interpolated because of what he perceived as multiple errors such as the disagreement of number as far as the "Evil One" is concerned, and, the introduction, for a second time, of Nicete's relationship with Herod here (cf. 8.2).[126] It is also argued that the role of the Jews in this contest of the disposal of the body of Polycarp seems anachronistic since "their role in early Christian persecution is slight."[127] Hence, these factors are seen to point to a later period when the cult of the martyrs was full-blown. However, most of the recent studies have questioned Campenhausen's conclusions that the document is interpolated.[128] As Holmes notes, the "thesis that the *Martyrdom* is a mid-third-century forgery is even less compelling, as it neglects the details that anchor the narrative in the second century but which a third-century forger would be unlikely to know or care about."[129] Thus, with the question of authenticity settled, it seems that in this document we have the earliest reference to the commemoration of the Christian saints.[130]

It has been suggested that in inaugurating the commemoration of the dead saints, Christians were adopting the existing Greco-Roman "cult of the heroes," the Jewish cult of the dead as well as attempting to express

---

123. *Mart. Pol.* 18.2.

124. Ibid., 18.3.

125. For the argument that in the *Martyrdom of Polycarp*, we have the beginning of the Christian cult of the dead, see Sherman, *The Nature of Martyrdom*, 50.

126. Schoedel, *Polycarp, Martyrdom of Polycarp, Fragments of Papias*, 49–82.

127. Ibid., 75.

128. See, for example, Barnard, "In Defence of Pseudo-Pionius' Account," 192–204; Schoedel, *Polycarp, Martyrdom of Polycarp, Fragments of Papias*.

129. Holmes, *The Apostolic Fathers*, 301.

130. Rordorf, "Aux origines du culte des martyrs," 79. For a summary of the early acts of martyrs, see Barnes, "Pre-Decian Acta Martyrium," 509–31.

the communion with the saints already in heaven.[131] However, the Christian commemoration of their dead at this point in time shows significant differences with that of the Greeks and the Romans. These differences are accountable to the distinctive Christian view of death. First, as Baldovin notes, while normally the Greco-Roman commemoration at the graves of the dead took place at the deceased's actual birthday, for the Christians, this visit took place at "the day of their true birth, the birth into eternal life."[132] As we noted with Polycarp, this would be their actual day of death. As Schoedel notes, in the Greek cult of the dead, "a man's (natural) birthday was the most important day of commemoration," adding that "we are dealing with a Christian transformation of this in the Martyrdom of Polycarp."[133] These visits, as Augustine was to point out later, were to be joyful ceremonies whereby the living saints fellowshipped with the ones already in heaven.[134]

A second key difference between the commemorations of the dead by Christians and the Greco-Roman culture is that, as far as Christians were concerned, these commemorations were not merely family matters. Rather, the entire Christian community was involved. "What differentiated the Christian martyrs," writes Baldovin, "was the fact that their graves were visited not just by immediate family members but by the entire community."[135] The idea here, just as it was the case with the shift of the burial places from outside to inside the cities, was to point out the fact that both the living and departed saints form one community, the community of Christ, which is his body. But, again, this development was

---

131. Ibid., 95. For a discussion of the Greek Hero cult worship, see Nock, "The Cult of Heroes," 141–73, Ward-Perkins, "Memoria, Martyrs Tomb and Church," 20–37, Brown, "The Rise and Function of the Holy Man," 80–101.

132. Baldovin, "Relics," 9.

133. Schoedel, *Polycarp, Martyrdom of Polycarp, Fragments of Papias*, 76.

134. Coleman quotes Chrysostom as declaring: "On the anniversary days of commemorating the dead, they were used to make a common feast or entertainment, inviting both the clergy and people, but especially the poor and needy, the widows and orphans, that it might not only be a memorial of rest to the dead, but an odor of sweet smell to themselves in the sight of God, as the author under the name of Origen words it" (Coleman, *The Antiquities* 416). For the argument that we do not have a clear evidence of prayers being offered specifically for the dead in early Christianity, see Swete, "Prayer for the Departed," 119–21.

135. Baldovin, "Relics," 13.

to fully take place in the fourth and fifth centuries whereby it became part of the church's architectural design.[136]

Finally, as far as the purposes for these grave visits are concerned, there was a change from the Greco-Roman culture to Christianity. Toynbee notes that the Romans' cult of the departed had a double purpose: "it provided that the dead survived in the memory of relatives, descendants, and friends."[137] It also "sought to ensure, through the medium of devout attention to their [the departed's] mortal relics in the tomb, comfort, refreshment, and perennial renewal of life to their immortal spirits."[138] In other words, the commemoration was a kind of "support" system for the departed. However, as far as the early Christians are concerned, the focus shifted to the living and how the departed could be of help to them. From the earliest times, the remembrance of the dead was characterized by the power believed to be with the departed saints.[139] In addition to memorizing the dead, the living longed to somehow benefit from the power of the departed. Assistance was sought in such matters as the keeping of one's vows, healing and protection against evil. As the cult of the saints grew, they were seen as "specialists, and their specialization often related to their own lives and especially their sufferings."[140] Hence, we see a changed understanding concerning the role of the commemoration of the dead is from the Greco-Roman emphasis on what the living can for to the dead to the Christian emphasis on how the power of the dead can be utilized by the living.

CONCLUSION

In this chapter, I have argued that the selection and adaptation of the early views of death by second-century Christians to present a distinctively Christian concept of death that is commensurate with the level of

---

136. As McCane notes, "this emerging Christian distinctiveness certainly did not stop at symbolism. By fifth and sixth centuries, Christians in Palestine had brought the remains of corpses right into their church buildings, and performed public worship in a proximity to the human dead which would have been profoundly disturbing to the Jewish feeling" (McCane, *Roll Back the Stone*, 121). For a discussion of the connection between Christian death and icons, see Grabar, *Christian Iconography*, 31–54.

137. Toynbee, *Death and Burial*, 61.

138. Ibid., 61–62.

139. Baldovin, "Relics," 10.

140. Ibid., 10–11.

progressive revelation that they had at the time extends not only to the views themselves, but also to the attitudes towards and treatment of their dead. While Christians conducted key funerary rites, just like the Jews and the Greco-Romans, in them, we see marked differences in terms of the meaning and function of these rites. As noted above, all their funerary rites were based on the belief that the departed are now fellowshipping as they await the resurrection. Death, Christians insisted, is a joyful and not a sad event. These attitudes were extended to the disposal of the dead bodies, whereby, as we noted, there was a progressive change from viewing the bodies as pollutants, as was the case with the Jewish and Greco-Roman cultures, to viewing them as part of the extended the community of God. Thus, no longer were the dead to be cremated or buried far from the living outside the city. Instead, they were to be welcomed as part of the community of God. Finally, the commemoration of the dead, which started most probably with the annual visitation of the burial place of Polycarp of Smyrna, would eventually, in the medieval times, develop into an elaborate cult of the dead. But this is beyond our exploration here.

CHAPTER 5

Conclusion

THIS STUDY AROSE FROM the realization that there is a gap in the treatment of the subject of death in the thought of second-century Christians. This is not the case either with the same subject in other key periods of church history or other subjects in second-century Christianity. Due to the rapid changing nature of the differing situations that second-century Christians lived, their views of death are also diverse.

The question that we have been asking is simply this: what is death according to the second-century Christians? However, as soon as one asks this question, it becomes clear that the answer must take into account the fact that second-century Christian thought entails different occasions, is expressed through varying terminology, and, to a large extent, involves a discursive conversation with its immediate cultural milieu (Judaism and Greco-Roman cultures, to be specific). In addition to these variables, second-century Christians are also operating with emerging documents that were eventually to be recognized as the word of God and known as the New Testament. Thus, in one's attempt to understand their concept of death, it is necessary to take all of these variables into consideration.

To introduce the study, we noted that a number of scholars on the subject have emphasized one of these variables at the expense of the others. On one end of the continuum are those scholars who argue that second-century Christian concepts of death present a complete contrast to the already-existing views of the same. These tend to see the views of the fathers of the church as offering a radically different concept of death, especially to the Greek idea of the immortality of the soul. On the other end of the continuum, there are scholars who understand second-century Christian concepts of death as completely Hellenized. Presented in differing versions, this is the view that second-century Christian concept of death is the final stage in the development that started during the poetic age, running through the heroic age, and culminating in early Christianity. According to this view, what we have in second-century in terms of the concept of death is actually a Christianized version of Platonic [Orphic] idea of the immortality of the soul. There are two enduring Greek paradigms of understanding death that have continually been applied to second-century Christian concept of death, especially where death was a result of martyrdom. These are the noble death and the false death concepts that became prevalent in the culture a few centuries before the birth of Christ. According to the former, Christian martyrs understood their deaths within the legacy of the vicarious deaths whose participants died for honor and fame either in defense of their country or their principles. They were expected to be rewarded with the gift of immortality or otherwise for what was perceived to be an unjustifiable death. The second paradigm focuses on the martyriological literature, arguing that this literature is structured like the Greek false death concept where the deaths never really take place. The commonality between these and Christian deaths is that both see death as the gateway to the resurrected bodies. However, while the false death legends are not real, Christian deaths are.

It became necessary, at this point, to come up with an interpretive paradigm that helps us understand the conception of death among second-century Christians that fully takes into account their rapidly changing situations as indicated by the different terminology and metaphors used as well as the possibility of an internal development of the concept of death as the century wore on. I proposed the "adaptation and modification" motif as a meaningful interpretive grid to help us define death in the second century. Through this grid, the study argued that amidst their challenges, second-century Christians borrowed and modified existing views of death, adapting and modifying them in light of the level of the progressive revelation that they had, to construct a distinctively Christian concept of death.

The study then explored these existing views of death. From the Old Testament, second-century fathers adopted primarily the idea of death as sleep (κοιμάω) as well as the concept of the survival of the soul after leaving the body at death. But instead of using the idea of death as sleep in a literal manner, as some scholars like Oscar Cullmann have suggested, the

Fathers use it metaphorically, emphasizing the concept of death as a calm conscious rest as one waits the upcoming morning (the resurrection). As the non-martyriological Apostolic Fathers insist, this understanding of death should inspire us to live good spiritual lives as we look forward to participating in that rest, a rest that the departed apostles are enjoying right now. Hence, rather than an anthropological metaphor, the Fathers use it to make a sanctification argument.

For an understanding of the state of the individual after death, second-century Christians turn to the Old Testament, the New Testament documents, as well as the culture. While not necessarily making direct quotations, for example, the martyrs adopt Pauline language in describing their deaths in such terms as, "sacrifice," "resurrection," "*imitatio Christi*." Specifically, with the rise of martyrdom, these and similar terms become prevalent as the key metaphors for death. Of these terms, the concept of death as "sacrifice" (περίψημα) has generated most discussion. While some scholars see Ignatius of Antioch, who uses this term to describe his death (see, for example, *Rom.* 2.2; 4.2b; *Eph.* 8.1; 18.1; 21.1; *Tral.* 13.3; *Smyr.* 10.2; *Pol.* 2.3; 6.1), as indicating that he saw his death as having meritorious value the same way that Christ's death was, the context indicates otherwise. In other words, this research has shown that second-century Christians use this and other terms in a modified manner to refer to their calling to follow Christ even when that demands death. But, judging from the stark differences that these fathers see between the value of their death and that of Christ, it is impossible to see how one can justifiably arrive at a conclusion that suggests their deaths are meritorious in the same way Christ's was.

A different theological climate emerges in the second half of the second century. With the onset of challenging groups both inside and outside the church, Christian apologists and polemicists offer responses that define death in a manner which seeks to fit it within the larger program of God's reconciliation with the fallen creation. In so doing, the second-century Christian apologists join with Orphic Platonism in rejecting earlier views held by Stoicism and Epicureanism (even Pythagoreanism) that death is a descent to nothingness (annihilationism). However, in contrast to the Platonists, who held that the soul is immortal by nature, the apologists argued for a modified concept of the immortality of the soul. The soul, according to them, is not eternal in that it does not have a beginning. Rather, it begins to exist the moment an individual is created by God. Where and in what form the soul will spend its eternity depends on whether or not it knows God, they insist.

In agreement with several groups of Gnosticism, the apologists held that death is the departure of the soul from the body. However, in contrast to some key strands of Gnosticism like the Valentinians, who held that the soul flees from the body never to come back to it again since the body is the prison of the soul (either teaching a spiritual resurrection or no resurrection at all), the apologists taught a future resurrection. It is in the writings of the apologists and polemicists that the concept of resurrection (material resurrection in some cases), is fully explored. Since neither the dead body nor the fleshless soul can feel either pain or joy, these writers speak of the need for the rejoining of the body and the soul in the future for dual purposes of rewarding and punishing the dead. However, in the meantime, the body must be dissolved in the crucible of the earth in order to put an end to its continuing in sin and prepare it for the attainment of immortality. In the thought of the apologists and polemicists, therefore, we have a grounding of death within God's re-creative program.

Finally, the study argued that the same adaptation and modification is also evidenced in the attitudes towards the dead as well as the practical aspects of dealing with the dead. In conformity with the Jews, for example, second-century Christians performed certain funerary rites upon their dead. Both also practiced inhumation of the dead instead of cremation of mummification. However, in contrast to the Jews, Christians modified their attitudes and treatment of the dead to a level commensurate with their theology of death at the moment. Jewish mourning styles—usually accompanied by sackcloth, ashes and excessive wailing by women and professional mourners—were discarded in Christianity. These were deemed inconsistent with the Christian hope faith and hope and the expectation of the resurrection. Gradually, bodies were no longer buried outside the city since they were no longer considered as pollutants to the living. Rather, they became part of the living community of God, being interred either in the church compounds or city cemeteries (the catacombs).

The same attitude is seen as second-century Christians borrow and modify the attitudes and treatment of the dead. Like the Greeks and the Romans, Christians conduct funeral rites on their dead. In contrast to them, however, Christian funerals were conducted in broad daylight and in public. Instead of being viewed as an affliction, because of the death and resurrection of Jesus Christ, death was now viewed by Christians as a joyful event. And, while in the culture cremation was the standard method of disposal of the dead, gradually Christians adopted inhumation as the only proper method of disposing their dead. Whether this change was prompted by their theology or not remains a matter of scholarly debate. We argued, however, that there are possible reasons to suggest that indeed theology played a role in this gradual change. Change is also seen in the places of the disposal of the dead. As noted above, while the Greeks and Romans disposed the dead outside the city, Christians eventually domesticated their dead by disposing the bodies inside their cities. Since the body of Christ is united, whether in heaven or on earth, they reasoned, why insist on separating them here on earth? This communion extended to the Christian post-burial commemoration of the dead. While adopting the practice of annual visitation of the graves of the dead on their birthday, Christians started to visit these graves during the actual death date of their departed. After all, they reasoned that this was their actual birthday in which these believers were born in heaven (cf. *Mart. Pol.* 18.3). And, instead of using these visits as an occasion to serve the dead, as was the case in the culture (the cult of the dead), at least by this time in the history of Christianity, Christians were concerned with commemorating their dead and fellowshipping with the living. Of course, this practice would undergo significant changed during the medieval times, but this time period is beyond our scope here.

On a theological methodology level, this thesis offers yet one more response to Adolf Harnack's thesis on the interaction of early Christianity with Greek thought. As argued in both *Lehrbuch der Dogmengeschichte* and *What is Christianity?* Harnack saw Christian theology in the second century as having united itself to Hellenistic philosophy, a unification that led to "perverse metaphysical reflection and dogmatic definition."[1] As noted in chapter 2, in his conclusion, Harnack made the scathing argument that:

> the Gospel entered into the world, not as a doctrine, but as a joyful message and as a power of the Spirit of God, originally in the forms of Judaism. It stripped off these forms with amazing rapidity, and united and amalgamated itself with Greek science, the Roman Empire and ancient culture, developing, as a

---

1. Bingham, "Develoment and Diversity," 49. See Harnack, *Lehrbuch der Dogmengeschichte*, Harnack, *What is Christianity?*

counterpoise to this, renunciation of the world and the striving after supernatural, a life, after deification.[2]

However, as I have demonstrated in this study, Harnack's argument that the gospel rapidly stripped itself of the forms of Judaism and united itself with Greco-Roman forms is not necessarily true. In other words, what happened was not a "rubber-stamping" of the Greek concepts by Christians. As I have demonstrated with this study of the "Christianization" of the Greco-Roman concepts of death, second-century Christians engaged in a highly critical modification of the existing views of death, judging them on the basis of their differing occasions and the level of progressive revelation that they had in order to construct a distinctive Christian view of death. Because of the formative nature of this time period in the history of Christianity, it is not a stretch to argue that the same approach was evidenced in many other areas of Christian belief.

One of the areas where more study is still needed is the question of the application of the concept of death in other areas of early Christianity. One area that comes to mind is the question of doctrinal development. Caroline Bynum suggested that the Pauline metaphor of a seed (1 Cor 15:44) was used by the apologists and polemicists to argue for both change and continuity.[3] The basic idea, especially with Irenaeus and Tertullian, was that there is continuity between the dead body and the resurrected body, for it is "what falls [that] must rise."[4] But, of course, there is an "alteration of quality," an alteration that the Fathers accounted for on the basis of the knowledge and power of God.[5] While attempts have been made to show how the belief in the resurrection functioned in the formation of the early Christian community, it seems an exploration that connects death to the development of Christian doctrine would be much welcome.

---

2. Harnack, *History of Dogma* 7.272.
3. Bynum, *The Resurrection of the Body*, 57.
4. For a discussion of the development of this formula, see Eijik, "Only that Can Rise," 517–29.
5. Bingham, "Development and Diversity," 63–64.

Bibliography

PRIMARY SOURCES

The Apostolic Fathers: A New Translation and Commentary. 6 vols. Edited by R. M. Grant. New York: Nelson, 1964–68.

Athenagoras. *Legatio and De resurrectione.* Translated by William R. Schoedel. Oxford: Clarendon, 1972.

Attridge, Harold W., and Elaine Pagels. "The Tripartite Tractate: Introduction." In *Nag Hammadi Codex I (The Jung Codex) Introduction, Texts, Translations, Indices*, edited by Harold W. Attridge, 159–90. Nag Hammadi Studies, vol. 22. Leiden: Brill, 1985.

Bihlmeyer, Karl. *Die apostolischen Väter.* Neubearbeitung der Funkschen Ausgabe. Tübingen: Mohr Siebeck, 1924.

Dibelius, M. *Der Hirt des Hermas.* Vol. 4. Handbuch zum Neuen Testament: Die Apostolischen Väter. Tübingen: Mohr Siebeck, 1923.

Ehrman, Bart D., ed. *The Apostolic Fathers.* Vol. 1, *I Clement, II Clement, Ignatius, Polycarp, Didache.* Loeb Classical Library, vol. 24. Cambridge: Harvard University Press, 2003.

Eusebius. *Ecclesiastical History.* Translated by C. F. Cruse. New updated ed. Peabody, MA: Hendrickson, 1998.

Goodspeed, E. J. *The Apostolic Fathers: An American Translation.* New York: Harper, 1950.

Hesiod. *The Homeric Hymns and Homerica.* Edited by T. E. Page. Loeb Classical Library. Cambridge: Harvard University Press, 1964.

Holmes, M. W., ed. *The Apostolic Fathers.* Grand Rapids: Baker, 2007.

———. *The Apostolic Fathers: Greek Texts and English Translations.* 3rd ed. Grand Rapids: Baker Academic, 1992.

Homer. *The Illiad with an English Translation.* Translated by A. T. Murray. Loeb Classical Library. London: Heinemann, 1965.

Isenberg, Wesley W. "The Gospel according to Philip: Introduction." In *Nag Hammadi Codex II,2–7, together with XIII,2, Brit. Lib. Or. 4926(1), and P. Oxy. 1, 654, 655*, edited by Bentley Layton, vol. 1, *Gospel according to Thomas, Gospel according to Philip, Hypostases of the Archon, and Indexes*, edited by Martin Krause, James M. Robinson, and Frederick Wisse, vol. 22, 131–41. Leiden: Brill, 1989.

Kirsopp, Lake. *The Apostolic Fathers*. 2 vols. Loeb Classical Library 24–25. Cambridge: Harvard University Press, 1912–13.

Lightfoot, J. B. S. *Ignatius, S. Polycarp. Part 2 of The Apostolic Fathers*. 2nd ed. 2 vols. London: Macmillan, 1889–90.

Lightfoot, J. B., and J. R. Harmer, eds. *The Apostolic Fathers: Revised Greek Texts with Introductions and English Translations*. 1891. Reprint. Grand Rapids: Baker, 1984.

Meyer, Marvin, ed. *The Nag Hammadi Scriptures*. New York: HarperOne, 2007.

Musurillo, Herbert. *The Acts of the Christian Martyrs*. Oxford: Clarendon, 1972.

———. *The Acts of the Pagan Martyrs: Acta Alexandrinorum*. Oxford: Oxford University Press, 1954.

Peel, Malcolm L. *The Epistle to Rheginos: A Valentinian Letter on the Resurrection: Introduction, Translation, Analysis and Exposition*. Philadelphia: Westminster, 1969.

———. "The Treatise on the Resurrection: Notes." In *Nag Hammadi Codex I (The Jung Codex) Notes*, edited by Harold W. Attridge, 137–215. Nag Hammadi Studies, vol. 23. Leiden: Brill, 1985.

Rius-Camps, J. *The Four Authentic Letters of Ignatius, the Martyr*. Orientalia Christiana analeta 213. Rome: Pontificium Institutum Orientalium Studiorum, 1980.

Roberts, Alexander, and James Donaldson. *Ante-Nicene Fathers: The Writings of the Fathers Down to A.D. 325: Hermas, Tatian, Athenagoras, Theophilus, Clement of Alexandria*. vol. 2. 1885. Reprint. Peabody, MA: Hendrickson, 1994.

———. *Ante-Nicene Fathers: The Writings of the Fathers Down to A.D. 325: The Apostolic Fathers: Justin Martyr, Irenaeus*, vol. 1. 1885. Reprint. Peabody, MA: Hendrickson, 1994.

———. *Ante-Nicene Fathers: The Writings of the Fathers Down to A.D. 325: Latin Christianity: Its Founder, Tertullian I. Apologetic; II. Anti-Marcion: III. Ethical*, vol. 1. 1885. Reprint. Peabody, MA: Hendrickson, 1994.

Schoedel, William R. Athenagoras: *Legatio and Resurrectione*. Oxford: Oxford University Press, 1972.

———. *Ignatius of Antioch: A Commentary on the Letters of Ignatius of Antioch*. Hermeneia. Philadelphia: Fortress, 1985.

———. Polycarp. *Martyrdom of Polycarp, Fragments of Papias*. *The Apostolic Fathers: A New Translation and Commentary*, vol. 5. Edited by R. M. Grant. Camden, NJ: Thomas Nelson, 1967.

Scopello, Madeleine, and Marvin Meyer. "The Gospel of Philip." In *The Nag Hammadi Scriptures*, edited by Marvin Meyer, 157–86. New York: HarperCollins, 2007.

Snyder, Graydon F. *The Shepherd of Hermas*. Vol. 6. *The Apostolic Fathers*. Edited by R. M. Grant. Camden, NJ: Thomas Nelson, 1968.

Thomassen, Einar. "The Interpretation of Knowledge: NHC XI,1." In *The Nag Hammadi Scriptures*, edited by Marvin Meyer, 651–62. New York: HarperCollins, 2007.

———. "The Treatise on Resurrection: NHC I,4." In *The Nag Hammadi Scriptures*, edited by Marvin Meyer, 49–51. New York: HarperOne, 2007.

———. "The Tripartite Tractate: NHC I,5." In *The Nag Hammadi Scriptures*, edited by Marvin Meyer, 57–101. New York: HarperCollins, 2007.

———. "The Valentinian School of Gnostic Thought." In *The Nag Hammadi Scriptures*, edited by Marvin Meyer, 790–94. New York: HarperOne, 2007.

Thomassen, Einar, and Marvin Meyer. "The Gospel of Truth: NHC I,3; XII,2." In *The Nag Hammadi Scriptures*, edited by Marvin Meyer, 31–47. New York: HarperCollins, 2007.

Wilson, Robert McLachlan. *The Gospel of Philip: Translation from the Coptic Text with an Introduction and Commentary*. New York: Harper & Row, 1962.

Zahn, Theodor. *Ignatius von Antiochien*. Gotha: Perthes, 1873.

SECONDARY SOURCES

Adair, John A. "Paul and Orthodoxy in Justin Martyr." PhD diss., Dallas Theological Seminary, 2008.

Allies, Mary H. *Treatise on Images: St. John of Damascus on the Holy Images, Three Sermons on the Assumption*. London: Thomas Baker, 1898.

Allo, È.-B. *Saint Paul. Seconde épître aux Corinthiens (ÈB 45)*. Paris: Gabalda, 1937.

Armstrong, A. H., and R. A. Markus. *Christian Faith and Greek Philosophy*. New York: Sheed and Ward, 1960.

Bailey, Robert Edson. "Is Sleep the Proper Biblical Term for the Intermediate State." *Zeitschrift für die neutestamentliche Wissenschaft und die Kunde der älteren Kirche* 55 (1964) 161–67.

Bakker, Hendrik Adrianus. "Exemplar domini: Ignatius of Antioch and His Martyrological Self-concept." PhD diss., Rijksuniversiteit te Groningen, 2003.

Baldovin, John F. "Relics, Martyrs, and the Eucharist." *Liturgical Ministry* 12 (2003) 9–19.

Bammel, Hammond. "Ignatian Problems." *Journal of Theological Studies* 33 (1982) 62–97.

Bandstra, Barry L. *Genesis 1–11: A Handbook on the Hebrew Text*. Baylor Handbook on the Hebrew Bible. Waco, TX: Baylor University Press, 2008.

Barnard, L. W. *Athenagoras: A Study in Second Century Christian Apologetic*. Theologie historique, vol. 18. Paris: Beauchesne, 1972.

———. "The Background of St. Ignatius of Antioch." *Vigiliae christianae* 17 (1963) 193–206.

———. "In Defence of Pseudo-Pionius' Account of Saint Polycarp's Martyrdom." In *Kyriakon: Feitschcrift Johannes Quasten*, vol. 1, edited by P. Granfield and J. A. Jungmann, 192–204. Münster: Aschendorff, 1970.

———. "The Heresy of Tatian—Once Again." *Journal of Ecclesiastical History* 19 (1968) 1–10.

———. "Justin Martyr's Eschatology." *Vigiliae christianae* 19 (1965) 86–98.

———. *Justin Martyr: His Life and Thought*. Cambridge: Cambridge University Press, 1967.

Barnes, Timothy David. *Early Christian Hagiography and Roman History*. Tübingen: Mohr Siebeck, 2010.

———. "Pre-Decian Acta Martyrium." *Journal of Theological Studies* 19 (1968) 509–31.

Barr, James. "Is God a Liar? (Genesis 2–3)—and Related Matters." *Journal of Theological Studies* 57 (2006) 1–22.

———. *The Garden of Eden and the Hope of Immortality*: The Read-Tuckwell Lectures for 1990. London: SCM, 1990.

Bass, Justin W. "The Battle for the Keys: Revelation 1:18 and Christ's *descensus ad inferno.*" PhD diss., Dallas Theological Seminary, 2011.

Bauer, Walter. *Die Briefe des Ignatius von Antiochia und der Polykarpbrief. Die apostolischen Väter.* Suppl. vol. of Handbuch Neuen Testament, vol. 2. Tübingen: Mohr, 1920.

———. *Orthodoxy and Heresy in Earliest Christianity.* Edited by Robert A. Kraft and Gerhard Krodel. London: SCM, 1972.

———. *Rechtgläubigkeit und Ketzerei im ältesten Christendum.* Tübingen: Mohr, 1934.

Bauer, Walter, W. F. Arndt, F. W. Gingrich, and F. W. Danker, eds. *A Greek-English Lexicon of the New Testament and Other Early Christian Literature*, 3rd ed. Chicago: University of Chicago Press, 2000.

Baumeister, Theofried. "Anytos und Meletos können mich zwar töten, schaden jedoch können sie mir nicht." In *Platonismus und Christentum*: Festschrift für H. Dörrie, edited by Horst Dieter Blume and Friedhelm Mann, 58–63. Jarbuch für Antike und Christentum Ergänzungsband, 10. Münster: Aschendorff, 1983.

Benz, Ernest. "Christus und Sokrates in der alten Kirche (Ein Beitrag zum altkirchlichen Verständnis des Märtyres und des Martyriums)." *Zeitschrift für die neutestamentliche Wissenschaft* 43 (1951) 195–244.

Bertholet, Alfred. *Die israelitischen Vorstellungen vom Zustand nach dem Tode.* 2nd ed. Tübingen: Mohr, 1914.

Bhabha, Homi. *The Location of Culture.* London: Routledge, 1994.

Bihlmeyer, Karl. *Die apostolischen Väter, Neubearbeitung der Funkschen Ausgabe.* Tübingen: Mohr, 1924.

Bingham, D. Jeffrey. "Development and Diversity in Early Christianity." *Journal of Evangelical Theological Society* 49 (2006) 45–66.

———. *Pocket History of the Church.* Downers Grove, IL: InterVarsity, 2002.

Birkeland, H. "The Belief in the Resurrection of the Dead in the O.T." *Studia Theologica* 3 (1945–50) 60–78.

Bloch-Smith, Elizabeth. *Judahite Burial Practices and Beliefs about the Dead.* JSOTS 123. Sheffield, UK: Sheffield Academic Press, 1992.

———. "The Cult of Death in Judah: Interpreting the Material Remains." *Journal of Biblical Literature* 111 (1992) 213–24.

Bolt, Peter G. "Life, Death, and the Afterlife in the Greco-Roman World." In *Life in the Face of Death: The Resurrection Message of the New Testament*, edited by Richard N. Longenecker, 51–79. Grand Rapids: Eerdmans, 1998.

Bommes, Karin. *Weizen Gottes: Untersuchungen zur Theologie des Martyriums bei Ignatius von Antiochien.* Theophaneia: Beitrage zur Religions- und Kirchengeschichte des Altertums, 1971.

Bonhoeffer, Dietrich. *The Cost of Discipleship.* New York: Macmillan, 1963.

Bousset, Wilhelm. *Kyros Christos: A History of the Belief in Christ from the Beginnings of Christianity to Irenaeus.* Translated by John E. Steely. Nashville: Abingdon 1970.

Bovon, Francois, and Eric Junod. "Reading the Apocryphal Acts of the Apostles." *Semeia* 38 (1986) 161–71.

Bower, R. A. "The Meaning of ΕΠΙΤΥΓΧΑΝΩ in the Epistles of Ignatius of Antioch." *Vigiliae christianae* 28 (1974) 1–14.

Bowersock, G. W. *Fiction as History: Nero to Julian.* Sather Classical Lectures. Berkeley: University of California Press, 1994.

———. *Martyrdom and Rome.* Cambridge: Cambridge University Press, 1995.

Braun, Willi, ed. *Rhetoric and Reality in Early Christianities*. Studies in Christianity and Judaism/Ètudes sur le christianisme et la judaisme, vol. 16. Waterloo, Ontario. Published for the Canadian Corp. for Studies in Religion/Corporation canadienne des *Sciences religieuses* by Wilfrid Laurier University Press, 2005.

Brent, Allen. *Ignatius of Antioch and the Second Sophistic: A Study of an Early Christian Transformation of Pagan Culture*. Tübingen: Mohr Siebeck, 2006.

Brown, Peter. *The Body and Society*. New York: Columbia University Press, 1988.

———. *The Cult of the Saints: Its Rise and Function in Latin Christianity*. The Haskell Lectures on History of Religions: New Series, No. 2. Chicago: University of Chicago Press, 1981.

———. "The Rise and Function of the Holy Man in Late Antiquity." *Journal of Roman Studies* 61 (1971) 80–101.

Büchsel, Friedrich. "ἀνίστημι, ἐξανίστημι, ἀνάστασις, ἐξανίστημι." In *Theological Dictionary of the New Testament*, edited by Gerhard Kittel, translated by Geoffrey W. Bromiley, vol. I, Α–Γ, 368–73. Grand Rapids: Eerdmans, 1964.

Buckley, Jorunn Jacobsen. "A Cult-Mystery in The Gospel of Philip." *Journal of Biblical Literature* 99 (1980) 569–81.

Bultmann, Rudolf. "θάνατος, θνῄσκω, ἀποθνῄσκω, συναποθνῄσκω." In *Theological Dictionary of the New Testament*, edited by Gerhard Kittel, vol. 3, 7–25. Grand Rapids: Eerdmans, 1972.

Burkert, Walter. *Greek Religion*. Cambridge: Harvard University Press, 1985.

Bynum, Caroline. *The Resurrection of the Body in Western Christianity, 200–1336*. Lectures on the History of Religions, vol. 15. New York: Columbia University Press, 1995.

Calvin, John. *Genesis. The Crossway Classic Commentaries*. The Crossway Classic Commentaries. Wheaton, IL: Crossway, 2001.

Campenhausen, H. von. *Die Idee des Martyriums in der alten kirche*. Göttingen: Vanderhoeck & Ruprecht, 1936.

———. *Ignace d'Antioche, Polycarpe de Smyrne Lettres*. Sources Chréstiennes. Paris: Cerf, 1958.

Cassuto, U. *A Commentary on the Book of Genesis: Part 1: From Adam to Noah Genesis I–VI 8*. Translated by Israel Abrahams. Jerusalem: Magnes, 1972.

Cavalin, Hans Clemens Caesarius. *Life After Death: Paul's Argument for the Resurrection of the Dead in I Cor 15: Part I: An Enquiry into the Jewish Background*. Coniectanea biblica: New Testament Series 7:1. Lund, Sweden: Gleerup, 1974.

Chadwick, Henry. *Early Christian Thought and the Classical Tradition: Studies in Justin, Clement and Origen*. Oxford: Oxford University Press, 1966.

———. "Justin Martyr's Defence of Christianity." *Bulletin of the John Rylands Library* 47 (1965) 275–97.

Charles, R. H. *Eschatology: The Doctrine of a Future Life in Israel, Judaism, and Christianity: A Critical History*. London: Schocken, 1899.

Coleman, Kathleen. "Fatal Charades: Roman Executions Staged as Mythological Enactments." *Journal of Roman Studies* 80 (1990) 44–73.

Copleston, Frederick. C. *A History of Philosophy*. Vol. 1: *Greece and Rome From the Pre-Socratics to Plotinus*. London: Burns, Oates & Washbourne, 1947.

Corwin, Virginia. *St. Ignatius and Christianity in Antioch*. New Haven: Yale University Press, 1960.

Cranfield, C. E. B. *The Epistle to the Romans*, vol. 1. International Critical Commentary. Edinburgh: T. & T. Clark, 1975.

Croix, G. E. M. de Ste. "Why Were the Early Christians Persecuted?" *Past and Present* 26 (1963) 6–38.

Cullmann, Oscar. *Christ and Time: The Primitive Christian Conception of Time and History*. Translated by Floyd V. Filson. Philadelphia: Westminster, 1964.

———. *Immortality of the Soul or Resurrection of the Dead? The Witness of the New Testament*. New York: The Macmillan, 1958.

———. "Immortality of the Soul or Resurrection of the Dead: The Witness of the New Testament." In *Immortality and Resurrection: Death in the Western World: Two Conflicting Currents of Thought*, edited by Krister Stendahl, 9–53. New York: Macmillan, 1965.

Cumont, Franz. *After Life in Roman Paganism*. New Haven: Yale University Press, 1922.

Daley, Brian E. *The Hope of the Early Church: A Handbook of Patristic Eschatology*. Cambridge: Cambridge University Press, 1991.

Daniel-Rops, H. *The Church of the Apostles and Martyrs*. London: Dent & Sons, 1960.

Daniélou, Jean. *The Theology of Jewish Christianity*. Vol. 1. The Development of Christian Doctrine before the Council of Nicaea. London: Darton, Longman and Todd, 1964.

Davies, Douglas. *The Theology of Death*. London: T. & T. Clark, 2008.

Davies, Jon. *Death, Burial and Rebirth in the Religions of Antiquity: Religion in the First Christian Centuries*. London: Routledge, 1999.

Davis, Stevan L. "The Predicament of Ignatius of Antioch." *Vigiliae christianae* 30 (1976) 175–80.

DeConick, April D. "The Rite Mysteries: Sacramentalism in The Gospel of Philip." *Vigiliae christianae* 55 (2001) 225–61.

Delitzsch, Franz. *A New Commentary on Genesis*, vol. 1. 1888. Reprint. Minneapolis: Klock and Klock, 1978.

Desjardins, Michael R. *Sin in Valentinianism*. Society of Biblical Literature: Dissertation Series. Atlanta: Scholars, 1990.

Dewart, Joanne E. McWilliam. *Death and Resurrection*. Message of the Fathers of the Church, vol. 22. Wilmington, DE: Glazier, 1986.

Dhorme, P. "L'idée de l'au-delà dans la religion hébraique," *Revue de l'histoire des Religions* 124 (1941) 113–42.

Dodd, C. H. "The Mind of St. Paul: A Psychological Approach." *Bulletin of the John Rylands Library* 17 (1933) 3–17.

Droge, Arthur J. *Homer or Moses? Early Christian Interpretations of the History of Culture*. Hermeneutische untersuchungen zur theologie, vol. 26. Tübingen: Mohr, 1989.

———. "Justin Martyr and the Restoration of Philosophy." *Church History* 56 (1987) 303–19.

Droge, Arthur J., and James D. Tabor. *A Noble Death: Suicide and Martyrdom among Christians and Jews in Antiquity*. San Francisco: HarperSan Francisco, 1992.

Dunn, James D. G. *Unity and Diversity in the New Testament: An Inquiry into the Character of Early Christianity*. Philadelphia: Westminster, 1977.

Edwards, M. J. "On the Platonic Schooling of Justin Martyr." *Journal of Theological Studies* 42 (1991) 17–34.

Eijik, Ton H. C. Van. *La résurrection des morts chez les Péres apostoliques*. Théologie historique: Collection fondée par le cardinal Daniélou Dirigée par Charles Kannegiesser, vol. 25. Paris: Beauchesne, 1974.

———. "Only That Can Rise Which Has Previously Fallen: The History of a Formula." *Journal of Theological Studies* 22 (1971) 517–29.

Elliot, J. K. "Imitations in Literature and Life: Apocrypha and Martyrdom." In *The Routledge Companion to Early Christian Thought*, edited by D. Jeffrey Bingham, 87–105. London: Routledge, 2010.

England, Archie Waits. "An Investigation of Resurrection Language and Imagery in the Old Testament in Light of Its Ancient Near Eastern Literary Background." ThD diss., Mid-America Baptist Theological Seminary, 1994.

Erickson, Millard J. *Christian Theology*. Grand Rapids: Baker, 1985.

Ellis, Peter. *The Yahwehist: The Bible's First Theologian*. Notre Dame: Fides, 1968.

Elze, Martin. *Tatian und seine Theologie*. Forschungen zur Kirchen- und Dogmengeschichte, vol. 9. Göttingen: Vandenhoeck & Ruprecht, 1960.

Fascher, Erich. "Sokrates und Christus: Eine Studie 'zur aktuellen Aufgabe der Religionsphänomenologie' den Andenken Heinrich Fricks (†31.12.52)." *Zeitschrift für die neutestamentliche Wissenschaft* 45 (1954) 1–41.

Felton, D. "The Dead." In *A Companion to Greek Religion*, edited by Daniel Ogden, 86–99. Blackwell Companions to the Ancient World. Oxford: Wiley-Blackwell, 2010.

Féret, Pére. "La mort dans la tradition biblique." In *Le mystére de la mort et sa célébration*, edited by Roguet Claude Aymon-Marie, 15–133. Paris: Cerf, 1951.

Ferguson, John. *Clement of Alexandria*. New York: Twayne, 1974.

Fischel, H. A. "Martyr and Prophet." *Jewish Quarterly Review* 37 (1947) 265–80.

Forbes, Chris. "Paul's Principalities and Powers: Demythologizing Apocalyptic?" *Journal for the Study of the New Testament* 82 (2001) 61–88.

Foster, Paul. "The Relationship between the Writings of Justin Martyr and the So-called Gospel of Peter." In *Justin and His Worlds*, edited by Sara Parvis and Paul Foster, 104–12. Minneapolis: Fortress, 2007.

Frazier, T. L. *Holy Relics: The Scriptural and Historical Basis for the Veneration of Relics of the Saints*. Ben Lomond, CA: Conciliar, 1997.

Frend, W. H. C. *Martyrdom and Persecution in the Early Church*. Oxford: Blackwell, 1965.

Gaca, Kathy L. "Driving Aphrodite from the World: Tatian's Encratite Principles of Sexual Renunciation." *Journal of Theological Studies* 53 (2002) 28–52.

Gaffron, H. G. "Studien zum koptischen Philippus-evangelium unter besonderer Berücksichtigung der Sakramente." PhD diss., Rheinische-Friedrich-Wilhelms Universität, 1969.

Garland, Robert. *The Greek Way of Death*. New York: Cornell University Press, 2001.

Gasparro, G. *Enkrateia e antropologia*. Rome: Institutum patristicum augustinianum, 1984.

Gavin, F. "The Sleep of the Soul in the Early Syrian Church." *Journal of the American Oriental Society* 40 (1920) 103–20.

Gibbon, E. *The History of the Decline and Fall of the Roman Empire*. 7 vols. Edited by J. B. Bury, vol. 2.111. London: Methuen, 1909.

Gillman, J. "A Thematic Comparison: 1 Cor 15:50–57 and 2 Cor 5:1–5." *Journal of Biblical Literature* 107 (1998) 439–54.

Glancy, Jennifer A. "Boastings and Beatings (2 Corinthians 11:23–25)." *Journal of Biblical Literature* 123 (2004) 99–135.

Gleason, Maud W. "Truth Contests and Talking Corpses." In *Constructions of the Classical Body*, edited by J. I. Porter, 287–313. Ann Arbor, MI: University of Michigan Press, 1999.

Glimm, F. X., J. M. F. Marique, and G. G. Walsh. *The Apostolic Fathers. Fathers of the Church* 1. Washington, DC: Catholic University of America Press, 1947.

Goldsmith, Dale. "De Resurrectione." *Journal of Religion* 45 (1965) 256–57.

———. "The Function of Jesus' Resurrection in Ignatius and the Early Church." PhD diss., University of Chicago, 1973.

Goodenough, E. R. *The Theology of Justin Martyr: An Investigation into the Conceptions of Early Christian Literature and Its Hellenistic and Judaistic Influences*. Jenna: Frommann, 1923.

Gonen, Rivka. "Burial in Canaan of the Late Bronze Age as the basis for the Study of Population and Settlements." PhD diss., Hebrew University of Jerusalem, 1979.

Gousmett, Christopher John. "Shall the Body Strive and Not be Crowned?: Unitary and Instrumentalist Anthropological Models as Keys to Interpreting the Structure of Patristic Eschatology." PhD diss., University of Otago, 1993.

Grabar, André. *Christian Iconography: A Study of Its Origins*. Princeton: Princeton University Press, 1968.

Grant, Robert. M. "Athenagoras or Ps.-Athenagoras?" *Harvard Theological Review* 47 (1954) 121–29.

———. *Greek Apologists of the Second Century*. Philadelphia: Westminster, 1988.

———. "The Heresy of Tatian." *Journal of Theological Studies* 5 (1954) 62–68.

———. "The Mystery of Marriage in the Gospel of Philip." *Vigiliae christianae* 15 (1961) 129–40.

Greenberg, L. Arik. *My Share of God's Reward: Exploring the Roles and Formulations of the Afterlife in Early Christian Martyrdom*. Studies in Biblical Literature, vol. 121. New York: Lang, 2009.

Greenspoon, L. J. "The Origin of the Idea of Resurrection." In *Traditions and Transformation: Turning Points in Biblical Faith*, edited by B. Harpen and J. D. Levenson, 247–321. Winona Lake, IN: Eisenbrauns, 1981.

Greshake, Gisbert, and Gerhard Lohfink. *Naherwartung-Auferstehung-Unsterblichkeit: Untersuchungen zur christlichen Eschatologie*. Queastiones Disputatae 71. Freiburg-Basel-Vienna: Herder, 1982.

Groh, Constance DeYoung. "Agents of Victory: Mary and the Martyrs in the Writings of Irenaeus of Lyons." PhD diss., Northwestern University, 2000.

Gundry, Robert H. *Sōma in Biblical Theology: With Emphasis on Pauline Anthropology* Cambridge: Cambridge University Press, 1976.

Hallote, Rachel S. *Death, Burial, and the Afterlife in the Biblical World: How the Israelites and Their Neighbors Treated the Dead*. Chicago: Dee, 2001.

Harnack, Adolf. *Lehrbuch der Dogmengeschichte*, 3 vols. Freiburg: Mohr, 1886–90; ET *History of Dogma*. Translated from 3rd German ed. 7 vols. Translated by N. Buchanan et al.; London: Williams and Norgate, 1894–99.

———. "Sokrates und die alte Kirche." In *Reden und Aufsätze*, vol. 1, 1.29–48. Gießen: Töpelmann, 1903.

———. *What is Christianity?* Translated by Thomas Bailey Saunders. 2nd ed. New York: Putnam's Sons, 1903.

Harris, M. J. "2 Corinthians 5:1–10: Watershed in Paul's Eschatology?" *Tyndale Bulletin* 22 (1971) 32–57.

———. "The Interpretation of 2 Cor 5:1–10 and Its Place in Pauline Eschatology." PhD diss., University of Manchester, 1970.

———. "Resurrection and Immortality in the Pauline Corpus." In *Life in the Face of Death: The Resurrection Message of the New Testament*, edited by Richard N. Longenecker, 147–70. Grand Rapids: Eerdmans, 1998.

Harrison, P. N. *Polycarp's Two Epistles to the Philippians*. Cambridge: Cambridge University Press, 1936.

Hastie, George Kimpton. "The Doctrine of Hades in the New Testament." ThM thesis, Dallas Theological Seminary, 1950.

Hastings, James. *Dictionary of the Bible*, 5 vols. Edinburgh, T. & T. Clark, 1904.

Healey, John F. "Death, Underworld and Afterlife in the Ugaritic Text." PhD diss., University of London, 1977.

Heidel, A. *The Gilgamesh Epic and Old Testament Parallels*. Chicago: University of Chicago Press, 1949.

Henten, J. W. van. *The Maccabean Martyrs as Saviours of the Jewish People*. Leiden: Brill, 1997.

Henten, Jan Willem van, and Friedrich Avemarie. *Martyrdom and Noble Death: Selected from Graeco-Roman, Jewish and Christian Antiquity*. London: Routledge, 2002.

Hick, John. "Present and Future." *Harvard Theological Review* 71 (1978) 1–15.

Hill, Charles E. *Regnum Caelorum: Patterns of Future Hope in Early Christianity*. Oxford: Clarendon, 1992.

———. *Regnum Caelorum: Patterns of Millennial Thought in Early Christianity*. 2nd ed. Grand Rapids: Eerdmans, 2001.

Holtzmann, Heinrich Julius. *Lehrbuch der neutestamentlichen Theologie*. Tübingen: Mohr, 1897.

Hopkins, Keith. *Death and Renewal. Sociological Studies in Roman History*, vol. 2. Cambridge: Cambridge University Press, 1983.

Hunt, Emily J. *Christianity in the Second Century: The Case of Tatian*. London and New York: Routledge, 2003.

Hurst, Eric C. "The Destiny of the Individual in the Thought of the Old Testament." *Review and Expositor* 58 (1961) 296–311.

Illman, K. -J. "מות." In *Theological Dictionary of the Old Testament*, edited by G. Johannes Botterweck, Helmer Riggren, and Heinz-Josef Fabry, trans. Douglas W. Stott, 185–209. Grand Rapids: Eerdmans 2004.

Isacson, Mikael. "Follow Your Bishop! Rhetorical Strategies in the Letters of Ignatius of Antioch." In *The Formation of the Early Church*, edited by Jostein Adna, vol. 1, 322–23. Wissenschaftliche Untersuchungen zum Neuen Testament, vol. 83. Tübingen: Mohr Siebeck, 2005.

Jaeger, Werner. "The Greek Ideas of Immortality." In *Immortality and Resurrection: Death in the Western World: Two Conflicting Currents of Thought*, edited by Krister Stendahl, 97–114. New York: Macmillan, 1965.

Jefford, Clayton N. *Reading the Apostolic Fathers: An Introduction*. Peabody, MA: Hendricksen, 1996.

Jenks, Gregory R. "Paul and His Mortality: Imitating Christ in the Face of Death." PhD diss., Dallas Theological Seminary, 2012.

Jeremias, Joachim. "ᾅδης." In *Theological Dictionary of the New Testament*, edited by Gerhard Kittel, translated by Geoffrey W. Bromiley, vol. 1, 146–49. Grand Rapids: Eerdmans, 1964.

———. "Παράδεισος." In *Theological Dictionary of the New Testament*, edited by Gerhard Friedrich and Gerhard Kittel, vol. 5, 765–73. Grand Rapids: Eerdmans, 1973.

Johnston, Philip. S. "Death and Resurrection." In *New Dictionary of Biblical Theology*, edited by T. Desmond Alexander and Brian S. Rosner. Leicester, UK: IVP, 2000.

———. *Shades of Sheol: Death and Afterlife in the Old Testament*. Downers Grove, IL: IVP, 2002.

Joly, Robert. *Le dossier d'Ignace d'Antioch*. Brussels: Université de Brussels, 1979.

Kellermann, Ulrich. *Auferstanden in den Himmel: 2 Makkabäer 7 und die Auferstehung der Märtyrer*. Stuttgart: Verlag Katholisches Bibelwerk, 1979.

Kelley, Nicole. "Philosophy as Training for Death: Reading the Ancient Christian Martyr Acts as Spiritual Exercises." *Church History* 75 (2006) 723–47.

Kerferd, G. B. *The Sophistic Movement*. Cambridge: Cambridge University Press, 1981.

Khomych, Taras. "A Forgotten Witness: Recovering the Early Church Slovanic Version of the *Martyrdom of Polycarp*." In *Martyrdom and Persecution in Late Antique Christianity: Festschrift Boudewijn Dehandschutter*, edited by J. Leemans, 123–33. Bibliotheca ephemeridum theologicarum lovaniensium, vol. 241. Leuven: Université Catholique de Louvain, 2010.

Kim, Eun Chul. "Cult of the Dead and The Old Testament Negation of Ancestor Worship." *Asia Journal of Theology* 17 (2003) 2–16.

King, Karen L. *What is Gnosticism?* Cambridge: Belknap, 2003.

Koester, Helmut, and James M. Robinson. *Trajectories through Early Christianity*. Philadelphia: Fortress, 1971.

Koltun-Fromm, Naomi. "Re-imagining Tatian: The Damaging Effects of Polemical Rhetoric." *Journal of Early Christian Studies* 16 (2008) 1–30.

Kromholtz, Bryan Louis. "Resurrection in Death in the Theology of Karl Rahner and Hans Urs von Balthasar." MA thesis, Graduate Theological Union, 2000.

Kyriakakis, James. "Byzantine Burial Customs: Care of the Deceased from Death to the Prothesis." *Greek Orthodox Review* 19 (1974) 37–72.

Laeuchli, Samuel. "The Drama of Replay." In *Searching in the Syntax of Things: Experiments in the Study of Religion*, edited by Maurice Friedman, T. Patrick Burke, and Samuel Laeuchli, 69–126. Philadelphia: Fortress, 1972.

Lane, William L. "Living a Life of Faith in the Face of Death: The Witness of Hebrews." In *Life in the Face of Death: The Resurrection Message of the New Testament*, edited by Richard N. Longenecker, 247–69. Grand Rapids: Eerdmans, 1998.

Latourette, Kenneth Scott. *A History of Christianity*. New York: Harper, 1953.

Lauwers, Michel. *La mémoire des ancêtres, le souci des morts: morts, rites et société au moyen âge (Diocèse de Liége, XIe–XIIIe siécles)*. Théologie et historique 103. Paris: Beauchesne, 1997.

Leclerq, Henri. "Incineration." In *Dictionaire d'archéologie chrétienne*, vol. 7, pt. 1, edited by Cabrol, Fernand, and Henri Leclerq. Paris: Letouzey et Ané, 1926.

Leupold, H. C. *Exposition of Genesis*, vol. 1. Grand Rapids: Baker, 1942.

Levenson, Jon L. *Resurrection and the Restoration of Israel: The Ultimate Victory of the God of Life*. New Haven: Yale University Press, 2006.

Lewis, Nicola Denzey. "Apolytrosis as Ritual and Sacrament: Determining a Ritual Context for Death in Second-Century Marcosian Valentinianism." *Journal of Early Christian Studies* 17 (2009) 525–61.
Lewis, Theodore J. *Cults of the Dead in Ancient Israel and Ugarit*. HSM, vol. 39. Atlanta: Scholars, 1989.
Liefeld, Walter. Luke. In *The Expositor's Bible Commentary*, edited by Frank E. Gaebelein and J. D. Douglas. Grand Rapids: Zondervan, 1984.
Lieu, Judith. *Image and Reality: The Jews in the World of the Christians in the Second Century*. Edinburgh: T. & T. Clark, 1996.
Lightfoot, J. B., and Fenton John Anthony Hort. "The Chronology of St. Paul's Life and Epistles." In *Biblical Essays*, 15th ed., 213–33. Peabody, MA: Hendrickson, 1994.
Lilla, Salvatore R. *Clement of Alexandria: A Study in Christian Platonism and Gnosticism*. Oxford: Oxford University Press, 1971.
Lincoln, Andrew T. *Paradise Now and Not Yet: Studies in the Role of the Heavenly Dimension in Paul's Thought with Special Reference to his Eschatology*. Cambridge: Cambridge University Press, 1981.
Lincoln, Bruce. "The Rape of Persephone: A Greek Scenario of Women's Initiation." *Harvard Theological Review* 72 (1979) 223–35.
Lionel, Swain. "The Bible and the People: Eternal Life in the Old Testament." *Clergy Review* 52 (1967) 105–7.
Livingston, James C. *The Enlightenment and the Nineteenth Century*. vol. 1. *Modern Christian Thought*. Minneapolis: Fortress, 2006.
Lods, Adolphe. *La croyance à la vie future et le culte des morts dans l'antiquité israélite*. Paris: Fischbacher, 1906.
Loewe, John. "An Examination of Attempts to Detect Developments in Paul's Theology." *Journal of Theological Studies* 42 (1941) 129–42.
Longenecker, Richard N. "Is There Development in Paul's Resurrection Thought?" In *Life in the Face of Death: The Resurrection Message of the New Testament*, edited by Richard N. Longenecker, 171–202. Grand Rapids: Eerdmans 1998.
Lotz, John-Paul. *Ignatius and Concord: The Backgrounds and Use of the Language of Concord in the Letters of Ignatius of Antioch*. Patrisric Studies. New York: Lang, 2007.
Lüdemann, Hermann Karl. *Die Anthropologie des Apostels Paulus und ihre Stellung innerhalb seiner Heilslehre: Nach den vier Hauptbriefen*. Kiel: Universitäts-Buchhandlung, 1872.
Lunde, J. "Heaven and Hell." In *Dictionary of Jesus and the Gospels*, edited by Joel B. Green and Scot McKnight, 3–127. Downers Grove, IL: IVP, 1992.
Lundhaug, Hugo. "'These are Symbols and Likenesses of the Resurrection': Conceptualizations of Death and Transformation in the Treatise on the Resurrection (NHC I,4)." In *Metamorphoses: Resurrection, Body and Transformative Practices In Early Christianity*, edited by Turid Karlsen Seim and Jorunn Økland, 189–205. Ekstasis: Religious Experience from Antiquity to the Middle Ages, vol. 1. Berlin: de Gruyter, 2009.
Lyman, Coleman. *The Antiquities of the Christian Church*. New York: Gould, Newman & Saxton, 1841.
Lyman, Rebecca. "Hellenism and Heresy." *Journal of Early Christian Studies* 11 (2003) 209–22.

———. "Justin and Hellenism: Some Postcolonial Perspectives." In *Justin Martyr and His Worlds*, edited by Sara Parvis and Paul Foster, 160–68. Minneapolis: Fortress, 2007.

———. "Natural Resources: Tradition without Orthodoxy." *Anglican Theological Review* 84 (2002) 67–80.

———. "The Politics of Passing: Justin Martyr's Conversion as a Problem of Hellenization." In *Conversion in Late Antiquity and the Early Middle Ages: Seeing and Believing*, edited by Kenneth Mills and Anthony Grafton, 36–60. Rochester, NY: University of Rochester Press, 2003.

Malinine, Michael, et al. *De resurrectione*. Zürich and Stuttgart: Rascher, 1963.

Marsden, George. *Reforming Fundamentalism: Fuller Seminary and the New Evangelicalism*. Grand Rapids: Eerdmans, 1987.

Martin-Achard, Robert. *From Death to Life: A Study of the Development of the Doctrine of the Resurrection in the Old Testament*. Translated by John Penney Smith. Edinburgh: Oliver and Boyd, 1960.

Matera, F. J. "Apostolic Suffering and Resurrection Faith: Distinguishing between Appearance and Reality (2 Cor 4, 7–5,10)." In *Resurrection in the New Testament: Festschrift J. Lambrecht*, edited by R. Bieringer, V. Koperski, and B. Lataire, 387–405. Leuven: Leuven University Press, 2002.

Matheson, Geroge. *The Spiritual Development of St. Paul*. New York: Whittaker, 1897.

McCane, Byron R. *Roll Back the Stone: Death and Burial in the World of Jesus*. Harrisburg, PA: Trinity, 2003.

McCue, James F. "Orthodoxy and Heresy: Walter Bauer and the Valentinians." *Vigiliae Christianae* 33 (1979) 118–30.

McGinn, Bernard. *The Foundations of Mysticism: Origins to Fifth Century*. London: SCM, 1991.

McNamara, Daniel Norman. "Ignatius of Antioch on his Death: Discipleship, Sacrifice, Imitation." PhD diss., McMaster University, 1977.

McNamara, Martin, ed. *Apocalyptic Eschatological Heritage: The Middle East and Celtic Realms*. Dublin: Four Courts, 2003.

Mellink, Albert Osger. *Death as Eschaton: A Study of Ignatius of Antioch's Desire for Death*. Amsterdam: University of Amsterdam Press, 2000.

Merrill, E. H. "שְׁאוֹל." *New International Dictionary of Old Testament Theology and Exegesis*, edited by W. A. VanGemeren, vol. 4. Grand Rapids: Zondervan, 1997.

Metts, Roy. "Death, Discipleship and Discourse Strategies: 2 Cor 5:1–10—Once Again." *Criswell Theological Review* 4 (1989) 57–76.

Meyers, Eric M. "Secondary Burials in Palestine." *Biblical Archaeologist* 33 (1970) 2–29.

Miguel, Otto. "Zur Lehre vom Todesschlaf." *Zeitschrift für die neutestamentliche Wissenschaft und die Kunde der älteren Kirche* 35 (1936) 285–90.

Moberly, R. W. L. "Did the Interpreters Get it Right? Genesis 2–3 Reconsidered." *Journal of Theological Studies* 59 (2008) 22–40.

Morey, Robert A. *Death and the Afterlife*. Minneapolis: Bethany House, 1984.

Morris, K. R. "Pure Wheat of God or Neurotic Deathwish? A Historical and Theological Analysis of Ignatius of Antioch's Zeal for Martyrdom." *Fides et historia* 26 (1994) 24–41.

Mourelatos, Alexander P. D. "Orphism." In *The Cambridge Dictionary of Philosophy*, edited by Robert Audi, 636–37. Cambridge: Cambridge University Press, 1999.

Muhlhern, Alice. "The Roman Catacombs." *Restoration Quarterly* 26 (1983) 29–38.

Nasrallah, Laura Salah. *Christian Responses to the Roman Art and Architecture: The Second-Century amid the Spaces of Empire*. Cambridge: Cambridge University Press, 2010.
Neil, S., and T. Wright. *The Interpretation of the New Testament 1861–1986*. Oxford: Oxford University Press, 1988.
Newman, John Henry. *An Essay on the Development of Christian Doctrine*. London: Pickering, 1845.
Nichols, Terrence. *Death and Afterlife: A Theological Introduction*. Grand Rapids: Brazos, 2011.
Nickelsburg, George W. E. *Resurrection, Immortality, and Eternal Life in Intertestamental Judaism and Early Christianity*. Expanded ed. Harvard Theological Studies 56. Cambridge: Harvard University Press, 2006.
Nock, A. D. "Cremation and Burial in Roman Empire." *Harvard Theological Review* 25 (1932) 321–59.
———. "The Cult of Heroes." *Harvard Theological Review* 37 (1944) 141–74.
Ogle, Marbury B. "The Sleep of Death." *Memoirs of the American Academy in Rome* 11 (1933) 81–119.
Orr, James. *The Progress of Dogma*. Old Tappan, NJ: Revell, 1901.
Osborn, Eric. *Irenaeus of Lyons*. Cambridge: Cambridge University Press, 2001.
Osei-Bonsu, Joseph. "Does 2 Cor 5:1–10 Teach the Reception of the Resurrection Body at the Moment of Death?" *Journal for the Study of the New Testament* 28 (1986) 81–101.
Osiek, Carolyn. *The Shepherd of Hermas: A Commentary*. Hermeneia. Minneapolis: Fortress, 1999.
Pagels, Elaine. *Beyond Belief: The Secret Gospel of Thomas*. New York: Random House, 2005.
———. *The Gnostic Gospels*. New York: Random House, 1979.
———. "The 'Mystery of Marriage' in the Gospel of Philip Revisited." In *The Future of Early Christianity*, edited by Birger Pearson, 442–54. Minneapolis, MN: Fortress, 1991.
———. "The Mystery of the Resurrection: A Gnostic Reading of 1 Corinthians 15." *Journal of Biblical Literature* 93 (1974) 276–88.
———. "Ritual in the Gospel of Philip." In *The Nag Hammadi Library after Fifty Years*, edited by Anne McGuire, 280–91. Leiden: Brill, 1997.
Parvis, Sara, and Paul Foster, eds. *Justin Martyr and His Worlds*. Minneapolis: Fortress, 2007.
Peel, Malcom L. *The Epistle to Rheginos: A Valentinian Letter on the Resurrection: Introduction, Translation, Analysis and Exposition*. Philadelphia: Westminster, 1969.
———. "Gnostic Eschatology and the New Testament." *Novum Testamentum* 12 (1970) 141–65.
Pelikan, Jeroslav. *The Shape of Death: Life, Death, and Immortality in the Early Fathers*. New York: Abingdon, 1961.
Perkins, Judith. *Roman Imperial Identities in the Early Christian Era*. Routledge Monographs in Classical Studies. London: Routledge, 2009.
Peters, Ted. "Resurrection: What Kind of Body?" *Ex Auditu* 9 (1993) 57–76.
Pfättisch, Joannes M. "Christus und Sokrates bei Justin." *Theologische Quartelschrift* 90 (1908) 503–23.

Pfleiderer, Otto. *Der Paulismus. Ein Beitrag zur Geschichte der urchristlichen Theologie.* Leipzig Fues, 1873.

Praxton, S. *Christianizing Death: The Creation of a Ritual Process in Early Medieval Europe.* Ithaca, NY: Cornell University Press, 1990.

Preiss, Theodor. "La mystique l'imitation du Christ et de l'unité chez Ignacé d'Antioche." *Revue d'historie et de philosophie religieuses* 17 (1938) 197–241.

Prusak, Bernard P. "Bodily Resurrection in Catholic Perspectives." *Theological Studies* 61 (2000) 64–105.

Pyne, Robert Allen. "The Resurrection as Restoration: A Thematic Study in Paul's Theology." ThD diss., Dallas Theological Seminary, 1990.

Quasten, Johannes. *The Beginnings of Patristic Literature*, vol. 1. Utrecht and Antwerp: Spectrum 1950.

Rad, Gerhard von. "ζάω." In *Theological Dictionary of the New Testament*, edited by Gerhard Kittel, translated by Geoffrey W. Bromiley, vol. 2, 832–72. Grand Rapids: Eerdmans, 1964.

Rahmani, L. Y. "Ancient Jerusalem's Funerary Customs and Tombs: Part Two." *Biblical Archeologist* 44 (1981) 229–35.

Rainy, Robert. *The Delivery and Development of Christian Doctrine.* London: T. & T. Clark, 1874.

Rajak, Tessa. "Dying for the Law: The Martyr's Portrait in Jewish-Greek Literature." In *Portraits: Biographical Representation in the Greek and Latin Literature of the Roman Empire*, edited by M. J. Edwards and Simon Swain, 36–67. Oxford: Clarendon 1997.

Ratzinger, Joseph. *Eschatology: Death and Eternal Life.* Translated by Michael Waldstein. 2nd ed. Washington DC: Catholic University of America, 1988.

———. *Introduction to Christianity.* Translated by J. R. Foster. San Francisco: Ignatius, 1968.

Rebell, Walter. "Das Leidensverständnis bei Paulus und Ignatius von Antiochien." *New Testament Studies* 32 (1986) 457–65.

Rebillard, Éric. *The Care of the Dead in Late Antiquity.* Translated by Elizabeth Trapnell Rawlings and Jeanine Routier-Pucci. Cornell Studies in Classical Philology. Ithaca, NY: Cornell University Press, 2009.

Reeve, John W. "The Theological Anthropology of Theophilus of Antioch: Immortality and Resurrection in the Context of Judgment." PhD diss., University of Notre Dame, 2009.

Reichenbach, Bruce R. "Resurrection of the Body: Re-creation and Interim Existence." *Journal of Theology for Southern Africa* 21 (1977) 33–42.

Rewolinski, E. T. "The Use of Sacramental Language in the Gospel of Philip." PhD diss., The Divinity School of Harvard University, 1978.

Ricoeur, Paul. *Symbolik des Bösen: Phänomenologie der Schuld.* 2 vols., vol. 2. Freiburg-Munich: Alber, 1971.

Riddle, Donald. "The Martyr Motif in the Gospel according to Mark." *Journal of Religion* 4 (1924) 397–410.

Robertson, Archibald, and Alfred Plummer. *A Critical and Exegetical Commentary on the First Epistle of St. Paul to the Corinthians.* 2nd ed. International Critical Commentary. Edinburgh: T. & T. Clark, 1911.

Robinson, Henry Wheeler. *The Christian Doctrine of Man.* Edinburgh: T. & T. Clark, 1911.

Robinson, Thomas A. *The Bauer Thesis Examined: The Geography of Heresy in the Early Christian Church*. Lewinston, NY: Mellen, 1988.

Rohde, Erwin. *Der griechische Roman und seine Vorläufer*. 3rd ed. Edited by W. Schmid. Leipzig: Breitkopf & Härtel, 1914.

Rordorf, W. "Aux origines du culte des martyrs." In *Acts of Piety in the Early Church*, vol. 17, edited by Everett Ferguson, 79–95. New York: Garland, 1993.

Ross, Allen P. *Creation and Blessing: A Guide to the Study and Exposition of Genesis*. Grand Rapids: Baker, 1996.

Routledge, Robin L. "Death and Afterlife in the Old Testament." *Journal of European Baptist Studies* 9 (2008) 22–39.

Rowe, William V. "Adolf von Harnack and the Concept of Hellenization." In *Hellenization Revisited: Shaping a Christian Response within the Greco-Roman World*, edited by Wendy Helleman, 69–98. Lanham, MD: University Press of America, 1994.

Rudolph, Kurt. *Gnosis: The Nature and History of Gnosticism*. Translated by P. W. Coxon and K. H. Kuhn. San Francisco: HarperSanFrancisco, 1987.

Rush, Alfred C. *Death and Burial in Christian Antiquity*. Washington, DC: Catholic University of America, 1941.

———. "Death as a Spiritual Marriage: Individual and Ecclesial Eschatology." *Vigiliae christianae* 26 (1972) 81–101.

———. "The Eucharist: The Sacraments of the Dying in Christian Antiquity." *Jurist* 34 (1974) 10–35.

Sabatier, Auguste. *The Apostle Paul: A Sketch of the Development of his Doctrine*. [1870] London: Hodder and Stoughton, 1896.

Sanday, Peggy Reeves. *Divine Hunger: Cannibalism as a Cultural System*. Cambridge: Cambridge University Press, 1986.

Schep, J. A. *The Nature of the Resurrection Body: A Study of the Biblical Data*. Grand Rapids: Eerdmans, 1964.

Schlatter, Frederic W. "The Restoration of Peace in Ignatius's Antioch." *Journal of Theological Studies* 35 (1984) 465–69.

Schlier, Heinrich. *Religionsgeschichtliche Untersuchungen zu den Ignatiusbriefen*. Beihefte zur Zeitschrift fuer die neutestamentliche Wissenschaft und die Kunde der aelteren Kirche, vol. 8. Giessen: Töpelmann, 1929.

Schmidt, Brian B. *Israel's Beneficent Dead: Ancestor Cult and Necromancy in Ancient Israelite Religion and Tradition*. Tübingen: Mohr, 1994.

Schmidt, Jean-Claude. *Ghosts in the Middle Ages: The Living and the Dead in Medieval Society*. Translated by Teresa Lavender Fagan. Chicago: University of Chicago Press, 1998.

Schmiedel, Paul Wilhelm. *Die Briefe an die Thessalonicher und an die Korinther*. Freiburg: Mohr, 1892.

Schmithals, W. "Death, Kill, Sleep." In *New Testament Theology*, vol. 1: A–F, edited by Colin Brown, 429–41. Translated from *Theologisches Bergriffslexikon zum Neuen Testament*. Grand Rapids: Zondervan, 1986.

———. "Θάνατος." In *New Testament Theology*, vol. 1: A–F, edited by Colin Brown, 429–41. Translated from *Theologisches Begriffslexikon zum Nuen Testament*. Grand Rapids: Zondervan, 1986.

Schoedel, William R. "Are the Letters of Ignatius of Antioch Authentic?" *Recherches de science religieuse* 6 (1980) 116–201.

———. "Theological Norms and Social Perspectives in Ignatius of Antioch." In *The Shaping of Christianity in the Second and Third Centuries*, vol. 1 of *Jewish and Christian Self-Definition*, edited by E. P. Sanders, 30–56. Philadelphia: Fortress, 1980.

———. "Theophilus of Antioch: Jewish or Christian?" *Illinois Classical Studies* 18 (1993) 279–97.

Schwally, Friedrich. *Das Leben nach dem Tode: Nach den Vorstellungen des alten Israel und des Judentums einschliesslich des Volksglaubens Im Zeitalter Christi: Eine Biblisch-theologische untersuchung*. Giessen: J. Ricker'sche Buchhandlung, 1892.

Schweitzer, Albert. *Paul and His Interpreters: A Critical History*. Translated by W. Montgomery. 2 vols. London: A. & C. Black, 1912.

Seeley, David. *The Noble Death: Graeco-Roman Martyrology and Paul's Concept of Salvation*. JSNTSup 28. Sheffield, UK: JSOT, 1990.

Segelberg, Eric. "The Coptic-Gnostic Gospel according to Philip and Its Sacramental System." *Numen* 7 (1960) 189–200.

———. "The Gospel of Philip and the New Testament." In *The New Testament and Gnosis: Essays in Honour of Robert McL. Wilson*, edited by Alastair H. B. Logan and A. J. M. Wedderburn, 204–11. Edinburgh: T. & T. Clark, 1983.

Setzer, Claudia. *Resurrection of the Body in Early Judaism and Early Christianity: Doctrine, Community, and Self-Definition*. Leiden: Brill, 2004.

———. "Resurrection of the Body in Early Judaism and Christianity." In *Deuterocanonical and Cognate Literature Yearbook 2009: The Human Body in Death and Resurrection*, edited by Tobias Nicklas, Friedrich V. Reiterer, and Joseph Verheyden, edited by Friedrich V. Reiterer et al. Berlin: de Gruyter, 2009.

Sevrin, Jean-Marie. "Practique et doctrine des sacraments dans l'evangile selon Philippe." PhD diss., University of Louvain, 1972.

Sherman, James Edward. *The Nature of Martyrdom: A Dogmatic and Moral Analysis according to the Teaching of St. Thomas Aquinas*. Paterson, NJ: St. Anthony Guild, 1942.

Shipp, G. P. *Studies in the Language of Homer*. 2nd ed. Cambridge Classical Studies. Cambridge: Cambridge University Press, 1972.

Skarsaune, Oskar. "Justin and His Bible." In *Justin Martyr and His Worlds*, edited by Sara Parvis and Paul Foster, 53–76. Minneapolis: Fortress, 2007.

———. *The Proof from Prophecy: A Study of Justin Martyr's Proof-Text Tradition; Text, Type, Provenance, Theological Profile*. Novum Testamentum Supplements 66. Leiden: Brill, 1987.

Slusser, Michael. "Justin Scholarship: Trends and Trajectories." In *Justin Martyr and His Worlds*, edited by Sara Parvis and Paul Foster, 13–21. Minneapolis: Fortress, 2007.

Smelik, K. A. D. "The Witch of Endor: 1 Samuel 28 in Rabbinic and Christian Exegesis till 800 A.D." *Vigiliae christianae* 33 (1977) 160–79.

Smith, Christopher R. "Chiliasm and Recapitulation in the Theology of Irenaeus." *Vigiliae christianae* 48 (1994) 313–31.

Sonnemans, Heino. "Soul, Afterlife, Salvation." *Communio* 14 (1987) 248–61.

Sparks, Adam. "Was Justin Martyr a Proto-Inclusivist?" *Journal of Ecumenical Studies* 43 (2008) 495–510.

Spronk, Klaas. *Beatific Afterlife in Ancient Israel and in the Ancient Near East*. Alter Orient und Altes Testament, vol. 219. Neukirchener-Vluyn: Neukirchener, 1986.

Stählin, Gustav. "περίψημα." In *Theological Dictionary of the New Testament*, edited by Gerhard Friedrich, translated by Geoffrey W. Bromiley, vol. 6, 84–93. Grand Rapids: Eerdmans, 1968.

Stead, G. C. "In Search of Valentinus." In *The Rediscovery of Gnosticism: Proceedings of the International Conference on Gnosticism at Yale New Haven, Connecticut, March 28–31, 1978*, edited by Bentley Layton, 75–102. Leiden: Brill, 1980.

Stendahl, Krister. "Introduction." In *Immortality and Resurrection: Death in the Western World: Two Conflicting Currents of Thought*, edited by Krister Stendahl, 1–8. New York: Macmillan, 1965.

Sterling, Greg. "*Mors philosophi*: The Death of Jesus in Luke." *Harvard Theological Review* 94 (2001) 383–402.

Streeter, Burnett Hillman. *The Primitive Church*. New York: Macmillan, 1929.

Stroud, William J. "Ritual in the Chenoboskion Gospel of Philip." *Illiff Review* 28 (1971) 29–35.

Svigel, Michael J. "Second-Century Incarnational Christology and Early Catholic Christianity." PhD diss., Dallas Theological Seminary, 2008.

Swartley, Willard M. "The Imitatio Christi in the Ignatian Letters." *Vigiliae christianae* 27 (1973) 81–103.

Swete, H. B. "Prayer for the Departed in the First Four Centuries." In *Acts of Piety*, edited by Everett Ferguson, 118–32. Studies in Early Christianity, vol. 17. New York: Garland, 1993.

Teichmann, Ernst. *Die paulinischen Vorstellungen von Auferstehung und Gericht*. Freiburg and Tübingen: Mohr, 1896.

Thomas, Louis-Vincent. *Le cadavre: De la biologie à l'anthropologie*. Brussels: Éditions Complexe, 1980.

Thomassen, Einar. *The Spiritual Seed: The Church of the "Valentinians."* Leiden: Brill, 2006.

Thompson, Leonard L. "The Martyrdom of Polycarp: Death in the Roman Games." *Journal of Religion* 82 (2002) 27–52.

Thrall, Margaret E. *A Critical and Exegetical Commentary on The Second Epistle to the Corinthians: Introduction and Commentary on II Corinthians I–VII*, vol. 1 of 2. International Critical Commentary. London: T. & T. Clark, 1994.

———. "Paul's Understanding of Continuity between the Present Life and the Life of the Resurrection." In *Resurrection in the New Testament: Festschrift J. Lambrecht*, edited by R. Bieringer, V. Koperski, and B. Lataire, 283–300. Leuven: Leuven University Press, 2002.

Toews, Thomas W. "Biblical Sources in the Development of the Concept of the Soul in the Writings of the Fathers of the Early Christian Church, 100–325 C.E." PhD diss., Andrews University, Seventh-Day Adventist Theological Seminary, 2011.

Torrance, T. F. *The Doctrine of Grace in the Apostolic Fathers*. London: Oliver & Boyd, 1948.

Toynbee, J. M. C. *Death and Burial in the Roman World*. Ithaca, NY: Cornell University Press, 1971.

Trevett, Christine. "Ignatius and His Opponents in the Divided Church of Antioch." PhD diss., University of Sheffield, 1980.

———. "Ignatius 'To the Romans' and I Clement LIV–LVI." *Vigiliae christianae* 43 (1989) 35–52.

Tripolitis, Antonia C. "The Doctrine of the Soul in the Thought of Plotinus and Origen." PhD diss., University of Pennsylvania, 1971.

Tripp, D. H. "The 'Sacramental System' of the Gospel of Philip." In *Studia patristica* vol. 17/1, edited by Elizabeth A. Livingstone, 251–60. Oxford: Pergamon, 1982.

Tromp, Nicholas J. *Primitive Conceptions of Death and the Nether World in the Old Testament*. Biblical et orientalia (Sacra Scriptura antiquitatibus orientalibus illustrata). Rome: Pontifical Biblical Institute, 1969.

Turner, H. E. W. *The Pattern of Christian Truth: A Study in the Relations between Orthodoxy and Heresy in the Early Church*. London: Mowbray, 1954.

Vassiliades, Nicolaos P. "The Mystery of Death." *Greek Orthodox Theological Review* 29 (1984) 269–82.

Volz, P. *Die Eschatologie der jüdischen Gemeinde im neutest. Zeitalter nach den Quellen der robbinschen, apokalyptischen und apokryphen Literatur*. 2nd ed. Tübingen: Hildesheim, Georg Olms Verlag, 1934.

Ward-Perkins, J. B. "Memoria, Martyrs Tomb and Church." *Journal of Theological Studies* 17 (1966) 20–38.

Webb, Matilda. *The Churches and Catacombs of Early Christian Rome: A Comprehensive Guide*. Portland, OR: Sussex Academic, 2001.

Weiner, E., and A. Weiner. *The Martyr's Conviction: A Sociological Analysis*. Atlanta: Scholar's Press, 1990.

Weiss, Bernhard. *Lehrbuch der biblischen Theologie des Neuen Testaments*. Berlin: Hertz, 1893.

Weiss, Johannes. *The History of Primitive Christianity*. Translated by F. C. Grant *et al.* 2 vols. New York: Wilson-Erikson, 1936.

Wetter, Gilles P. *Altchristliche Liturgion I: das christliche Mysterium. Studie zur geschichte des abendmahles*. Forschungen zur Religion und Literatur des Alten und Neuen Testaments. Göttingen: Vandenhoeck & Ruprecht, 1921.

Wilamowitz-Moellendorff, Ulrich von. *Der Glaube der Hellenen*, vol. 2. Berlin: Weidmannsche Buchhandlung, 1931–32.

Williams, Michael A. "Realized Eschatology in the Gospel of Philip." *Restoration Quarterly* 14 (1971) 1–17.

Wilson, Robert McLachlan. *The Gospel of Philip: Translation from the Coptic Text with an Introduction and Commentary*. New York: Harper & Row, 1962.

Windisch, H. *Der zweite Korinther-Brief*. Göttingen: Vandenhoeck & Ruprecht, 1924.

Winslow, Donald F. "The Idea of Redemption in the Epistles of St. Ignatius of Antioch." *Greek Orthodox Review* 11 (1965) 119–31.

Wolfson, Harry Austryn. *Philo: Foundations of Religious Philosophy in Judaism, Christianity and Islam*, vol. 1. Cambridge: Harvard University Press, 1975.

———. "Immortality and Resurrection in the Philosophy of the Church Fathers." In *Immortality and Resurrection: Death in the Western World: Two Conflicting Currents of Thought*, edited by Krister Stendall, 54–96. New York: Macmillan, 1965.

———. *The Philosophy of the Church Fathers: Faith, Trinity, Incarnation*, vol. 1. Cambridge: Harvard University Press, 1956.

Wright, George Ernest. *The Old Testament against Its Environment*. London: SCM, 1962.

Wright, N. T. *The Resurrection of the Son of God. Christian Origins and the Question of God*, vol. 3. Minneapolis: Fortress, 2003.

Young, Frances. *Biblical Exegesis and the Formation of Christian Culture.* Cambridge: Cambridge University Press, 1997.

Zaehner, R. C. *At Sundry Times: An Essay in the Comparison of Religions.* London: Faber and Faber, 1958.

Index

absorption, 14, 32
Achamoth, 114, 120, 148
Achilles Tatus, 12
acta martyrum. See *acta sanctorum*
acta sanctorum, 94, 95, 97–98
Acts
    1:8, 95
    1:22, 95
    7:60, 60n27, 63, 64
    13:36, 63
    14:12, 57n15
    20, 103
Acts of Andrew, The, 94, 95
Acts of the Apostles, 98, 155
Acts of the Christian Martyrs, 55, 98, 155. See also *acta sanctorum*
Acts of John, The, 94, 95, 182
Acts of Justin and His Companions, 97–98
Acts of the Martyrs, 75
Acts of Paul, The, 94, 95, 97, 178
Acts of Peter, The, 94, 95
Acts of the Scillitan Martyrs, The, 97
Acts of Thomas, 94, 95
Adam, fall of, 4, 18, 24–26, 60–61, 147
Ad Autolycus (Theophilus), 179
Adversus haereses (*Against Heresies*; Irenaeus), 114, 122, 139, 146
Adversus Marcionem (*Against Marcion*; Tertullian), 155
afterlife, theological discussion on, 1–2
Alexander of Aphrodisias, 33
Amos
    2:1, 164

    9:2, 30
Anaxarchus of Abdera, 5–6
ancestor worship, 162. See also dead, veneration of
Andronicus, 182
animal men, 109
annihilationism, 193
anthropology
    Christian, 145
    dualistic, 112
    Valentinian, 111–12
Apocryphal New Testament, 94–95
Apologies (Justin Martyr), 130, 132, 133, 137
apologists, 90, 99, 193, 194, 196. See also Aristides; Athenagoras; Justin; Tatian; Theophilus of Antioch
    on death, 101–2, 126–28
    perspective of, 100–101
    on treatment of the dead, 178
Apology (Aristides), 128
Apology (Plato), 6, 7
apolytrosis, 19, 20, 106, 110, 114, 116, 125, 166n38
Apostolic Fathers, 19, 54–55
apotheosis, 41
apparent death, 11
Apuleius, 11
Aristides, 128, 179
Aristocles, 33n127
Aristotelians, 32, 33
Armstrong, A. H., 32, 33, 40–41
arrogance, suppression of, 127
astral bodies, 41

INDEX

Athenagoras, 101, 128, 143–46, 178–79
atonement, death and, 75
Augustine, 185, 188
Avemarie, Friedrich, 14–15n48, 38

Bailey, Robert Edison, 64
Baldovin, John F., 188
baptism, 59–60, 93n193
Barbeliots, 110
Barnabas, 55n6
Barnard, L. W., 131, 140–41
Barr, James, 24n79
Barth, Karl, 61
Basilidians, 102
Bauer, Walter, 67, 68, 73, 104–5
Baur, E. C., 103–4
bench tombs, 158
Bertholet, Alfred, 161–62
birthdays, death as, 90, 93, 94, 197
Bloch-Smith, Elizabeth M., 157, 158–60
body
    corruption of, in death, 148
    rejoined with the soul, 126
    resurrection of, in the future, 92
    soul attached to, after death, 179–80
    as soul's tomb, 151
    value of, 40
Bousset, Wilhelm, 107
Bowersock, G. W., 11, 13, 86n153, 92n186
Brent, Allen, 10
Brown, Peter, 156, 184
Bultmann, Rudolf, 43–44
burial clubs, 170
burial places, 158, 179, 183–85. *See also* catacombs
burial practices, 157, 164, 171
Burkert, Walter, 34, 35–36, 167, 168–69 [QY: Burkett on 34]
Bynum, Caroline, 11–12, 13, 14–15, 91–92, 175, 178, 196

Calvin, John, 25, 27
Campenhausen, Hans von , 73, 77, 78, 82n134, 187
cannibalism, 14
Cassuto, U., 25
catacombs, 175, 176, 184

Catholicism, 112
caves, burial in, 158
Celsus, 179
cemeteries, 184, 194
Chariton, 12
Chrism, rite of, 121–22
Christ. *See also* Jesus
    conscious fellowship with, 48
    death of, 56
    healing male-female separation, 121n109
    imitation of, 77–79
    passion of, 7, 85–94
    preaching to the dead, 59–60
    preaching to souls, 152–53
    as prototype of pneumatic man, 107
    redemption and, 109–10
    resurrected before death, 119
    resurrection of, 52, 56, 118
    suffering of, 84. *See also* Christ, passion of
Christian anthropology, 145
Christianity
    Alexandrian tradition of, 149
    catholic, 104
    cult of the dead in, 186–88
    doctrinal development of, 104
    early characteristics of, 104
    Hellenization of, 130, 192, 195–96
    Justin's defense of, 133
    philosophizing of, 130–31
Christian martyrdom, 96
Christians
    funerals of, 182
    obsession of, with relics, 186
    persecution of, 96n206
    treatment of the dead, 171–85
    viewing death as gain, 174, 184, 194–95
Christ and Time (Cullman), 2
Chronicles, First
    17:11, 31, 60n27
Chronicles, Second
    16:13, 31, 60n27
Chrysostom, 188n134
church, unity of, 55
churches, design of, 189

INDEX

Clement, First, 19–20, 55, 56–57, 60n26, 63, 155
Clement, Second, 60n26
Clement of Alexandria, 128, 149–53, 139
Clement of Rome, 55n6, 185
Clitophon, 12–13n41
coffins, 173
Coleman, Kathleen, 172, 173, 174, 182
collegium theory, 96n206
communio sanctorum, 185
comparative religion, school of, 77
Copleston, Frederick C., 131
Corinthians, First, 112
    2:6–8, 115n82
    6:14, 71n75
    7:39, 60n27, 63
    11:30, 63
    15, 113n
    15:3–4, 52
    15:6, 60n27
    15:12–5, 71n75
    15:17ff., 64
    15:20, 63
    15:22, 63
    15:25f., 116
    15:51, 60n27, 116–17
    15:54, 31n114, 48
    15:55, 52
    15:56, 117
Corinthians, Second
    4:14, 71n75
    5:1, 49
    5:1–4, 51
    5:1–10, 44–45, 46, 73
    5:4, 48
    5:5, 46
    5:8, 48, 51, 116
    12:14, 50
Cranfield, C. E. B.., 23
cremation, 20, 157, 164, 166, 167, 170, 174–81, 63–64
Cullman, Oscar, 2–3, 4n9, 7n22, 192–93
cult of the dead, 157–61, 164, 169, 182, 186–88, 195

Daley, Brian, 17n57, 17–18n59, 102, 122, 128, 138, 141, 143, 145n206, 154
Daniel
    12:2, 60n27
Daniel-Rops, H., 175–76, 184n113
Davies, Douglas, 176
Davis, Stevan L., 41–42
dead, the. *See also* cult of the dead
    burial of, 164. *See also* dead, disposal of
    Christian prayer over, 175n81
    Christians' treatment of, 171–85
    closing of the eyes, 166, 173
    commemoration of, 171, 181–82, 189
    considered as pollutants, 183–84
    contact with, 158, 159–60, 163
    disposal of, 156–57, 165, 170, 172–85
    dressing of, 169–70
    Greeks' treatment of, 165–69
    offerings to, 160, 161–62. *See also* sacrifice
    Old Testament treatment of, 157–65
    powers of, 158–59
    provisions for, 158
    Romans' treatment of, 165, 169–71, 189
    separation from, 169
    social locations for, 183–84
    treatment of, 185, 194–95
    veneration of, 157, 158, 162, 164
De anima (Tertullian), 149
death. *See also* false death; Noble Death
    apologists on, 20, 101–2, 126–28. *See also* Aristides; Athenagoras; Justin; Tatian; Theophilus of Antioch
    as *apolytrosis*, 110
    attitude toward, changes in, 18
    baptism and, 59–60
    beauty of, 3
    biblical definition of, 20–23
    as birthday, 90, 93, 94, 187, 197
    changed by God, 127
    Christianization of, 185, 196
    and Christ's resurrection, 118

Christians view of, ix, 2–3, 174
competing view of, ix
as destruction of the soul and body, 3–4, 142–43
as descent to nothingness, 33
destructive power of, 44
as discipleship, 19, 65–69, 81
dualistic approach to, 8
early church's concept of, 2
as eschaton, 89–90, 94
as extinction of life in the body, 113
fear of, 3, 22, 43, 44, 62, 163
as freedom from suffering, 136
functionality of, 126
in Greco-Roman culture, 32–34
Greek concepts of, ix–x, 4–5, 21–22, 43
Hebrew term for, 21, 28
Hellenized concept of, 4–5, 10–11
as imitation, 19, 77–79, 81, 82–94
Jesus' victory over, 52
martyr's concept of, 19, 64–99
metaphors for, 113
nakedness and, 51
New Testament's view of, 22, 43–53, 63
in the Old Testament, 21, 27–31
origin of, 23–27
paradoxical view of, ix
and the Passion of Christ, 79
paving way for resurrection, 127–28
personification of, as demon, 22
physical, 118
places for, 50–53. *See also* burial places; Hades; Paradise; Sheol
in Platonism, 34–43
polemicist's view of, 20, 126–27. *See also* Clement of Alexandria; Ireneaus of Lyons; Tertullian
as process, 91, 138, 148
as punishment, 135, 137
purpose of, in God's program, 127
as redemption, 117, 137–38
related to the future, 135
resurrection and, 49–50, 69–73, 81, 89, 95–96, 98, 148
Roman concept of, 42
as sacrifice, 19, 73–76, 80, 81
salvation and, 89, 98, 106, 137–38
salvific benefits of, 75–76, 78–79
separate from resurrection, 134, 137
separating body and soul, 145–46, 151, 153–55
sin and, 43–44, 147, 151–52
as sleep, 28, 31, 51, 55, 56–64, 192–93
as soul's ascent to the creator, 120–21
soul returning to origin after, 125
suppressing arrogance, 127
as temporary dissolution of the body, 142
terms used for, 120
theological discussion on, 1, 52
theology of, 99
Valentinian concept of, 105, 106, 110–26
virtuous living and, 55
Deconick, April D., 121n109
Delitzch, Franz, 24–25
demi-gods, 37
Demiurge, 108, 114–15
Democritus, 33, 154
descensus ad infernos, 154
destructive sacrifices, 167–68
Deuteronomy
32:39, 27, 31
32:50, 30
de Vaux, Roland, *Ancient Israel: Its Life and Institutions*. London: Longman and Todd, 1961.
devil, 91–92
Dewart, Joanne E., 57, 138–39
Dhorme, P., 161–62
Dialogue with Trypho (Justin Martyr), 129, 130, 133–34
Didache, The, 55n6, 60n26
digestion, 14
discipleship, 55, 65–69, 80, 81, 155
Discorides, 177–78
Docetism, 12
Dominitian, 96n206
Droge, Arthur J., 38, 131–32
Drusiana, 182
dualism, carried into death, 125
Dunn, James, 105

Ecclesiastes
  7:26, 29
  12:7, 29
Ecclesiastical History (Eusebius), 140
Eijik, Ton H. C. Van, 14, 70–71
ekphora, 166, 167
elect, 109, 113
Elliott, J. K., 95–96
Ellis, Peter, 162
Empedocles, 154
Encratism, 139, 140
Ephesians
  1:21, 115n82
  2:2, 115n82
  5:14, 60n27
  11:2, 71
Epictetus, 33
Epicureanism, 19, 32, 33, 193
Epiphanius, 139
Epistle to Diognetus, 55n6
Epistle to Rheginas. See *Treatise on the Resurrection*
Erickson, Millard J., 25
eschatology
  Christian, 152
  individual, 110
eschaton, death as, 89–90, 94
Eucharist, 74, 75, 87, 172n68, 182
Eusebius, 90n175, 103, 104, 139, 140, 181
expiatory sacrifice, 39
Ezekiel
  26:20, 30
  31:18, 31, 60n27
  32:20–32, 31, 60n27

false death, 5, 11, 12–15, 192
Felix, Minucius, 180–81
Felton, D., 166
Férét, Pére, 20–21
J. Fontaine, "Discussion" in *ACTES of the 11th International Congress of Christian Archeology*. Rome: Pontifical Institute of Christian Archeology, 1989.
foreign terms
  ἅδης, 22
  Θάνατος, 4, 21, 23, 38, 113
  κοιμᾶσθαι, 60–64, 173
  μάρτυς, 86, 95
  περιψάω, 79–80
  נֶפֶשׁ., 30
Fragments (Tatian), 141
Frend, W. H. C., 74–75, 96n206
funerary practices, 28, 42, 195–96
  Greek, 166–69
  Old Testament, 163
  Roman, 169–71

Galatians 6:7f, 117
Garland, Robert, 35, 36, 37–38, 165, 166, 168
Gavin, F., 61–62
Genesis
  2, 27
  2:7, 22
  2:17, 23, 24
  3, 25–26
  3, 27
  3:19, 26
  3:22, 24
  5, 27
  5:5, 24
  6:3, 26
  15:15, 30
  25:8, 30
  35:29, 30
  37:34f., 164
  37:35, 30
  49:33, 30
Gnosticism, 12, 77, 101, 104, 194. See also Valentinians
  categories of, 102–3
  salvation and, 106–7
gnostic theosophy, 147
God
  attaining, 68–69, 81, 84
  knowledge of, 127, 142
  sacrifice to, 87
Gospel of Philip, The, 106, 110, 118–22
Gospel of Truth, The, 106, 119n98, 122–24, 125
Gousmett, Christopher John, 62, 136
Grant, Robert, 100–101, 139–40, 145n206
graves

robbery of, 174–75
visitation of, 189, 195
Greco-Roman culture, death in, 32–34
Greeks
   on death, ix–x, 4–5, 21–22, 43
   philosophy of, development of, 131–32n155, 133
   treatment of the dead, 165–69
Greenberg, L. Arik, 5, 6, 8, 38–39, 86, 96n207
Greenspoon, L. J., 28

Hades, 35, 36–37, 50, 51–52, 134, 148, 149, 152–53, 154–55, 165
Hallote, Rachel, 157, 159
Harnack, Adolf., 104, 130, 133, 195–96
Harris, Murray J., 46–47, 48
Hebrews
   2:15, 43, 44
   12:22, 51
Hegel, G. W. F., 104
Heidel, A., 30
Heliodorus, 12
Hellenistic mystery religions, 77
Hellenization, 130–31
Henten, J. W. van, 14–15n48
heresy, 103, 104, 109
Hermas, 55n6
hero cult, 38, 187–88
Hero death, 38, 39
heroes, 37–38
Heroic age, 37
Hesiod, 37–38
Hesychius of Jerusalem, 79–80
Hick, John, 1
Hill, Charles E., 145
Hippolytus, 106, 108, 116n86, 139
holiness, 55, 56–57
Holmes, M. W., 55, 85, 82n134, 186, 187
Homer, 4, 21, 34, 35–37, 62, 168
Hope of the Early Church, The (Daley), 17n57, 17–18n59
Hopkins, Keith, 42, 171, 182
humility, 125, 127
Hunt, Emily, 139
Hymn to Demeter (Homer), 36

idols, 4

Ignatian Letters, 65–81
Ignatius of Antioch, 8–10, 13–14, 39, 49–50, 55, 64–81, 83, 88, 94, 117, 155, 185, 193
Iliad (Homer), 34, 35
Illman, 27–28 [QY: Need first name and add to references}
imitatio Christi, 8, 77–79, 82, 83, 85, 94, 193
imitation, 55, 65, 77–79, 81, death as, 82–94, 155
immortality, 6, 16, 23n75, 38, 40–41, 91
   acquisition of, 93
   astral, 41
   circle of, 149–50
   conditional, 25
Immortality of the Soul or Resurrection of the Dead? (Cullman), 2
incarnation, orthodox explanation of, 112n73
incipient resurrection, 48
Ingersoll, Caroline Haskell, 2n3
Ingersoll, George Goldthwaite, 2n3
Ingersoll Lectures on Human Immortality, 2
inhumation, 20, 166, 167, 170, 174–81
intermediate state, 89–90, 91, 136, 148
internment, Christian, 182
Interpretation of Knowledge,, The, 106, 125
Irenaeus of Lyons, 106–10, 114–15, 122, 127, 128, 146–49, 196
   accusing Tatian of heresy, 138–40, 141
   theology of, 141
Isaiah
   8:19, 159
   9:1 LXX, 22
   25:8, 31
   44:23, 30
   57:2, 60n27
   57:9, 30
   59:3–4, 60n27
Israel, burial types in, 158

Jaeger, Werner, 4–5, 34, 35, 40
James
   1:15, 117

Jefford, Clayton N., 54, 87, 90–91, 93, 94n196
Jeremiah
    2:33, 31, 60n27
    28:39, 31
Jesus. *See also* Christ
    death of, 3, 7n19, 176
    pre-Gospel accounts of, 13
    as revealer, 123
    spiritual resurrection of, 118
Jews, death rituals for, 183
Job
    3:11–14, 31, 60n27
    3:13, 29n105
    10:21–22, 30
    11:8, 30
    14:12, 31, 60n27
    17, 29n105 [QY: correct? Or should this be 3:17?]
    21:26, 31
    26:3, 57
John
    11:11, 63
    13:37, 79n118
John (apostle), 182
John of Damascus, 147n216
Johnston, Philip S., 20, 164
Judah, burial types in, 158
Judahite Practices and Beliefs about the Dead (Bloch-Smith), 157
Jude
    6–7, 51
Justin Martyr, 101, 128, 129–37, 144, 178
    on death, 134–36
    defending Christianity, 133
    work of, related to Greek philosophy, 131, 133

Kautzsch, Emil Friedrich, 162
Kellerman, Ulrich, 72
King, Karen, 102, 108
Kings, First
    1:21, 31, 60n27
    2:10, 31
Kings, Second
    4:32, 31, 60n27
    5:7, 31n114

Koester, Helmut, 105

Lamentations
    3:6, 28
last rites, 173
Latourette, Kenneth Scott, 175
Legatio (Athenagoras), 178–79
Lehrbuch der Dogmengeschichte (Harnack), 195
Liefeld, Walter, 50
Lethe (river of forgetfulness), 4
Letter to the Philippians (Polycarp), 81, 82–84, 93–94
Leucippe, 12–13n41
Levenson, Jon L., 30
Lewis, Nicola Denzey, 110, 115, 116, 118, 119–20, 124, 125–26
life force, departure of, 22
Lightfoot, J. B. S., 66n49, 67, 68, 73, 93
Liturgical Readings, 106
liturgy, 126
Loisy, Alfred, 101
Longenecker, 44–45n186
Lord's Supper. *See* Eucharist
Luke
    1:79, 44
    8:52, 60n27
    9:23, 81n130
    15:19–21, 88n166
    16:19–31, 50
    16:23, 50
    23:43, 50, 51

Maccabean martyrs, 39, 75
Maccabees, Second, 39, 71
    7, 72, 73
    7:9, 72
    7:36, 72
    12:43–44, 72n80
    12:43–45, 60n27
Maccabees, Fourth, 39
man
    created moral or immortal, 24–27
    creation of, 108
    dualistic view of, 114, 117
    immortality of, 5
    nature of, inward and incorruptible, 114

needing redemption, 107
threefold substances of, 109
Valentinian categories of, 107–9
Marcion, 82, 104, 139
Marcionism, 104
Marcionites, 102, 155
Marcosian death rite, 110
Marcosians, 114, 116n86
Marcus the Magus, 110n58
Mark, 7–8
    4:3, 56
    5:39, 60n27
    14:33, 7n19
Markus, R.A., 32, 33, 40–41
Martin-Achard, Robert, 20–21, 161–62
martyrdom, 5, 6, 13, 67, 192, 193
    baptism and, 93n193
    honor of, 88
    meaning of, 86
    resurrection and, 14
    as sacrifice, 74–75
    victory of, 91–92
Martyrdom of Apollonius, 97
Martyrdom of Perpetua and Felicitas, 97
Martyrdom of Polycarp, The, 79, 81, 85–94, 97, 186–87
martyriological fathers, 19–20
martyr motif, 7–8
martyrs, 38–39
    apocryphal acts of, 94–95, 97
    Christian, 96
    on death, 64–99
    deaths celebrated as birthdays, 93
    deaths of, significance of, 95–96
    doing theology, 99
    resurrection of, 71
Martyrs of Lugdunum, 97
material man, 107
Matthew
    4:16, 22, 44
    10:38, 89
    11:23, 51
    16:18, 51
    16:24, 81n130
    27:52, 63
    28:52, 60n27
McCane, Byron R., 183

McNamara, Daniel Norman, 66n49, 67, 75, 77
Mellink, Albert Osger, 9, 64–65n47, 68, 71, 79, 88, 89, 90, 94
Merrill, E. H., 30
Metamorphoses (Apuleius), 11, 12
metempsychosis, 22, 143
Meyers, Eric M., 122–23
Middle Place, 121
Middle Platonism, 131–32
Moberly, R. W. L., 24n79
Montanists, 141
mortality, 24–25, 127
mortuary decisions, 125–26
mourning rituals, 163, 164, 195
Mulhern, Alice, 176
mummification, 157
Muratorian Canon, 58n
mystery religions, 176–77

Nag Hammadi texts, 106, 122
Natalis, Caecilius, 180
Neoplatonism, 32, 41
Neopythagoreans, 105
nepeš, 21, 28
Nero, 97
New Testament
    abode of the dead in, 50–53
    death in, 22, 43–53, 63
    emergence of, 191
Nicetes, 186, 187
Nichols, Terrence, 1–2
Nickelsburg, George W. E., 73
Noble Death, 5–7, 9, 38, 86n153, 92, 96, 192
Nock, A. D., 174, 175, 176–77
non-martyriological fathers, 19–20
Numbers
    20:24, 30
    28, 30
    31:2, 30
nutrition, 14

Octavius (Felix), 180–81
Odyssey (Homer), 34, 62
Ogle, Marbury B., 31, 62–63

Old Testament
    death in, 27–31
    treatment in, of the dead, 157–65
On the Resurrection of the Dead
    (Athenagoras), 145, 178
On the Soul (Tertullian), 179–80
Oration to the Greeks (Tatian), 139–40,
    141–42
ordo defunctorum, 172–73n68
Origen, 57–58n15, 93n193
Orpheus, 41n
Orphism, 39–41, 192, 193
orthodoxy, 103–4
Osborn, Eric, 146
Osei-Bonsu, Joseph, 47–48
Osiek, Catolyn, 59

Pagels, Elaine, 104, 105, 113n
pain, 8
Papias, 55n6
Paradise, 50–51, 52, 147, 153
Parousia, 45n, 46–49, 71
Passion of Christ, 79
passions, control of, 120
Paul, 116, 133
    comparing Christ with Adam, 23
    facing death, 47
    Gnostic language of, 43
    letters of, 44–45, 46, 52, 56, 79, 88,
        152
    on Paradise, 50, 51
    on resurrection, 48, 49
Peel, Malcolm, 111, 112, 116–17
Pelikan, Jaroslav, 103, 142–43, 148,
    149–50, 156
perideipnon, 168
Perkins, Judith, 11, 12, 14–15
Petronius, 11
Peter, First
    3:19, 51n212
    3:19–20, 59n25, 152
    4:6, 59n25
Peter, Second
    3:4, 63
    3:7, 51
Philippians
    1:23, 48, 51
    1:29, 79n118
    2:27, 88
    3:8, 79n118
Philo, 32–33, 133
philosophy
    criticism of, 133
    Greek, development of, 131–
        32n155, 133
Philostratus, 9n31
Photius, 79–80
pit graves, 158
Plato, 4, 5, 6, 7, 132, 153, 154, 166
Platonism, 19, 33–43, 129–30, 150, 151,
    152, 192
Platonists, 3, 32, 132
Plea for Christians (Athenagoras),
    143–44
Pleroma, 121–22, 123–24
Pliny the Elder, 174
pneumatic man, 107–8
pneumatic resurrection, 111
polemicists, 90, 108, 126–27, 193,
    194, 196. *See also* Clement of
    Alexandria; Iraneaus of Lyons;
    Tertullian
Polycarp of Smyrna, 55, 79, 81–94, 117,
    146, 155, 186
    body of, final disposition of, 92–93
    execution of, 85n151, 90–91
    immortality and, 91
    relics from, 186–87
postapostolic period, 54
Praxton, S., 172n68
Preiss, Theodor, 8, 77, 78
priesthood, and the cult of the dead, 160
prose fiction, Christianity and, 11,
    12–14
prothesis, 166
Protrepticus (Clement), 150
Psalms
    3:6, 31, 60n27, 63
    4:9, 31, 60n27
    15:10, 31
    18:4, 29
    30:9, 31
    31:12, 28
    49:14, 29
    51;14:2
    55:23, 31

55:4, 29
87:6, 31, 60n27
88:4–6, 28
90, 26
143:3, 28, 30
psyche, departure of, 165–66
psychic man, 107
psychorrhagêma, 166
purgatory, 121
purification, death as, 91
Pyne, Robert Allen, 26–27
Pythagoreanism, 33, 113, 193
Pythagoreans, 32, 154

Quadratus, 55n6
Quintus, 85, 86

Rajak, Tessa, 86n153
Ratzinger, Joseph, 48
Realized Eschatology, 45n
Rebell, Walter, 9n29
Rebillard, Éric, 174, 180
recapitulation, doctrine of, 147
Rechtgl.ubigkeit und Ketzerei im ältesten Christendum (*Orthodoxy and Heresy in Earliest Christianity*; Bauer), 104–5
redemption
　Christ and, 109–10
　death and, 117, 137–38
　gnostic, 108
　man's need for, 107
Reeves, John W., 92n186
Refutation of All Heresies (Hippolytus), 116n86
Reichenbach, Bruce R., 61
relics, 186
religionsgeschichtliche model, 77
repose, 61, 173, 175n81, 185
Republic (Plato), 153
resurrection, 65, 69–73, 81, 193, 194
　already occurred, 117
　bodies in, 41
　chrism and, 121–22
　Christ's, 52, 56
　commemoration of, 93
　death and, 49–50, 118, 148
　death paving way for, 127–28
　death separate from, 137
　doctrine of, 111
　false death and, 11–12
　hope of, 152, 176
　incipient, 48
　martyrdom and, 14
　material, 15
　Orphic Platonism's rejection of, 40
　participation in, 84
　pneumatic, 111
　ridicule of belief in, 180–81
　separate in time from death, 134
　Sheol and, 30
　spiritual, 117, 118, 119
　and time since death, 89
resurrection body, reception of, 46–48
Revelation
　1:18, 52
　14:13, 64
　16:6, 95
　17:6, 95
　20:1, 53
　20:4–6, 95
　20:13, 52
　20:14, 52
Rhodon, 140
Riddle, Donald W., 7
Ringgren, Helmer, 27–28
R.I.P., 173
ritual bath, 165
Robinson, James, 105
Romans
　on death, 42
　treatment of the dead, 165, 169–71, 189
Romans (Letter to)
　4:17, 52
　5:12, 23
　5:12ff., 44
　5:12–21, 23
　6:1–11, 59n23
　6:5, 71n75
　6:20–23, 152
　6:21, 117
　6:23, 44, 117
　7:5, 117
　8:6, 117
　8:11, 71n75

8:13, 117
8:15, 44
8:38, 115n82
14:13, 61
16:14, 58n
Ross, Allen, 26
Routledge, Robin L., 30
royal cult of the dead, 161
ruah, 29
Rush, A. C., 62

sacramentalism, 126
sacraments, 118
sacrifice, 55, 65, 73–76, 80, 81, 94, 155, 159, 160–61, 167–68, 171, 193
    discipleship and, 80
    Polycarp's death as, 90–91
saints
    commemoration of, 187
    cult of, growing, 189
salvation, 75–76, 78–79
    death and, 89, 98, 106, 137–38
    gnostic, 108
    Gnosticism's perspective on, 106–7
    goal of, 122
    knowledge and, 109–10
    sexual abstinence and, 140–41
    story of, different levels of, 122–23
    Valentinians' view of, 106–7
salvator salvandus, 77
Samuel, First
    2:6, 31n114
    28, 159
Samuel, Second
    1:11f., 164
    12:23, 30
    13:31, 164
sanctification, 81, 193
Satan, 186
Satryica (Petronius), 11
Saturnilians, 102
Saturnus, 139
Schientod, 11
Schlier, Heinrich, 77–78
Schmidt, Brian B., 162
Schmithals, W., 26–27, 44
Schoedel, William, 55, 67, 68, 70, 78–79, 87, 91, 93, 145n206, 188

Second Sophistic phenomenon, 9–10
Sethians, 111
sexual abstinence, 140–41
Shape of Death, The (Pelikan), 156
Sheol, 22, 30–31, 51
Shepherd of Hermas, The, 19–20, 55, 57–60, 63, 155
Shipp, G. P., 36n148
sin, death and, 21, 43–44, 147, 151–52
Sirach
    46:20, 60n27
sleep, death and, 55, 56–64, 192–93
Slusser, Michael, 130
Smith, Wilbur, 141
Socrates, 3, 4, 6, 7, 22, 132
soma sema, 151
Sonnemans, Heino, 34
soteriology, Valentinian, 109
soul
    awaiting reuniting with their body, 135–36
    beginning of, 127, 142, 151, 193–94
    conscious existence of, after death, 136
    immortality of, 4–5, 16, 40–41, 101, 127, 145, 191–92, 193
    incorruptibility of, 93
    and the knowledge of God, 127
    leaving the body, 192
    liberation of, 22
    life of, after death, 19, 181–82
    mortality of, 142, 154
    preexistence of, 149–50
    re-creation of, 142–43
    recycling of, 143
    rejoined with the body, 126, 179–80
    resurrection of, in the future, 92
    returning to origin after death, 125
    returning to Pleroma, 123–24
    transmigration of, 22
    trial of, after death, 119
soul-flight, 19
soul sleep, 61–62, 64
Sparks, Adam, 130n147
spiritual body, 46
Spronk, Klass, 158, 161, 164
Stählin, Gustav, 80
Sterling, Greg, 5, 6–7

Stoicism, 32–33, 113, 132, 154, 193
Stromata (Clement), 150, 151, 152
suffering, 77–79, 83–84
Svigel, Michael J., 112, 118, 119
Swartley, Willard M., 68
Syrian church, 62, 64

Tatian, 62, 101, 128, 138–43, 149
Tertullian of Carthage, 128, 141, 149, 153–55, 179, 196
Theological Definition of the Old Testament, 21
Theophilus of Antioch, 128, 137–38, 179
theosis, 138
Thessalonians, First
    2:12, 88
    4:13–14, 63
    4:13–15, 60n27
    4:14, 71n75
    4:16, 64
    5:10, 48
Thomas, Louis-Vincent, 178
Thomassen, Einar, 122–23
Thompson, Leonard L., 85n151
Thracian, 41n
Thrall, Margaret E., 47, 49
Timaeus (Plato), 132
Timothy, First
    6:16, 22
Timothy, Second
    1:10, 52
    2:18, 111
Tinsley, E. J., 77
To Autolycus (Theophilus), 137–38
Toews, Thomas W., 152
Torrance, T. F., 75
Toynbee, J. M., 169, 170, 175, 189
Trajan, 96n206
Treatise on the Resurrection, The, 106, 110–17, 120, 125

Treatise on the Soul, A (Tertullian), 153–54
tree of life, 24–25
Tripartite Tractate, 106, 107, 108–9, 110, 124–25
Tübingen school, 103–4
Turner, Henry, 105
Tyrataeus, 4

unitary anthropology, 62

Valentinian Exposition, 106
Valentinian Gnosticism, 19, 20, 40
Valentinianism, anthropology of, 107, 108–9
Valentinians, 102, 105–6, 109, 139, 155, 194
Valentinus, 106, 111, 122, 139
Vassiliades, Nicholas, 18–19, 127
virtue, 55
von Rad, Gerhard, 25–26

Wetter, Gilles P., 74, 75
What Is Christianity? (Harnack), 195
Williams, Michael A., 119
Wilson, Robert McLachlan, 119–20
Winslow, Donald F., 75
witness, 55
Wittgenstein, Ludwig, 10
Wolfson, Harry A., 2, 16, 33, 133
worthiness, proving of, 88–89
Wright, G. E., 162

Xenophon of Ephesus, 12

Yahweh, cult of, centralizing, 160

Zahn, Theodore, 73, 75
Zeno of Elea, 5–6

www.ingramcontent.com/pod-product-compliance
Lightning Source LLC
Chambersburg PA
CBHW051637230426
43669CB00013B/2337